Morning Light

Morning Light

Triumph at Sea & Tragedy on Everest

Margaret Griffiths

*A story of George Griffiths written by his wife,
Margaret, based on tape recordings, letters,
diaries, conversations and reports*

Foreword by Pat Morrow

Rocky
Mountain Books
VANCOUVER • VICTORIA • CALGARY

Rocky Mountain Books
#108 – 17665 66A Avenue
Surrey, BC V3S 2A7
www.rmbooks.com

Rocky Mountain Books
PO BOX 468
Custer, WA
98240-0468

Library and Archives Canada Cataloguing in Publication

Griffiths, Margaret, 1920 –
    Morning light : triumph at sea & tragedy on Everest / Margaret Griffiths.

ISBN 978-1-897522-08-0 (bound)

    1. Griffiths, George—Family. 2. Griffiths, Blair. 3. Sailors—
Canada—Biography. 4. Mountaineers—Canada—Biography.
5. Sailing—Atlantic Ocean. 6. Mountaineering accidents—Everest,
Mount (China and Nepal). 7. Fathers and sons—Canada—Biography.
I. Title.

GV810.92.G75G75 2008   797.124'092   C2008-902780-9

Library of Congress Control Number: 2008930512

Printed and bound in Canada.

Rocky Mountain Books gratefully acknowledges the financial support of the Government of Canada through the Book Publishing Industry Development Program (BPIDP); the Canada Council for the Arts; and the province of British Columbia through the British Columbia Arts Council and the Book Publishing Tax Credit for our publishing activities.

BRITISH COLUMBIA ARTS COUNCIL
Supported by the Province of British Columbia

Canada Council
for the Arts

Conseil des Arts
du Canada

This book has been produced on 100% post-consumer recycled paper, processed chlorine free and printed with vegetable-based dyes.

Photo on page 242: Lony Rockafella

The verse quoted on p288 is from "Lux in Tenebris," by Katharine Tynan (1861–1931), in *Ballads and Lyrics by Katharine Tynan*. London: Kegan Paul, Trench, Trübner & Co., 1891.

I dedicate this book to the memory of my godson,
Robert Kenward.

Contents

FOREWORD

It has been a privilege to be counted as a friend by Margaret Griffiths, widow of sailor George Griffiths and stepmother of mountaineer/cameraman Blair Griffiths, both of whom she writes about so lovingly in this book.

I first met this remarkable woman through an email that arrived out of nowhere one early winter evening nearly three years ago:

Dec. 20, 2005:

> *Dear Pat Morrow, you don't know me but I feel from two years' research that I know you. My name is Margaret Griffiths and I have written a book, mainly from diaries, of the later life of my late husband George who received a seamanship award for his sail in a small boat from England to British Columbia. He arrived home to receive news of the death of his son Blair on the Khumbu Icefall during the first Canadian ascent of Mount Everest....*

She wondered if she could arrange to use one of my photographs of the icefall.

> *If you would like to glance through the manuscript first I could email it to you. I wish you and your family a very happy Christmas.*

Margaret Griffiths, Galiano Island, BC.

When the manuscript arrived, on first read I couldn't help but marvel at the high level of perception of a writer who had never been on the high seas, or even seen the Himalaya, yet had so perfectly captured the essence of what took both her husband and his son on their personal quests into the unknown.

I've long been a fan of the British climber/sailor/author Bill Tilman, and devoured his mountaineering and sailing books in my youth. I could see right away that Margaret Griffiths had created a highly literary work, in the tradition of Tilman, combining a high-end sailing adventure with the drama of life and death on the world's highest mountain, between the same covers.

Impressed, I made a few suggestions, mostly to do with the chronology in the section of her manuscript I knew the most about, our 1982 Canadian Mount Everest expedition. I was deeply moved by her account, as seen from the point of view of my fallen teammate Blair, and told her as much.

Jan. 9, 2006:

Dear Pat, I have altered the MS in line with your comments, and I am most grateful for the time you took. I didn't mean to bring back a flood of memories, but your team's victory snatched from defeat really was superb....

Blair was my stepson and we became close when George was on his long sail. We sat together in despondency, on the floor with a bottle of wine the night John Lennon died....

Thank you again. If you should come this way I would love to meet you.

Margaret.

We began to sign off every email to each other with "Hugs!" and looked forward to the day when we could make the hugs real.

Before too long, my wife and I got to meet Margaret on her home turf. At 87, she lives alone in the lovely home that she and George handcrafted on the rugged west coast of Galiano Island, a one-hour ferry ride from British Columbia's capital, Victoria.

Despite fighting an advanced form of macular degeneration, she came out to meet us as we walked down her cobbled lane. Tall and stately, with a warm British accent, she delivered the much-anticipated hugs as she welcomed us into her home.

Eventually we saw her in action at the computer. Forced by her failing eyesight to wear strong reading glasses, she needed additional enlargement in the form of a magnifying glass held up against the computer's glowing terminal. It was evident that the process of writing for her had become almost as painful and slow as carving hieroglyphics into a stone tablet.

Margaret's thorough research and intimate knowledge of her husband's life voyage made her secure in the knowledge that the sailing part of the book was as accurate as could be. For the mountaineering section, she drew story elements from the several books that have been produced by team members, as well as the unpublished personal diaries of Lloyd Gallagher, Peter Spear and Blair. When it came to verifying details of Blair's story in the context of the 1982 expedition, she sent versions of her manuscript to several team members.

In October 2007, in a touching scene at the 25th reunion of the team, held at the Whyte Museum of the Canadian Rockies in Banff, Margaret got a chance to meet many of those she had been writing about so painstakingly for the previous few years. At this event, which had drawn eight team members and one Sherpa, as well as a couple hundred supporters, a hush fell over the room when Margaret stood up and thanked the team for showing the courage it took to retrieve Blair's body from the icefall and give him a respectful send-off.

Against difficult odds, Margaret has lived her dream of completing this book. The interwoven destinies of two men and those they knew and loved now live on within its pages.

Pat Morrow
September 2008

ACKNOWLEDGEMENTS

In writing this story I am grateful for the support of my friends Audrey Thomas, Harold and Karen Callaghan and the late Jane Rule, all of whom encouraged me. I thank my grandchildren, Michael Thorne, who appears in the chapter "The Old Man and the Boy," Kika Thorne and Erik Anderson for their constant support. Michael and Erik typed my handwritten manuscript into the computer and Kika helped with the photographic images. It became a family affair.

I thank Shera Street and Gloria Olsen for finding the equipment to help me to finish the book when my eyesight presented difficulties.

I thank Christie McLaren for her thoughtful editorial work.

Climbers on the 1982 Canadian ascent of Mount Everest, along with Dr. Stephen Bezruchka, the altitude specialist, provided excellent information about the expedition after Blair's diary abruptly ended. Particular thanks to Pat Morrow for information, support and his spectacular photographic illustrations.

George Griffiths shared his voyage on his "little ship" *Kairos* through tape recordings made as he sailed. Although the background thunder of storms and the sound of the boat working cannot be captured in words alone, I believe his words do succeed in sweeping the reader along on his adventure. I am thankful for them. With help such as this, long after these adventures took place, I have tried to show the way it used to be in earlier times.

Kairos is now owned by Jack Schooley of Orcas Island in Washington State. From photographs of her restoration that Jack has sent me, I am grateful to know that she is receiving excellent care in her new life as *Able* of Friday Harbor.

INTRODUCTION

This is a story of a man who, in old age, lived his dreams. I hear him still, in the sea, in the wind.

George described himself as a very simple man. He was born in a red brick house in Portsmouth, England, in 1914 to Ena and George Griffiths. The dream of his that grew as years went by was to sail a small boat, alone, in self-reliance, propelled by the wind, steered by the sky, across the Atlantic. After he moved to western Canada, the dream included sailing home to British Columbia with the winds and currents used by the ancients. Many years later, at the end of this long sail, he was awarded the Alec Rose Trophy, given by Sir Alec Rose to members of Britain's Royal Naval Sailing Association for exceptional seamanship.

When George left on his voyage from England he was 66; he was 67 when he reached Canada. He was 71 when he climbed to the base of Mount Everest to lay down his burden of grief at the feet of the Goddess Mother of the World....

But his story should begin at the beginning. It is a story woven together from tape recordings, diaries, conversations and letters. He wrote marvellous letters, in which he talked of school and of life in the red brick house.

George's father joined the Royal Navy as a boy and rose rapidly through the ranks to a commission. He was intelligent, funny, entirely disciplined and seldom home. George's mother Ena was an energetic woman who knitted beautiful socks and scarves for the men away on ships in the First World War. George's earliest memory was of the day his mother left him and his heart broke.

An aunt had come to look after him. She said his mother would be back in 10 days. George, not quite three years old, had little concept of 10 days, but he waited faithfully, often standing on an armchair in the bay window of the "front room" of the red brick house, looking for his mother coming down the street.

His fidelity was rewarded only with betrayal. His mother came home with a girl baby in her arms, clearly a replacement for him, for she cooed over it and rocked it as she used to rock him. He must have been in some way unsatisfactory.

George was excluded from his mother's bedroom when the infant was fed. "We must be alone, just the two of us, when she has her dinner." George always had his dinner with his mother and aunt. Why couldn't this stupid baby?

One day when the new child had been fed and bathed and cooed over and left on a cushion in his mother's bedroom, George crept in and, with all the piled-up frustrations of a two-year-old, took his mother's large handbag and put it on the baby to squash it. Then he left home on his tricycle.

The aunt, still helping out, and drawn to the bedroom by the baby's strong objections, found young George two blocks away and brought him home in disgrace.

He thought his life couldn't get any worse, but it did. A few weeks later a strange man came to the house and got into bed with his mother.

George was told the man was Daddy and that he remembered Daddy. But he didn't remember. Daddy was away on a battleship in the war. This man wasn't on a battleship at all. He was walking around their house as if he owned it. Didn't this man know that only he, the child, had access to the warmth of his mother's bed when, first thing in the morning, he crawled in and they shared a cup of tea, his mostly milk? Now, the morning after Daddy arrived, his mother's bedroom door was closed to him.

But suddenly Daddy was standing beside his bed, wrapping his son in a blanket against the cold of the house before the fires were lit. In case he should trip on the blanket as he came downstairs, Daddy carried him to the "front room" window. Outside, the world was spread with a magic carpet of snow. Everything was beautiful: the street, the garden tree, the house across the road. Everything glistened, perfectly smooth except for the tracks of the pony and cart delivering the morning milk.

Daddy smelled slightly of pipe tobacco. He held the child in a tight embrace, cocooned in the warm blanket. In that moment shared with his father, George's heart was healed.

For his fourth birthday, George's aunt returned for a visit and brought a magnificent present. She gave him a sailboat with a moveable mainsail and foresail and a pennant on the masthead. It was the admiration of the children on the block as he walked beside his aunt to the park.

There they headed for the pond and he slipped his boat into the water. George reached to adjust the mainsail to the wind, already feeling instinctively the needs of a little ship under sail. Later, he didn't remember the cold impact of water as he fell in. He only recalled the humiliation of walking back home, his sailor suit dripping, past the other giggling children.

His mother was disheartened when she opened the front door.

"I might have known," she muttered.

"I only took my eyes off him for a moment, Ena," protested his aunt.

When he turned five, George's academic and spiritual education were entrusted to the infants' class of a school run by Jesuits. The Brothers moulded his character with care, paying particular attention to mortal sin. But George loved school, and in the Christmas play he was proud to be the front end of a camel.

George now wore a school uniform, much admired by his little sister Eileen. But at weekends his mother still dressed him in sailor suits, which she sewed herself. Hopefully she stitched on the sleeve the badge of a petty officer.

Childhood ended at age 12. George was to be trained for the sea. He left the warmth of the red brick house and reported to Naval Training College, HMS *Worcester*, a 50-gun frigate of 1,500 tons lent by the Admiralty and moored in the Thames. His father, keen, exacting and popular, continued to advance in rank in the Royal Navy, and George Sr. had ambitions for his son beyond the badges his mother had sewn onto his sailor suit.

On HMS *Worcester*, strong men reined in the young George's spirit. A 1930 newspaper advertisement for the elite naval training school read: "A disciplined school life. Before a man can command he must obey. To make a man of your son, apply to Secretary, Worcester." George, as a youth, tried to be everything people wanted him to be, and began to stammer. But he was not unhappy. He learned to row. He was excellent at sports. He studied the intricacies of charts, old and new, and he mapped the currents and winds of the world. He learned science and mathematics, and to read the sky. He learned navigation. He learned to tell the truth and to pray on Thursday nights that the friendships formed at the school would not be broken by sin or worldly cares. He learned "manning the yards," when the cadets rushed up ladders to stand in rows high on the yardarms of the training ship.

George learned to love the ocean for its moods and its beauty, and grew to be confident at sea. To boost his confidence on land, he bought a red MG sports car the year he graduated. That, along with a pair of plus-four trousers, and he felt ready for the world.

But this was the 1930s, the years of minimizing and disarming the Navy, the years of the Depression. George felt lucky to get a job as captain of a vessel in the North Sea fishing fleet; with a master's certificate, he was a Master Mariner, qualified to command ships. His father, since retiring from the Navy as Commander, had become captain of King George V's racing yacht *Britannia*, a very British ship with even the chair cushions designed as Union Jacks. George Sr. was uncertain about his son's red MG and tweed cap worn at an angle. The spirit so carefully moulded was becoming a trifle devil-may-care.

That George was keen on sports, fond of the outdoors, eager to stretch himself physically, his father appreciated. But the other side of him, the voracious reader and collector of old books, the interest in poetry, philosophy, religions and aboriginal beliefs, the photographer, the romantic, were all beyond his father's comprehension. When George quoted Camus after darkness fell – "The marvel of night, when the hope of love is one with the rain, the sky, and the earth's silences" – his father was, so to speak, all at sea.

When George's training was needed by the Royal Navy in the Second World War, and he served in the Battle of the Atlantic in 1941, there was a sharing again between father and son. But George spoke little of those hard and bitter years.

After he worked in the English Channel as a diver and frogman on the Pipeline under the Ocean, or PLUTO, which helped supply the invasion of Normandy in 1944, George's underwater training took him to Bermuda, at war's end, to command a salvage vessel operating in the Atlantic Ocean. In 1957 as a Lieutenant Commander, he left the Royal Navy and came to Canada, a homecoming for his Canadian wife with their two young sons, Blair and Mark.

George was now an immigrant, ready to take any job he felt able to do. From being in charge of men at sea, he became, as he described it, a virtual deckhand on a little boat that sailed the British Columbia coast carrying an appraiser who assessed property values for taxation. In the coastal wilderness there are many properties not accessible by road. Far from feeling hard done by, George revelled in the scenery, in the moods of the sea and the sky, and in the wildlife. Seldom was he seen without his camera. In reduced circumstances financially, he felt rich.

One day when he regretted not taking his camera was the time he met a bear on the trail. He was on his way to visit friends, tramping through the forest undergrowth from the boat moorage in the mouth of the Kleena Kleena River, where treed slopes holding mist dipped to the sea.

George had made friends, it seems, all the way up the coast, and now on his way to visit Bill and Lou in their house in the woods he stopped dead upon meeting the bear, and spoke quietly to it as he had been warned to do if he should be confronted by one. The animal faced him and eyed him, an unexpected stranger, when Lou came onto the deck.

"Come up, George. Nice to see you."

Couldn't Lou see there was a black bear on the trail?

"Don't mind the bear. That's Bruno. Just walk by him, he practically lives with us."

Bears that have bonded with humans can still be treacherous. And this bear smelled awful.

"Excuse me, Bruno," George said as he edged by, feeling that any animal that smelled like that should be asking his pardon, not the other way round.

On the deck of his friend's house, drinking tea with Lou, George said how sorry he was not to have brought his camera.

"There's tomorrow. Come back and we'll have more tea on the deck. Bill will be home, too."

The next day, George walked through the undergrowth, this time with his camera at the ready, and was delighted when Bruno came crashing out of the undergrowth into his camera sights.

"Hello," George greeted him. "Let's take you full face." The bear obediently faced him.

"Now, profile please, Bruno."

The bear turned away, confused.

"Come on up," shouted Lou.

"I'm photographing Bruno."

The bear didn't like all this shouting. He looked edgy.

"That's not Bruno. Bruno's 'round the back."

Those bear pictures were probably George's favourites from his wildlife album, but unfortunately the very early colour has faded with time.

While George was on the little boat he studied for examinations to become a property appraiser. Once he qualified, he worked for the British Columbia Hydro and Power Authority in a little grey room with sealed windows looking onto Vancouver Harbour. For the first time since childhood, he had turned his back on the sea, and his sense of self-reliance and oneness with Creation now became nurtured through mountain climbing. When his sons were old enough, he took them on his adventures.

One summer, in 1968, a friend who was planning a long holiday in Nova Scotia lent me her house on Salt Spring Island to care for and enjoy while she was away. Walking along the beach in the late afternoon I saw a man skimming pebbles with all the glee of a boy. When he turned to smile I thought I knew him.

"I've seen you before," I told him.

"I met you at our office Christmas party. George Griffiths."

I too worked for BC Hydro, in a little grey room similar to his but 13 floors lower. Apart from the raucous Christmas party, known as the "bum-pinchers' ball," we had never met. As a land supervisor, he was on this little island off Canada's west coast to look over the route planned for a new transmission line that would require several easements over private property. He was expecting to eat in a nearby café and I asked him back for a meal, warning him to expect nothing fancy.

Eating supper, we looked through the window at the darkening sky while the sea held onto the day. When darkness came we went outside to look at the night. He told me of the stars and named each one. Then he told me of his dreams and I knew they were entrusted to few people and I must carry them with care. As we talked I seemed to be seeing a caged bird beating its wings against the bars, and the cage would not open until retirement brought time for the dreams to be lived.

When George explained his plan to buy a little boat and single-hand her across the Atlantic, he observed that this was no great feat. It was often done, but he planned to equip his small vessel with only the basics. No newfangled electronic stuff.

"It can let you down," he explained. "You have to be self-reliant."

As I listened I was doing a little mental arithmetic. If he retired at 65 and spent time finding and fitting out his boat, and after crossing the Atlantic, sailed the Pacific back home to Canada, he would be an old man even when he first set sail. He read my thoughts and laughed.

"What slaves we are to chronological age. These things bully us."

I asked him about his family and he became despondent. He was full of self-doubt after a failed marriage, and missing his home and time with his two sons.

We left the subject and went for a last walk along the beach. As the wind strengthened and shreds of cloud blew across the moon, we ran into the rising wind, laughing. When we parted for the night he took my hand.

"Thank you for letting me be a boy," he said.

The next weekend we met and wandered around an art gallery. Together we bought a whale carved out of maple so smooth it looked as though the water was shining on its back. This was our first sharing but not our last.

I had been a widow for 11 years, and my children, Corinna and Michael, were grown. I was not looking for a new relationship, but some things come best into our lives when unsought. We married and walked into old age together, building a house of cedar on Galiano Island, off Canada's western mainland. The thought of this home would sustain George often on his long sail as he lived his dream.

For 10 years after we met and married he worked in his grey office and I in mine. Through the office window he looked down at the little boats like toys making for sea or coming home to Vancouver Harbour, and his heart went with them. One evening in the office he scribbled in his diary: "Working late. The sea and the sky are one, the colour of smoke, as evening comes. Little boats scurry home to harbour before nightfall. One day I will have my own little boat."

George began the research for his own little boat as the day of retirement approached, and it absorbed him. Some days his look was glazed as though his thoughts were totally elsewhere. One morning at breakfast I remarked: "I think we need a four-hole toaster. We're having rather a lot of visitors."

Without looking up, George answered, "The problem is they don't sail to windward very well." I pointed out that this kind of reply was getting difficult for meaningful conversation, and George promised to pay better attention. But he had already begun to live his dream, immersed in the study of various boats and their performance. He was looking for something basic. Complex technology, he said, is unreliable on a small boat in a storm. Simplicity is the most dependable.

On his retirement from BC Hydro in early 1979, George's colleagues gave him a party, binoculars and a floater jacket, and said farewell. He went later that year to England to look for his boat. He found her hidden from the world, lying under a tarpaulin. And he bought her, a little sloop called *Nymph of Lorne*, built by McGruer & Co. Ltd. in Scotland for the 1961 Boat Show in London. More than 60 years had passed since his aunt had given him his first little sailboat. This was the first real seagoing vessel George had ever owned.

He changed her name to *Kairos*. George had read Ivan Illich, and decided that his *Kairos* meant, as in Greek, the dividing line between stillness and activity. The dividing line between dreaming and decision. Some years later, after sailing *Kairos* first across the Atlantic and then the Pacific, George was awarded Britain's Alec Rose Trophy for exceptional seamanship. In England to receive the honour, he felt Sir

Alec's warm handshake. That is when he believed at last, in old age, that he really had lived his dream.

Those on an adventure, meeting a challenge, will invariably leave behind someone who waits. Too early in time for communication by satellite, George steered by the sky and kept in touch with me from the ocean by speaking into a tape recorder and mailing the tape when he got into port. This way I travelled with him, hearing his voice against the wind and the workings of the boat, sharing his journey of discovery within himself. In his long solitary nights on the companionway steps, watching through the porthole for the first rays of the new day, he came to realize that we all carry the hope of the morning light within us, no matter how long and dark the night. This thought sustained him through the grief that lay ahead.

When George was dying he told me that we shall meet again in the new day. As I write this story in my 88th year, I look forward to that bright morning.

I have written this account faithfully from tapes, diaries, letters, reports and conversations we had together, weaving it carefully like a special piece of cloth. It begins after George has left Cornwall, in England, to cross the Atlantic in little *Kairos* and come home again through the Panama Canal to Canada. He has run into a storm off Cape Finisterre, off the west coast of Spain. To be blown inside the shallow Bay of Biscay could spell tragedy.

Alone in the screaming wind he talks to me on the tape recorder...

The Oceans

OCTOBER 17, 1980 · Biscay, southwesterly gale, Force 8. Lundy, Fastnet and the Irish Sea northeast 6 to gale 8, locally severe gale 9. Squally showers ... I'm battened down on the edge of the Bay of Biscay. Can you hear the wind screaming in the shrouds? It's past one o'clock in the morning and bitterly cold. That was the radio weather forecast, and it's blowing Force 8, possibly Force 9. There is no moon tonight, just deep blackness, the shrill of the wind and the deep thunder of the sea. If I stick my head outside the cabin, saltwater flecks lash my face and eyes like whips. My little ship, a little over 28 feet over all and 21 on the waterline, moves well and finds some rhythm in this chaos. And I am in tune with her, listening to the sounds of her working.

It's two hours since I put on oilskins and harness and tied a flashlight to the coach-house roof while I got both sails down. All is secured and I'm just sitting this one out. With the leeboards up, lashed in my bunk, I watch the swinging shadows of the Tilley lantern, tied to restrict its movement. A full four days out from England and bound for Tenerife to begin the Atlantic crossing and then sail to Canada, I'm concerned about this loss of time because of weather.

At all costs I must not get blown inside the Bay.

I was late leaving Cremyll in Cornwall, later in the year than I had intended, because I was anxious to have all done and well done rather than fix some things on the way. I've only come 200 miles and that's no record. But I'm far enough out from shore that all ties to land have gone, and the roaring sea is my element. This pitching port bunk is my bed and above it is my bookcase, where I keep my heavy navigation and pilotage books, held in place by a wooden bar. The starboard bunk is piled high with provisions, tied well down. On the shelf above it is the radio, secured with a lashing.

The mahogany of the cabin panelling shines warmly in the light of the Tilley lamp, and in the corner is a little Pansy stove that burns charcoal. For extra light I have three gimballed bright brass oil lamps. It sounds cozy. But the boat below decks is full of condensation. My bunk is wet. My socks and clothes are wet.

The chill of my whole being tells me to hurry south as soon as possible to let a drying wind blow through the boat. But here we sit all battened down in the screaming darkness.

I dream. If this Iceland low moves down, I might be able to get a foresail up and pick up the westerlies. Then we'd really scoot south to the bright warming sun of the Spanish coast.

The boat is riding well and I listen for any unusual noise. I'm waiting for the dawn, that blessed morning light after the long dark. It will always come predictably, never late, never early, and so I wait on my step. Each night I watch. Sleep can come in the afternoon when shipping can see us. Night is for waiting and listening.

OCTOBER 18 · There is still a storm Force 9 warning on the radio and I am still on the edge of Biscay, snugged down in a wild sea that breaks over the cockpit.

About three o'clock this morning I took a short break from my watch and drowsed in my bunk with everything secure. Suddenly the sea and the wind together made a noise like an express train. With a bang the little ship went over and shuddered up again. The oil lamp above the stove went out and my head took a beating from a cascade of navigation and pilotage books from the bookcase above.

I rubbed my head and floundered in the dark amid the pile of books. The stove, which is not gimballed, had jumped up three to four inches as it swung upward, knocking out the lamp. If that was the angle of heel, we must have gone over about 80 degrees.

I waited for the dawn, that first blessed ray in the dark sky, wondering what damage I would find on deck. At first light I secured my harness and battled the wind to make a tour of inspection. The only result of the knock-down is a broken lashing on the dodgers! Stout little ship!

The boat continues riding well and I listen to the sea. You can generally hear the big waves crest. Hold on now! It's past. Here comes another! Woof! We slid over. We rise to the top of the world with the crest just under the boat, then down into the dark grey trough and up, in a wind that wrenches at my clothing if I go on deck. She's a good little boat and has taken only a little water into the bilge. I scarcely need to pump her out. The wetness is all in the cabin!

I have a problem eating. If I don't eat I may become lethargic, but I can't cook with so much movement in the boat. I'm really living on cereal and powdered milk with honey. But I think hot soup would warm me, and I'll clean some of the condensation out of the little cups on the stove and put on the pressure cooker.

Through the porthole I see grey cloud banked on a black ocean, but there is a break in the sky. An onshore wind would put me right into the Bay, which would be disastrous, but in fact the wind is taking me, hove-to, in the direction I want to go.

I can see a glimpse of the sun and at noon I'll get a couple of sun-shots and find out exactly where we are. When things quiet down I'll get some sail up. We'll go quickly toward Spain, toward the sun, the drying winds.

It's still blowing Force 8 and very cold.

OCTOBER 19 · Still after storm. By dark last night the wind had died away. After screaming sea, we are silent.

I hoisted the genoa (or jenny) and main, but we scarcely moved in the stillness, and I lashed them again. Now, without wind, we make no progress southward toward the sun.

As I keep watch through the night, I plan my chores for tomorrow. In the knock-down I lost my bread knife. The boom has a split at the end and must be lashed. And the rudder has started to act up. If I run the engines a few minutes that will top up the batteries.

As I keep watch on the companionway step under the lantern, looking through the porthole the dark sky is turning red, then deep red, angry and beautiful, and I rest here alone, a small part of the universe, watching the first light stain the ocean under a sky the colour of blood. There will be a storm later, but now my heart thrills to the majesty of the moment.

OCTOBER 20 · In the early light I looked at the gathering storm and found the rudder was jammed amidships. I sat in the cockpit and thought: "Here am I in the middle of the Bay of Biscay, with a sou'wester brewing by the look of the sky, and I can't steer."

In my aloneness I have developed two voices. Authority is something of a tyrant, and Submission tends to argue but always gives in. Authority said: "Here's a fine kettle of fish – but never panic at sea." Submission said obediently: "No, sir," and then added defiantly: "I wasn't going to."

I sat very quietly.

Then I began to notice that every now and again the tiller would jump back, and when it did it caught the self-steering. This must be making the steering jam. I tried putting a soft wedge behind the tiller to stop it jumping. When that seemed to make a difference I held it in place with yards and yards of cellotape. Now we're steering well, moving south on a reefed main, and very happy.

It's 9:00 a.m. and I've worked around the boat for three hours. I still can't find the bread knife – it's shot underneath somewhere. I'm going to have a monumental breakfast and then prepare some stew in the pressure cooker for tonight. I still have my oilskins on and they're wet. I've put protective canvas over the bunk but the cushions have

5

become damp. I've put the blankets in plastic bags but they're damp. I bless my woolly hat. Wet through it may be, but it still keeps the old head warm. The wind is southerly Force 6. I got the jib up with a fight and *Kairos* is doing three to four knots, very bumpy and tiring. The wind is moaning, the sea confused, the foredeck covered in water and spray.

But I've found the bread knife!

OCTOBER 21 · Last night I longed to climb into my bunk to try to find warmth. Authority said, "Don't you get into that bunk, Griffiths," and Submission answered, "No, sir, I wasn't going to." So I'm keeping watch in the darkness, sitting on my step with a cold bottom. Until 4:00 a.m. there's a bit of a moon, a special treat, a companion in my world.

Bang! We just hit a hole. The wind has really piped up and we're going like a train on a well-reefed main and a very small jib. I wait for the dawn, that hope of the new day.

OCTOBER 22 · Dawn came faintly pink, the morning was overcast, and now we have one of those dirty fall days. I have been busy with chores. My sweater is cold and damp, my hair is on end and Authority thinks me a very unkempt sailor. I ignore him.

I have made my stew for tomorrow. I usually cook up some soybeans and when they are soft I add something tasty like Marks and Spencer's canned curried chicken. All my tins are colour-coded, so that when the labels come off in the dampness life won't be full of surprises.

The condensation in the cabin is worse, dripping onto my charts. My bread has gone bad and I gave it to some terns who refused to eat it. I have plenty of Ryvita.

"Griffiths, you drink some nice hot soup," says Authority.

"Don't want hot soup, sir," says Submission, and drinks it anyway. I need my good body, my strength, my skill. If I neglect myself at sea it would be disrespectful to the sea that can take me at any time if I am stupid, or forgetful, or take her lightly. But I have always felt at home on the water.

Here in my strong little ship, the first I have owned, with the wind to propel me and the sky and the horizon to steer by, I am never alone. I talk to myself. To Authority. To Margaret, who I know is always with me, on the tape recorder. I talk often to the boat. The boat and I are becoming one. Even when I'm dozing in the afternoon I know if something isn't right with her, if the rhythm alters, if sounds and motions change, or if another vessel is nearby. At sea you develop an extra sense. The boat and I are both doing our best and I speak not of "I" but "we." We have become a team in which her sounds give me her messages.

As the day wears on Authority hands out various instructions. "You must get a bearing with the RDF on Finisterre."

"Yes, sir."

"You must make better speed southward, to the warm drying winds."

"I'll try, sir." And to show willing I put off as long as possible taking down the jib. On we fly, like a bird.

As night falls I'm still on a well-reefed main and a very small jib, approaching the Spanish Coast. The wind is such that I should be farther out to sea, but I'll keep my watch and we'll hang on as we are until daylight.

I watch for the dawn. Soon the first few rays will flood the sky and lift my heart.

OCTOBER 23 · Three eggs are boiling in the teakettle as we run down the Spanish-Portuguese coast. I'm past Finisterre. I got my bearing on the RDF yesterday and I'm 50 or 60 miles out from land.

Daylight gets later every day as we slip further into winter. This morning brought one of those dirty fall days, grey and overcast, with no sight of land.

My world is small and my problems narrow. Shall I take off my oilskins and stretch out comfortably on the bunk, knowing I am in water too deep for fishboats and out of shipping lanes? Or shall I leave the oilskins on, in case there is an emergency? The decision is made. With a gale warning and the wind piping up, the oilskins and boots stay on and I don't stretch out. I have reefed the main, ready for the gale, and when it blows harder I'll take down the mid-jenny.

Early today there were other people in my little world, giving a strange feeling. Another sailboat appeared on my empty ocean, five or six miles inside me on exactly the same course. She was much bigger and faster than we are and soon vanished into the grey haze ahead. I wondered who she was, where she came from, how many she carried and whether they wondered about me.

OCTOBER 24 · More company! I was soaking my dried soybeans ready for the evening stew when I saw two Dutch naval vessels astern. When they deliberately turned toward me and came in closer I hoisted my flag, the red maple leaf. Young men, mostly born since the Second World War, cheered and called and cheered again. More men came running onto the deck, waving to me, and two men were filming. I believe it must be a wave to my Canadian flag for the Canadian liberation of Holland, because although we may forget, I'm told the Dutch people never will.

I watched them sail on. The shouting grew fainter, the ships grew smaller. Still I watched. They had gone and I was alone, and still I watched. The air had been full of human voices.

Authority scolded me, giving orders, and still I watched where the two vessels had faded away in the grey late autumn afternoon.

"You're standing dreaming because other men appeared in your world like a mirage and called to you," nagged Authority. "You have to press on as hard as you can to get south. Get busy."

Submission said, "Yes, sir, I'll check my position."

At 4:30 in the afternoon I got some good sights and was pleased with them until I realized they put me well behind my estimated position. Then I felt depressed. Authority scolded and the wind died. I lowered the genoa and lashed it to the rail. The main is noisy, slatting around in a big sea on a windless day. A weather forecast will help me to decide whether to lower the main and stop the noise or try to sail. Authority is silent on the subject.

OCTOBER 25 · I fixed my position at dawn. It was a clear sky and I could see Sirius, the moon and Venus clearly. The wind piped up and the weather forecast gave southwesterly wind five to six with occasional gale. Now we're pressing on hard with a reefed main. The mid-genoa has developed a slit in the patch and needs repair as soon as it can be made. Night falls early as it comes close to winter. I'm going along well at four to five knots under a beautiful sky full of stars.

OCTOBER 26 · All my world last night was flooded with moonlight, and we pounded along on a silver-flecked sea, close-hauled on the port tack at a list of 25 degrees. The weather forecast gave Force 6 to 8 gale, and Authority told me to eat something while I could still cook. I felt lethargic and couldn't think of food, and I defied him, skipping supper altogether. Keeping watch on my step, I waited for the day.

Daylight brought a bad sign – a sky that looked as though it had been scratched by a hand. Trails right across the sky seemed to be from planes going into Madeira. I found them good company!

The wind is about six-plus, and as we kept up speed during the day, my spirits rose and I ate some stew. I felt very happy and optimistic, making excellent time now toward Tenerife. I have just got a very good sun-sight and I'm pleased with my position. The wind is steady and I'm continuing close-hauled.

OCTOBER 27 · Today I wept.

I had spent the morning happily attending to chores in spite of a 25-degree list and the boat pounding. I cleaned the stove, ran the engine for a short time, which charged the batteries, and I filled the oil lamps. I was eating a late lunch of dried apricots and nuts with Ryvita, happy that the wind was holding steady. It was hard, bumpy going with the sea right on our nose. Suddenly, there was a deafening bang and the boat seemed to jump up in the water. I rushed on deck without my harness. Both my twin backstays, which help to support the mast, were sinking in the sea.

I dashed forward, still without my lifeline, to try to save the mast and got down both mainsail and foresail. With all the speed I could, I lashed them. Then I secured all halyards aft, to try to hold up the mast.

I shackled the topping lift out of the horse and hauled tight on the mast winch. I worked quickly but still the early winter dark had almost come before I felt the mast was really secure.

Now I'm very tired; I'll wait for the light, the inspiration of the new day, before effecting temporary repairs. There is so much to do if I am not to lose the boat. I've given myself a list of instructions.

My feelings and emotions must be held on a tight rein. I must eat. And I must sleep.

OCTOBER 28 · I didn't sleep. I tied the swinging lantern very tightly to keep it still, and lying in my bunk as the boat drifted I quietly worked out step by step the best way to handle the situation so that I can hope to save *Kairos*. Confidence came with the new day. At first light I had a good breakfast of three eggs and Ovaltine. I knew now in my head what I must do, and it was all finished before 7:00 a.m.

I tightened up both cap shrouds. Then I got up the spare shroud and shackled it to the port backstay bottle screw and topping lift. I hauled taut on the topping lift – the shackle was just two inches short of the masthead block. I bulldogged the downhaul of the topping lift to a bottle screw shackled to a spare lug in the chainplate (bless Theo Mashford at Mashford's Boatyard for insisting on the spare lug). After experimenting, I secured the spinnaker halyards to a becket held taut with a handy billy secured to the starboard quarter.

I looked the mast over and felt sure it was alright, and the temporary rig would hold it securely if I spared it all I could. With reefed main and inter-genoa we made sail. The sea was flat calm with a big swell. My sights put me much further back than I had dead-reckoned, and I cannot believe we drifted so far in the wrong direction in the short time we were disabled.

There is no wind. I must decide on a plan, and the best seems to be to sail for Gibraltar. I feel there will be less hassle there with Customs, and I don't want to try to effect repairs in a language I can't speak or understand.

So, Gibraltar it is, and the challenge is going to be rounding Cape St. Vincent with the slowness of this temporary rig. Although I pray for more wind, the last thing that should happen now is to be off the Cape in a Force 9 sou'wester.

The early evening brought big black clouds, blacker than thunder, banking in the west. The horizon was dark and grey. I changed down to the inter-jenny and reefed the main. The weather forecast warned of the coming gale.

At midnight I got two good sights of the moon and Venus. Then long feathers of cloud blew across the moon. I watched the sky, made a cup of Ovaltine and I'm sitting in my crippled ship, waiting for the storm.

OCTOBER 29 · It blew hard all last night and I hoisted the storm jib. The temporary rigging appears to be holding well. Water and spray are everywhere. At first light the wind died and I cleared a tangled log-line from the self-steering paddle, hanging over the stern and getting very wet. The wind now is cyclonic, blowing a little from the north, then dying, leaving ugly swells and everything banging about.

The sails are slatting and the Aries self-steering not coping. I have only made good 15 miles since the morning sights and have been hand-steering two hours. I should have the genoa up but I'm fearful for the mast. I feel very low indeed. The dream. The reality! Then a fly walked over my head and I smiled. Spanish fly!

A big bulk carrier passed me on the starboard side. I must keep a good lookout. I have no radar reflector now – it was on top of the mast and I lost it. It's doubtful if radar screens would pick up a small wooden boat with all this sea clutter.

At midnight there was a fair weather report. The night was quite beautiful and I could smell the land. I must round Cape St. Vincent before the weather breaks. Perhaps I should risk the mast a little. I decided to do that and hoisted the main with two rolls.

OCTOBER 30 · A forecast for continuing fair weather came in loud and clear. I went wild and used half a kettleful of warm water and had a wash-down in the cockpit. Then I cooked my soybean stew for tonight in the pressure cooker and washed the pressure cooker in my used washing water.

Sights at ten o'clock this morning placed me 60 degrees West of Lisbon. I debated whether to alter course and run in, but stayed with my plan to continue on to make Gibraltar for repairs. If the weather turns against me I can always run back. I'm now sailing with the genoa, hoping to reach the latitude of Cape St. Vincent before the weather breaks.

I need to know my position but I took an hour to work out one sight. What's the matter with me?

As the light faded there was a gale warning and I took an extra roll in the main and changed down to the inter-genoa. But an hour later the wind had died. The air was heavy and sultry. Big black clouds piled up to the west. The forecast predicted the wind would veer northwest and that would blow us around Cape St. Vincent. I gave thanks.

I looked over my little crippled ship with her temporary rig, bow lights lashed with tape because the bolts had pulled out of the wet wood chocks, scars on the foredeck, tattered dodgers, all brasswork green, lashed rudderhead, weathered topsides. Then I added to yesterday's bean stew a tin of asparagus soup and another of my favourite curried chicken. I followed this with Ryvita and honey. Then I dozed.

OCTOBER 31 · When the alarm clock rang at three o'clock this morning, I looked out at a blood-red dawn. With the wind Force 3 to 4 from the south, I changed the foresail up to the genoa. Standing at the foot of the mast I could see the mast top bending from the force of the sail. This is the limit of wind strength on the genoa. At all costs I must not lose the mast now, as we try to round the Cape.

In early afternoon, just as I was waiting for the promised north-westerly wind, thinking I cannot weather the Cape with the wind as it is, there was a shift of a point or two and we are now making good a course of 150 degrees. This is just what we need. I'm a little slow backing into the short steep seas, but most grateful. On picking up Cape St. Vincent on the RDF, I celebrated with a good meal of corned beef, carrots and spices.

Now, running hard through a night as black as the inside of a sweep's hat I'm approaching main shipping lanes and must keep a good lookout. With the boat starting to pound I got the genoa down to save the mast. The log-line is wrapped again five or six times around the self-steering and I need a third hand to hold the flashlight. I can't clear it.

NOVEMBER 1 · The forecast is gales for Finisterre and Trafalgar. With no moon, torrential rain, and the wind increasing, I felt I had no wish, in the first hours of the morning, to take the main down, but it had to be done. It could be tricky with no proper topping lift, but all went well. With confidence, at dawn, I tackled the log-line, still wrapped around the self-steering paddle. Doubly secured with both lifeline and main sheet, I climbed over the stern onto the self-steering framework and cleared some turns around the paddle, but not all. The water up to my waist was not cold. Climbing aboard, I finished the job with a boat-hook. By 9:35 a.m. I was running fast before Force 6 to 7 northerly winds, but became depressed because I was finding it difficult to get sights, and I must establish my position. Then, looking to windward I saw a rainbow, a shout of joy in the sky and my spirits rose again. It was an omen. I ran all day before the northerlies and as daylight faded I altered course to round the Cape. I should see the light on Cape St. Vincent before dawn.

As I keep watch a coaster passes me close to port. The stars are out, the sky is clearing and I am still running before the wind.

NOVEMBER 2 · Just after midnight I saw the loom of Cape St. Vincent light. I hope the wind does not go easterly.

As I sat on my step, keeping watch and waiting for the promise of daylight, the sun rose yellow with purple-tinted clouds, and I saw a light on the port side. One, two, three, four. Cape St. Vincent! We're around it! Rain and wind suddenly changed to a pleasant morning and seven gannets skimmed the water close astern with a grace that lifted my heart. I have seen so few birds....

My navigation is slipping. Early this morning I got good sights of Venus and Sirius but it takes an effort now to complete the plot. I must get some sleep during the day to keep good watch at night. There are many ships about and I appear to be north of outward-bound shipping lanes out of Cadiz.

The sea now has big swells and we are getting rain again before the wind. I pray the wind will not go easterly tonight.

As darkness comes I can see the loom of Santa Maria light and we shall soon be in the lee of the African coast.

NOVEMBER 3 · I have been standing on deck dreaming, with the rain running off my oilskins. When I get to Gibraltar I can have a shower. Warm water will run over my shoulders and down my back, and there will be hot steaming coffee and a white tablecloth. I'd like to wear a clean shirt when I go ashore. I'm on my second shirt now from the dirty laundry bag, but I do have a clean one left for harbour.

Authority, who hasn't had much to say lately, suddenly snaps out: "Griffiths, get moving, you're gazing into space again. You know it won't be easy to weather Cape Trafalgar and you should be worrying."

To spite him I cat-napped until I suddenly picked up the radio station in Cadiz, very loudly, on my RDF. Tomorrow I will see Cadiz.

NOVEMBER 4 · It was a dirty dawn with driving rain and squalls and black, banking clouds. Watching the shoreline I still have some sea-room for the next four to five hours, but the wind is backing to the south and I am heading north of east. This is getting dangerous. As I keep watch the wind turns anticyclonic and the broadcast came in loudly, giving a gale warning.

In the early afternoon I saw through the glasses the buildings in Cadiz. A big bulk carrier and a small coaster are jibbing around in the harbour, perhaps waiting for the weather to moderate. The water is shallowing sharply and the waves pile up with steep fronts. One swamped the cockpit and left me spluttering.

I'm only two miles off the breakwater and I'm unhappy about this position in relation to the gale warning. I decided to risk the mast a little more and hoist the jenny and shake the reef out of the main. Just after lunch I came about onto the port tack and before dark I ran the engine for three-quarters of an hour to get some offing from the coastline. On this tack I should have some sea-room if it blows southeasterly. As I ate my supper I watched the twinkling lights of Cadiz.

But I'm tired. I had hoped to be in Gibraltar early this morning, but I still have 200 miles to go in busy shipping lanes. Oh Lord, please give me a fair wind.

NOVEMBER 5 · I'm keeping watch on my step at one in the morning.

The boom was slatting and I decided to take the sail down. This proved a real pantomime because I have no topping lift. *Kairos* is tired and fed up and kept changing tacks. With a very small foresail she wouldn't heave to properly. In the end I lowered the boom to the rail and got it into the crutch by brute force. Then I wrestled with the madly flapping sail. Exhausted, I lay down at three o'clock for an hour's sleep and set the alarm. I must not have heard it, for I had the longest sleep since leaving Cornwall. I woke at nearly eight o'clock in the morning with a start to see broad daylight. I remembered! The close shoreline! The gale warning! I shot up on deck.

What I found was a lovely bright sunny morning with the boat taking care of herself perfectly, right on course in a light wind. I put up the big jenny to make better speed. I feel rested and happy. The cabin is beginning to dry out as the warm air blows through. I stood a while this morning with the sun on my face.

Then Authority was at it again, nagging, but Submission stood up to him. "Look at this mess," Authority said. "You think you're going to sail into harbour looking like a seaman with a sordid-looking cabin like this?"

"It isn't bad at all, sir," argued Submission with a bit of spirit, but he began to tidy up. First he squared up the chart table, then he organized the cabin and the starboard bunk that held so much of the stores. He filled up the batteries, filled and trimmed the lamps and cleaned the stove.

The wind stayed steady northwest. With an ease that delighted me we weathered Cape Trafalgar and entered the Straits of Gibraltar in the evening. The Straits make for difficult sailing. The wind died right away and left us slatting around on a flat sea listening to the useless flapping of the main. I'm so close to bringing my crippled vessel into port, and edgy in case things go against me now. So near, yet so far.

We need more wind to weather Tarifa, but too much wind in the form of a southeast gale will blow us back out to sea. I wait to see which way the wind will blow, like a gambler waiting for the wheel to spin.... Here comes a puff, taking me in the right direction.

As I keep watch the wind strengthens and we are abeam of Tarifa light, making steady progress now under a reefed main and mid-genoa. I can see in the blackness of early winter the street lights and moving car lights of Tarifa.

It's a dirty night, blowing and raining, with the wind taking me under reefed main and genoa exactly where I want to go. So close to shore and in shipping lanes I must not sleep. It is my voice, and not that of Authority, that says aloud: "Stay awake. Stay alert."

November 6 · It's four o'clock in the morning and I'm watching in the darkness, sitting in the cockpit in the rain.

I must not sleep.

Dawn will soon show in the east, a pink flush on grey cloud, the light after darkness.

I have sat here all night and the driving rain runs in little rivers down the front of my oilskins. When I look up, water cascades down my back from my sou'wester and rain beats on my face.

I am looking up now. There's a red light blinking high in the sky. I don't know what it is. It may be a radio tower. I don't know.

There it goes again, Dash dot dot. Dash dot dot dot.

My eyes ache and I'm very tired. I'm slow. I don't know what that light is at all. More water trickles down my neck as I look up again.

Dash dot dot. Dash dot dot dot. GB?

GB! Slowly it sinks in. GB!

Gibraltar!

We've saved the little ship.

At dawn the rain seemed to be easing a little. At 9:15 a.m. I saw the runway, the breakwater and the mouth of the marina all at once. By 10:30 I had secured at the berth.

Two Spanish Customs officials came down. They looked at *Kairos* with her green brasswork, split-ended boom and jury rig, and she looked proud.

"Last port?"

"Cremyll in the U.K."

"You must be a good sailor," said one, shaking his head, and that was the highest commendation I could ask for.

I patted *Kairos* on the transom. "I'm very glad to be here," I told him. This was very true indeed, but after being entirely alone I was surrounded by many voices. After the roar of the sea I felt strangely bombarded by sound. I had been part of the rhythm of the universe and now I was part of a system of forms and regulations.

I was exhausted and suddenly longed unreasonably for a glass of milk. Access to Spain from Gibraltar was completely shut off by a large green gate. There was no fresh milk on the Rock. People came down to look at *Kairos* as a curiosity, and one kindly fellow offered me a white liquid made of chemicals imported from Belgium. It passed for milk.

I wanted to get a message to Margaret, my wife, companion and love who waits for me. I was overdue for my first landfall and she would be worrying. I had avoided injury through all the storms of Biscay, but now in the harbour I had twisted my knee badly leaping upward from the boat to the wharf. I could hardly walk. After phoning I would sleep and rest. I wrote in my diary: "Port after storm. Rest after toil."

The only public telephone was in the Town Hall and I staggered up to the old building on a hill. There an elderly gentleman dealt bravely with a lineup of people trying to place international calls. In a tiny room he would phone Madrid through a hand-held telephone, but would have difficulty hearing the operator because of the babble of people in the lineup trying to get his attention in languages he could not understand.

He told Madrid: "Mr. Griffiths wants a collect call." Pause. "*Si*. The charges will be reversed." Pause. "The call is to Mrs. Griffiths." Pause. "No. They are not here together. They are apart. They are in different places. Mr. Griffiths is beside me. Mrs. Griffiths is in Canada. *Si*." The lineup shuffled anxiously and my knee throbbed. I was told I could have three minutes because of the demand on the phone line.

Margaret answered her phone at three o'clock in the morning British Columbia time. She was lying awake. "You're safe! I'm so thankful. You were so overdue. The operator who just asked me if I would accept a call from Mr. Griffiths in Gibraltar will never remember. But I shall never forget." The people in the lineup became impatient. I said I was fine and would mail my tape straightaway. Margaret said she would make one for me and I asked her to make it full of little everyday things at home. My three minutes was up.

My sleep was without anxiety, long and lovely after I had said goodnight to Margaret as I always do, and had given thanks that I had managed to make harbour where I can be among friends.

In the morning I got in touch with Harry Manners, a representative of the Royal Naval Sailing Association. He came aboard with the most warm greeting and kind concern and delivered me to the care of his Boat Officer. The Boat Officer insisted I have dinner that night at his house.

I dug out a white shirt and my blue blazer. Both were covered in thick green mould. I attacked them with a scrub brush and got it all off but I smelled funny all the evening. I wallowed in the luxury of a tablecloth with silver knives and forks while my hosts behaved most graciously, as though all their guests smelled mouldy.

The next day we motored *Kairos* over to the dockyard, and there the mast was lifted ashore by a small crane. Repair will need new parts, which must come from England, and I am waiting with patience while an east wind blows through the boat's ports and hatches, drying everything out in the mild sunshine after rain.

Patience is something I have luckily already learned. I tried at a store to get new globes for the cabin oil lamps. "Yes, we're agents. But we haven't any." Six other shops had none, and with all my preparation before leaving, hindsight now tells me how wise it would have been to stock up on globes.

I have done my laundry with difficulty. The local radio frequently interrupts its pop music to announce that area four, or one, or six, is about to lose its power in 10 minutes' time. When this leaves Gibraltar's one laundromat cut off in mid-wash or mid-dry, a small crowd expresses extreme displeasure in several languages.

I have been here now over a month, waiting, drying everything out, gaining strength, mending my knee, getting repairs to the rigging, genoa and dodgers. With all defects made good I shall only have to get stores aboard. Meanwhile, life on the Rock is claustrophobic and I have nothing to do. I sit waiting, And I listen over and over to the tape I received in the mail from Margaret.

"It's a new morning," I hear her voice say, "a wonderful morning because you are safely in Gibraltar. It feels like Christmas, full of gifts! Last week wasn't like this. But now the whole house has new meaning because I know you've come safely into harbour.

"I'm looking across the bay from the kitchen window to the rock where the cormorants stand. They're all very straight and snobbish with their beaks in the air, and behind them the grassy bank is orange because the maple leaves have fallen and the wind hasn't blown them away under the shelter of the trees. The sky is grey cloud with two eagles circling. One of the sea lions is back and makes obscene noises under the kitchen window. I wonder if the male comes first and the ladies meet him later.

"The birds are swarming before migrating. The antics of the woodpecker and the soft winter gleam of the goldfinch are all joyous on this lovely day.

"It was so long before I heard from you, and I knew from friends in England that there were storms off Biscay and Finisterre. Waiting was hard. Now I shall put out extra sunflower seeds for the chickadees because you are in Gibraltar. I phoned Blair at the CBC to tell him his Dad is safe but he wasn't at work 'til later. I left a message for him: "George is in Gibraltar." The receptionist said, "That sounds very exotic, madam. Is it code for 'There's a bomb at the CBC?'"

"The news in Canada is all about Trudeau bringing the Constitution home from England. The cartoonists are having a ball with the information that Canadian lawyers are in London showing Margaret Thatcher their briefs.

"I've made new curtains for the living room. I hope you'll like them. They make the room warmer. I keep busy and don't feel lonely except when I see your clothes hanging in your closet. I got an organizer for your shoes but liked it better when they were in a heap.

"I have the kettle on for tea. Some day before too long you'll join me for a cup. I have the fire lit. The house is at peace. A ferry has gone by, silver in the winter sun. I've planted crocuses by the front door. They will be welcoming in the spring.... I'll wait for your phone call before you leave again. My thoughts are with you wherever you are..."

I lie here and think of home and the little things that make for living and loving.

It's almost two years now since my mystified peers at the British Columbia Hydro and Power Authority properties division heard that my retirement dream was to single-hand the Atlantic in a small boat, which I would then sail home to Canada. They gave me their blessing and a floater jacket. Some said goodbye on my last day of work as though they would never see me again. My younger son Mark drove me to Seattle, and with excitement and last-minute confusion I caught a plane to England and began to search for my little ship.

Nymph of Lorne lay under a canvas at Burnham-on-Crouch. Her mast and rigging were stored in a shed. She had been built by McGruer in Scotland for the London Boat Show 18 years before. She had a splined mahogany hull that showed under varnish the kind of workmanship we will seldom see again. Every detail was precise and she was strong. At 28.7 feet long she was beautifully proportioned. My search was over. I bought her on August 17, 1979 and changed her name to *Kairos*. From then on *Kairos* and I formed a partnership of a strength I cannot describe.

In my inexperience in fitting out for single-handed sailing I then made a series of miscalculations. I took her to a boatyard at Burnham to prepare for the Atlantic crossing, intending to sail within weeks. I was impatient to start my long sail by September 1979. I knew little then of going slowly and accepting what the Fates send.

In the months of August and September, boatyards give their employees their holiday time. I was straining at the bit to get to Plymouth by September 12 to store up and prepare to leave for the Canaries, my landfall being Tenerife. But I still had to learn to go slowly, to wait and wait again.

I lived in lodgings in Burnham-on-Crouch and worked each day on *Kairos* with help from the boatyard. With a portable light held within a few inches, I chipped away at the rust on the keel. Pressed for time, I was impatient when I found that one job always seemed to lead to another. To fit the stern pulpit (for she had none) we had to dismantle the entire fuel tank and pipes. After careful measurement by the yard a new Taylor paraffin stove was ordered, and it fitted well. However, when gimballed the stand was three-quarters of an inch too wide for the existing space, and I was unwilling to make holes in the bulkhead. I decided on a non-swinging stove, the stove that was later to do that jump that put the light out during my knockdown in the Bay of Biscay.

Because of late summer holidays taken in Burnham, the bow rollers could not be regalvanized for at least two weeks. And the sailmakers were on vacation and unable to start on the new suit of sails I had planned. Red sails, as Margaret and I had decided over the phone, would be fitting for an older, mahogany-hulled vessel.

I was operating faster than the boatyard employees and the people in the town. By October the little ship I was working so feverishly to restore was again dirty and forlorn. The engine was in bits, the cabin's newly sanded floorboards were up and lying in the shed, the freshly washed sail cover was full of finger marks. I was learning the hard way to take time when you have 100 things to do; otherwise they will have to be redone and your list will grow to 200.

I grew increasingly impatient and anxious to leave. I decided that any work outstanding could be finished in Tenerife, in the Canary Islands. It could be reached in 18 days from Sutton Harbour in Plymouth, according to my estimate.

On November 11, I bowed my head in reverence to fallen comrades, and then *Kairos* and I set sail for Sutton Harbour, where I could take on stores.

There, I waited for fair winds ... and sailed with the first easterly.

A day out from Sutton Harbour the wind changed. Black clouds blew in. A sudden strength of the sea broke over the little boat and smashed the forehatch. A lurch sent me spinning and injured my shoulder. I came back into port at Sutton Harbour, intending to repair myself and the boat.

Now patience and wisdom were beginning to dawn. I slowed down.

Margaret came to England and stayed with me while my shoulder healed. As we talked it became clear to both of us that long-range planning is the major part of any distance sailing. Preparation cannot be rushed. Nothing should be left to be done on the way.

At last I had the sense to put in to Mashford's Boatyard in Cremyll, Cornwall. And there, where Mashford Brothers Ltd. had for years prepared boats for long-distance sailing – *Chichester, Rose, Lewis* and most of the racing boats entered in the OSTAR, or Observer Single-Handed Trans-Atlantic Race – I relaxed and drew on all the benefits of that experience. I took all the time needed to have my little boat in first-class condition for the entire journey back to Canada, with no work but ordinary repairs along the way.

Kairos was in Mashford's yard for almost a year, from fall 1979 to October 1980.

By letter I kept Margaret involved in the process and planning.

On a cold winter day in December, Margaret sent me a telegram at the boatyard to say that my sister Eileen was terminally ill, and I hurried back to Canada to sit beside her in the hospital in Edmonton, Alberta. We talked of old times and she still managed to smile. She died on a day the snow was thick and the river was frozen. After the funeral I returned grieving to *Kairos,* in her shed at the Cremyll yard, where I greeted her, my old friend, still propped up on her staging. I began work again, mourning for Eileen.

Now I was working differently, going with time instead of against it, and the work was good for sadness. Now, instead of lodgings, I lived aboard, in the shed, to get used to organizing my little space.

It was lonely in the shed at night. Just Rat and me. Rat came out after supper into the darkness, and his little rodent eyes glistened in the beam of my flashlight as he pushed the paint cans around on the cement floor.

Other boat owners worked in the shed during the day, but only I slept there. I saw no signs of Rat's family. We were both alone. And I was learning stillness within. I had decided that this boating game is one of philosophical acceptance of whatever trials have been assigned to those who go down to the sea in small boats. I felt at peace with the world. I told Rat about it. I told him about Margaret and the island where we live, and about Eileen, and he always stopped what he was doing and listened.

The boatyard came noisily alive at 7:30 a.m. About nine o'clock the people working on the boat next to me would arrive at the shed and switch on their radio. They had planned to be away from port six weeks after putting into the yard, but after five weeks were still waiting for two small parts to repair a fuel pump. The engine was out for an overhaul, and the pieces on the ground were of great interest to Rat at night.

Duet, a lovely old yawl, was in the yard with a broken mast. Coming down the English Channel in a lop, her bowsprit dug into the water and speared a large fishing net. In the jar her topmast came down.

I watched the boats come wearily into the yard, for vessels and crew to be mended and sheltered, some with patience, some fretting over time and wind and tide.

I had put myself entirely in the hands of the Mashford Brothers. They were confident that I had a good little boat, and when I asked Boy (aged 60) if the new part had arrived for the engine, and it had not, he remarked that I had at last adopted the right attitude. No fretting or panicking. Just wait. "When at last you are ready, wait again for that spell of easterlies, and don't push her."

Now the March winds had blown themselves out and the cool Cornish spring of 1980 gave way to what would be described as one of the wettest and windiest summers on record. Although I never feel alone at sea, lying on land alongside nothing but a stone wall at night seemed sometimes to erode my spirit.

I developed a routine in the shed. Up at 7:00 a.m. and hear the news (nothing ever about Canada). Breakfast of cereal and an orange, which cost nearly two pounds with the exchange against me. Work until noon. Bread-and-cheese lunch. Work till 5:00 p.m. Then there would be the rush to the yard washroom for what was left of the hot water to wash, shave and do the laundry. The evening was a time of leisure and letter-writing, often to Margaret, and cherishing her letters to me. After a special treat to eat, bed at 9:30, listening to Rat pushing the paint tins.

Most of my rewards to myself were in the form of food. One day, winkles at the market, followed by fresh strawberries. I had wondered about the strawberries – most expensive. But Theo Mashford said I had been working hard, and I decided he was right and I deserved

25

them. Another day I fished around in my little cheese tin and found some Stilton. My treat for the day! I had eaten most of it and enjoyed it immensely before I remembered the Stilton was finished last week. I had eaten mouldy old white cheddar.

I was practising cooking nourishing food that would store well on a long sea voyage – dried peas and beans in a stew with onions and garlic. Lots of rice. I labelled, crated and stored the food in the quarter berth, and practised crossing it off my list as I ate it. But the day I saw on my list a tin of crab in No. 2 crate was the day I realized my organization was faulty. Getting at No. 2 crate involved moving all the tools off the temporary chart table over the quarter berth, and pulling out No. 1 crate and a cardboard box. Driven hard by the expectation of crab for supper, I reached in and hauled out No. 2 crate from the very back of the quarter berth. No crab!

I had eaten it and not crossed it off. I ate beans out of a saucepan.

I dreamed often of a white tablecloth. My dream was realized one evening when a dentist, a captain in the Royal Navy, took me back to his nearly 300-year-old house to have dinner. The dining room was pleasant with a high ceiling, long chintz-curtained windows, and a red carpet almost covered by five yellow Labrador dogs. I returned happily to my little ship in the shed. "Hello, Rat!" I called at the top of my voice. "I've had a lovely evening with a white tablecloth!"

The next day I learned that Rat had been joined by Badger, who was living in the big rocks and playing noisy havoc at night with the garbage. A big cage was made and baited, and the following morning a sorrowful-looking Badger was entrusted to a lady expert on moving badgers. She promised everyone he would be happy and we told him what the lady had said before she took him away.

I was now beginning to feel all my 66 years as I climbed on and off the staging with my tins and brushes. My decision that as little work as possible would be done to the boat between leaving Cremyll and arriving in Canada led to another decision: that a varnished hull is no good in the tropics. I must scrape it down entirely and give the mahogany twenty coats of Deks Olje, a Scandinavian oil that treats and preserves the wood instead of simply covering it.

My list of little jobs to be done was also growing longer instead of shorter. I pinned up another page of instructions on the bulkhead. Check the shrouds, all the bulbs, the methylated spirits and paraffin, mark the cable and shackles to be rewired, devise a stowage plan. With more weight on deck, the heavy items must be stowed lower. But I was only 21 feet on the waterline. Could I, I wondered, get one of the spare anchors into the bilge? Painting, marking and cataloguing the food tins would be a longer job.

Advice and experience was rich and plentiful at Mashford's. "Go easy, boy," said Theo Mashford. "Get every little detail the way you want it before you leave the yard." So I took my time to go over the boat, checking the sheet leads, renewing both the main halyards and getting the No.1 jib cut down to storm size. Everything must be basic, nothing newfangled, nothing that would cease to operate and leave me stranded through mechanical or electrical failure. I would not even have shackles on the clews of the sails, for these can fly back in a storm and do an injury.

It was one evening when light was fading and I was struggling with the cove stripe – that narrow decorative band around the gunwale strake – that I met Jerry, an ex-shipwright from the Navy. He became my constant support, but it was said that the way he drank he should have been dead by all normal statistics. He looked sadly and solemnly at my struggle with the cove stripe. "We'll fix that, George," he said, and returned with a little bottle of golden liquid. "Do I put it on with a brush?" I asked.

"No, stupid, you drink the fucking stuff."

Day after day I scraped and sanded. I applied coat after coat of oil until the hull shone.

"She be handsome, my lover, she be," proclaimed a stout Cornishman as he walked by.

Harry, from the Missions for Seamen, came to bless the boat. Harry was full of trouble. His wife, he said, was "difficult." She wanted the lady church warden, who she thought was carrying on with the vicar, replaced by a more sensible woman who she felt sure had never carried on with anybody.

It was after the boat had been blessed by Harry that Theo Mashford recommended that the engine piston should be replaced. The floorboards came up and the engine casing was dismantled. The engine looked naked, forlorn, disembowelled. The cabin took on a sordid and unloved appearance. And I was driven out. I told Rat I would have to leave, and I found a bed-and-breakfast in a village on the bus route five miles away.

I found deep content in a large old house going rapidly to seed, with darkened oil paintings covering the wallpaper, with cracks in the ceiling, and which was as cold as charity in the bedroom. In the freezing bathroom I wallowed in a hot bath. There was an evening meal in a pleasant dining room, with shining silver on the white tablecloth and a little bell to ring. In answer, the next course would arrive on a tea tray while I sat in heaven, alone at the head of the table, in my logger socks and stained but washed trousers. I described it all to Jerry when I got back to the yard, and he responded in colourful language.

I was renewed and somewhat carried away by my brief retreat into the world of tablecloths and hot baths, and decided I could afford the luxury of laying a teak deck. This, I thought rightly, would strengthen the boat ... and wrongly, that it would not take long. The man laying the deck broke his ankle fishing off the rocks, so the senior apprentice worked alone. The storeman didn't order enough caulking compound and supplies were slow. August 1980 became September, and the rain pelted down on the tin roof of my shed and poured out of the gutters onto the concrete slipways. We were in a depression from the Atlantic that seemed unending.

All the major deck fittings now lay beside the boat and Theo Mashford went out of his way to collect caulking compound from Falmouth. He declared the chain plates to be the key to all the rigging and he strengthened them. "Now you can face any storm," he said.

The weather banged tree branches on the roof of the boatshed until one night I shone my flashlight to see if there might be a prowler. No one. Even Rat was asleep. The tree cracked and pounded in the dark.

In early September there was a strong gale. In the harbour, a Colin Archer, a Norwegian-type cutter on a buoy, started to drag. The lifeboat stood by while the whole trot of buoys pulled together in a tangled bunch, and a catamaran broke its moorings and was carried away. A small sloop lost its mast and it was found later by the police boat. My tree walloped madly on the boatshed roof.

I was ready, I felt, for anything the weather could serve up for *Kairos* and me. All gear was thoroughly tested and inspected, the rudder-head strengthened, all mast fittings were covered with galvanized paint, with white paint over top. I bought spares of everything that I thought would be hard and expensive to buy on the journey – shrouds, paint, grease, batteries. The hull, hatches, cockpit seats, deckhouse, mast and boom were all treated with Deks Olje, coat on coat, ready for the little ship to face the tropics. And the weather remained terrible, with lows constantly sweeping in from the Atlantic.

Anyone who had sailed the Caribbean became anxious to advise me.

"Buy all the flags you need between here and Canada now," advised a man on a boat that had just come into the yard. "Don't get them as you go. If you don't fly the courtesy flag when you get to some islands, the boarding official will tell you it's mandatory and will produce one from his briefcase for an extortionate amount. If you argue, your stay can be made unpleasant. So nobody argues."

I bought flags for Spain, Portugal, Grenada, Tobago, Barbados, Holland, Panama, the U.S.A., France, Venezuela and Ecuador. "Keep clear of the Colombia coast," advised the owner of a newly arrived sloop. "Officials are bad and boats are pirated." I told myself *Kairos* was too small and insignificant for the drug trade, and single-handed yachtsmen are known to lack worldly goods. I talked to Jerry about it, and he had many colourful and discouraging stories.

We put *Kairos* in the water and stepped the mast on a still day in late September, later in the year than I would have wished. Then the wind blew again and a boat moored nearby parted one stern line and narrowly missed bashing my hull, while the other stern line fouled my wind vane and broke it.

I took on stores to make a dash as soon as the weather broke. Then I checked my list again. Paint, tools, lamp wicks, needles, bulbs, warps, spare rigging, blocks, paper towels, Nivea cream for a backside that has sat too long, toothpaste, pencils, sunglasses, vegetable scraper, oil, greases, turpentine, dustpan, brushes, batteries for radio, direction finder, tape recorder, flashlights, sea beam, quartz clock, little alarm clock, methylated spirits for the Tilley lamp and stove, sail needles, thread, cutters in case the rigging goes, nuts, bolts, screws, nails, glue, sandpaper, plotting sheets, chlordane to kill cockroaches in the tropics.

The boat had been checked from stem to stern and checked again. I must reach the Canaries in time to be across the Atlantic to the West Indies before the hurricanes start brewing. Once across, there are plenty of "hurricane holes" to make for. But in the open sea a hurricane will advance at about 15 knots and a small sailboat doesn't have the speed to get out of the track.

Sitting in the water, bobbing in the wind and straining on her lines, stored up and heavy, little *Kairos* waited in the middle days of October 1980. I wanted to get through Biscay before November. I spoke to the long-range weather office in London. This was shaping up to be the worst October on record. "Strong westerlies for the next five to seven days," it said. "Worst summer since 1907," claimed the radio. "Glory be, it's stopped raining," said a man strolling by.

Then one day *Kairos* harnessed the east wind and sailed away.

Here in Gibraltar I have found a haven. Most boats are going to Greece or the West Indies, and some crews try to find work ashore to replenish their dwindling funds. But for some it's a place of broken dreams, perhaps for lack of money, or incompatibility. Some masts carry a sad "For Sale" sign swinging in the wind.

A magnificent sailing yacht tied up near *Kairos* has a constant falling-out among the crew. The police have been called twice, and the owner is stranded because his wife has flown back to Texas and frozen all his assets.

It is said that a captain who is not entirely sure of himself can become a shouting tyrant through sheer panic. An inexperienced crew can become a liability. A chosen companion can become a stranger in a small space under adverse conditions. The wife of the captain of a nearby sloop has refused to step on the boat ever again.

Many boats are here under repair. A British Merchant Navy master who bought a new boat thinking he would have no trouble with her has been here four months waiting for engine parts. He has become patient. Another big yacht has just arrived from Greece on her way to delivery in South Africa. Her steering went, her engine is faulty, and she split her mainsail.

But there are cheerful faces around too. The young people here are mostly on an adventure, carefree, attractive, tanned, Swiss, French, and many Germans. They may wonder about this ancient mariner also on an adventure. The young Frenchman on the boat next to mine is going to Dakar to see his friends, then to Brazil for Carnival, then to the West Indies to leave the boat and fly back to France to work as a charter skipper until he has enough money to sail again.

Several boats are waiting like me to get to the Canaries. A New Zealander with a cockney lad as crew on a pretty Friendship gaff sloop came aboard *Kairos* to borrow my charts to make tracings. He says his navigation is so shaky he'll just make for the first island he sees.

The marina is a wonderful meeting of nations, and the town is a place of contrasts. Young tourists from the north of England walk past the shops alongside older North African women in the long traditional cloak and hood, white cloth tied around the face, big black eyes staring impersonally. In narrow Main Street every other shop is stocked with Japanese radios and assorted electronic equipment. Nearly all the shops are owned by people from India. Some came via the United Kingdom and have opened little coffee bars that offer depressing snacks under glass that remind me of British Rail.

The young people on the streets chatter and laugh, switching easily from English to Spanish, sometimes in mid-sentence. They hang out around buildings with casements and thick, thick walls, and they dream of driving some battered car on Gibraltar's 11 miles of road.

Listening to Margaret's voice on her tapes, I think a lot about when I will get back to Canada, with *Kairos* sea-weary and travel-stained. The pristine white paint in the cabin is already becoming darkened with stove oil and light fumes, and the beautiful hull shows early signs of battering from the weather. I have dreamed of how it will be when I settle down at home. I send my idyll to Margaret.

"We will find a rich and fulfilling life, with me growing vegetables and you growing flowers, with swifts skimming the water, and our other birds. There will be halcyon days sailing quietly together. Without wealth we will have all we need: books, music, sunshine, rain, and wood fires, all the sea and sky, the running stream. Life will be golden and there will be a white tablecloth. We shall have solitude of space and solitude of sea." So I dream.

I inflict on everyone around me, like Gracie's harp, my photographs of our home on Galiano Island. Invariably they will ask, "Why did you leave?" I don't know how to reply.

I keep another picture in plastic, a snapshot taken on my return after being away for a short time and on arriving home finding Spring had come to the bay. Margaret stood in the driveway. That's how it will be. It tugs at my heart.

Margaret's taped stories of everyday life there, and in the background the nostalgic sound of the ship's horn announcing a ferry is entering Active Pass on its way from Vancouver Island to the mainland, all give me pause for soul-searching. Why am I here? With my greatest treat a newspaper parcel of fish and chips with a little Union Jack impaled in the batter? Why, in my 68th year, am I sailing halfway around the world? And why do I want to achieve this solo crossing of the Atlantic? Is it because I was trained to the sea from boyhood? In later years the call back to the sea is too great? Perhaps a little, but not all.

As a boy of 12 in England I was placed by my sailor father in naval college. My father was never without a neatly knotted tie and shoes that shone like mirrors. He would eye my shoes critically. "If you can't shine on top, boy, shine down below" were the words he impressed on me for life.

Some private schools in the days of my boyhood were run on the five Cs: cleanliness, cold showers, caning, Christianity and chastity. At HMS *Worcester* a sixth could have been added: celerity. The last boy up the rope ladder got a swipe with a knotted rope that could hit or miss the testicles. We learned to be clean and shiny and quick – and some of us might also be sterile.

I became as a boy confident at sea, able to read the clouds, the tides, the flight of birds, the ruffling and shelving of the waves, as well as the art of sailing and navigating. Yes, the call will always be there.

But I know there are also inner reasons for this voyage. It is a journey alone into doubt and fear about myself. Perhaps before knowing how to love and be loved by others we must first learn to stand alone. How often do we escape into relationships because we are afraid to be alone? How often can we find ourselves in silence and feel companioned? I know that on this trip, solitary in the immensity of the sea and sky, touching the water and the face of God in some mysterious manner, I will come to understand and possibly love myself, without narcissism. Only then can one wholly love another.

I have been asked if I have been lonely at sea. No. At one with the ship and the ocean there is a feeling of being in tune with all the spiritual and physical aspects of the sea, even when things seem to be going drastically wrong.

Looking back on the sail here to Gibraltar from Cremyll, it was in fact a truly wonderful experience. Despite the discomfort and worry about the little ship and getting her through, I know now that I learned peace in the quiet.

Margaret, always so close to me: I shall be changed when I come back, but I believe I shall be a better man. All the pettiness of everyday life, all the resentment and frustrations and guilt over little things seem to have been washed away in that clean fresh air. Alone with the universe, the sun, the moon and the stars friendly in their predictability, the company of a few birds and fewer ships, there was – and will be – time to sort myself out. There are so many things in the past that have brought worry, upset, fear; things that try to stay with me and rerun through my mind. Out there on the great ocean I realized how stupid it all was, and what is important in my life. In the simple words of Ezra Pound, "What thou lovest well remains, the rest is dross…"

The radio is playing. "God rest ye merry gentlemen, let nothing you dismay. Remember Christ our saviour was born on Christmas Day."

The year has nearly gone. It's time for me to leave Gibraltar. God bless all at home this Christmastime, and peace on earth, good will toward men.

4 BOUND FOR TENERIFE

CHRISTMAS EVE, 1980 · I am alone on a calm ocean on a night full of bright stars, perhaps like the bright star that heralded the Christ Child. All day I have waited for wind, with the sails flapping and slatting around, and at 7:00 p.m. I lowered the main to stop the noise, leaving the jib up while I hand-steer to catch any little breeze. With the odd light zephyr, *Kairos* is sailing slowly but steadily with no sound but the sea slipping by as I wait for the dawn, sitting in the cockpit, watching for shipping.

Yesterday there was a forecast for light easterly winds, so I rushed around Gibraltar doing last-minute shopping – potatoes, carrots, onions. All the fresh fruit, green vegetables and milk are beyond the gate that bars the road into Spain. I bought Christmas presents to leave for the delightful children of the German couple who clean the washrooms. Then I quickly bent on the sails, put up the big jenny and main, got everything squared up and lashed down on deck, slipped the lines and quietly stole away in the gathering darkness. My landfall is to be Los Cristianos on the island of Tenerife, and from there I will cross the Atlantic to Barbados.

I set sail under the big jenny and main and came down the Spanish side of the Straits of Gibraltar. There is always a strong westerly tide going in the Straits, and with an easterly wind stronger than forecast there was a short, vicious little sea. I got down as far as Tarifa, on the Spanish westerly end of the Straits, and then shot across until I was close to Cape Spartel, on the African side. Then I looked at the wind clouds gathering in the dark sky, and stood out to sea. When it began to blow really hard I took four turns in the main and changed down to the small jib. The African coast is not a good place to be caught on. It's low and there are shoals, so I decided to make still more sea-room in case the wind went to the sou'west. Then, well out to sea in the darkness, I was ready for the storm.

But the wind died right away.

CHRISTMAS DAY · This morning there was still no wind when dawn dyed the ocean crimson. We still slipped along slowly, catching the odd warm zephyr, making very poor progress to the Canaries. I polished up the inside of the boat for Christmas morning, got the stove – my friend Smoky Stover – really shining, washed the pressure cooker, filled the lamps, ran the engine and swept the cabin. There was very little shipping about. All the fish boats are in port for Christmas. I'm off main shipping lanes but might possibly see the odd liner going down to the Canaries. When a large bulk carrier did thump its way past quite near me I stood and waved and shouted Happy Christmas, but received no response. Its name was Icon. I couldn't see its port of registry but it wasn't Russian.

A mile or so away I watched another ship, an autoline vessel looking like a floating warehouse. Then I was alone.

I celebrated Christmas lunch by cutting a cake made for me by my friend Mabel Oates in Cremyll. Then I opened a packet of nuts I had saved for Christmas, but they somehow slipped from my fingers and fell on the floor. I got the dustpan and pointed it this way and that. The nuts rolled with the movement of the ship as we slipped along, and although I got most of them, some are no doubt still hiding to roll out quietly onto the cabin sole and catch me unawares. They may be the greatest hazard of the voyage!

In the early evening I lit all the oil lamps and the cabin looked festive for Christmas Day. The wind freshened to Force 3 to 4 and I sailed under jenny and main, hanging on with this sail combination as long as I could to make up for the time loss in windless fair weather. As the night wore on the wind increased and soon we were dashing along and pounding. My Christmas dinner was bean stew. I lurched and spilled half onto the bunk.

At midnight I decided to ease things a bit, because suddenly there was a fair amount of shipping around. Very unwillingly I left the warmth of the bright Christmas cabin, and in my oilskins faced the wind and stinging spray. There was a brilliant moon, and I got down the jenny, got up the working jib and put a roll in the main.

Now we're jibbing along comfortably at about two-and-a-half to three knots. If the wind stays like this I'll use the first flush of morning light to hoist the small jenny and let her go. Then I can sleep as daylight comes, when other ships can see me.

It's been a Christmas Day to remember, happy on the windswept sea, feeling the good thoughts of Margaret and those I love. A blessed Christmas to you all!

DECEMBER 26 · Today was a wonderful day. Perhaps sailing at its best. We bowled along before a steady northeast breeze Force 4, in bright sunshine under a sky with large, woolly clouds. In spite of a big swell which makes us swing, the self-steering is acting well after giving us trouble on the first day out from Gibraltar. In the very light winds, it wasn't coping. I wonder if the windvane, which was custom-made at Mashford's and not standard, may be a little heavy. The paddle seems very deep in the water. But I must remember we have a lot of weight on board, which will make us low. I've got a lot of paraffin, meth, diesel, extra sails. Thirty gallons of water is 300 pounds, and I'm carrying heavy tinned food.

I'm reflecting now on deep matters, sitting on my step, keeping watch, munching Mabel's Christmas cake and waiting for daybreak. I have brushed my hair without quite knowing why, but it is still Christmas. Hoping to make up the time I lost in the first windless 48 hours, I've been hanging onto the small jenny and main with the wind still northeast Force 4. But now as evening comes it's very black to windward. I should have light from a bright moon tonight if I have to change sails.

DECEMBER 27 · Toward dawn the wind freshened, and with the swell and sea at about 12 feet with a couple of breaking crests in the cockpit, we were having a wild ride. At daybreak I got a shot of Sirius and the moon, but with the motion of the boat I was too unsteady and I don't think the shot was very good. I don't want to go forward for fear of floundering and losing the sextant.

By daybreak the small jenny was flapping very badly and shaking the mast, so I tightened the sheet right in and she's practically flat. Even with this sail area we're doing about four knots.

Now morning light shows very dark clouds but I can see bits of pale blue sky. On we fly, and although I'm shouting into the tape recorder you may not hear me over the thunder of sea and wind!

DECEMBER 28 · I have fretted all day about my position. Before the early dusk this evening I went forward onto the coach-house roof and lashed myself to the mast. The wind screamed and buffeted but I got a really good sight. *Kairos* was swinging around, down to look into the dark belly of the wave, then up. Now I have unlashed myself and feel very happy with the sight and my position. There's a 40-fathom bank about 120 miles ahead of us on the tack we're on now, and I have to be careful to stay clear. The sea will be large over that and with the swell we're already at 15 feet and cresting.

Encouraged by such a good sight I measured off when I'll expect to be in Los Cristianos. With wind and sea in constant uproar I didn't attempt to cook, but ate a cold supper and settled down to read Ivan Illich by the light of the oil lamp.

Then one of the self-steering lines broke with a sound like thunder.

The ship swung right over. I heard the boom run across with a crash. *Kairos* began to roll like a mad thing, beam-on to the sea, still going like a train.

I dashed into the cockpit without oilskins and struggled the sails down. The moon went out (Sod's Law) but luckily I do my halyards up one particular way all the time, so I know at night which way to let them go. It blew harder with driving rain, and I got the boom down and into the crutch. Now we're hove-to.

With the washboards up, sails down, tiller lashed, I might as well take off my boots and sweater until daylight comes at about 6:30. I'll sleep if I can. In the morning I'll be able to see the damage and hopefully fix it.

As I lie down in the bunk, Authority starts to fret, as he does in crises.

"You can't sleep 'til you have a plan," he says.

"Well, sir, if I can't fix the self-steering I'll have to hand-steer until dark. Then I'll heave to. I'll also have to heave to to get sights. If we're running, it will be hard even to hand-steer with the wind on the quarter."

Having given Authority my worst scenario to keep him quiet, I'm going to close my eyes.

DECEMBER 29 · Hove-to and swinging in a world of chaos, I slept little. As dawn pinked the edges of the dark cloud, I had a look at the break in the self-steering. I think I can fix it, but it's almost in the water. I'll have to strip and go over the stern to rethread the line through the tiller. And I can't do that until the weather moderates.

Having inspected the damage it seems like a good idea to have breakfast while still hove-to. The next priority is to get sights, because we must be near that 40-fathom bank....

By the time I'd fixed my position the wind was screaming, and going over the stern to fix the self-steering was out of the question.

I experimented with a lash-up of shock cord on the tiller to give me modified steering, and cautiously set sail with only the small jenny. We seem to be going to westward. Perhaps the Canary current is working on us. But I would have thought it would take us south, not west.

As it grew dark I took a wind measurement on the ventometer. It was up to 30. That's at sea level and so you really have to add another 30 degrees. Ah-ooh! We're just rolling our insides out, more or less broadside. The glass is falling. She's blowing a full gale, alright. I'd better heave to again.

DECEMBER 30 · It was a bad night full of motion, and daylight showed a dirty-looking sky with hard edges on the black cloud. I hoped in vain the odd spot of rain might knock the sea down a bit. I doubt I can fix the self-steering in this weather and have decided to continue with the shock-cord steering lash-up and see how she will go with just the small jib. I want very much to get south.

All morning I felt lethargic, deeply concerned about the weather and the steering, and I just sat on the bunk and stared at nothing. Authority was unrelenting and intolerant of inactivity.

"Look at the sordid mess in the cabin," he snapped.

"I don't want to look at the cabin, sir." Then Submission made a hot drink and put on clean underwear to brighten himself up.

We ran along well all day and as dark came we were dropping down to leeward toward the Salvage Isles – probably well named, as I think they're unlighted. I knew I had to get to windward, and hoisted the main with a prayer that the lash-up self-steering would take it, and so far it's working on this tack, but it's the losing tack, downwind. *Kairos* won't go dead before the wind on this self-steering modification, and I tried using the bearing-out spar. But while I wrestled with it the boat gave a flip and I lost it over the side. All my efforts to get it back were in vain and perhaps it will be found tossed up on some beach by someone who needs just such a spar. I'll have to get another in Tenerife.

Listen! I've picked up the Canary radio. A young tenor is singing in English "... and I bought a little puppy, to give to you on Christmas Day..." The band reaches a crescendo against the drumming of the wind and on we go, through the rain, westward with the wind nor-nor-east.

As the night wears on I'm not holding quite the course I want, but after spending about an hour and a half playing with the sail trim and the shock-cord lash-up, we're steering clear of the Salvage Isles and she's going along more or less in the right direction. There are one or two ships around. It's tiring single-handed in shipping lanes because you must stay alert at night, and during the day you need time to work out sights and wait for opportunities for sights.

If it hadn't been for the break in the self-steering line we'd be home free by now! But I'm not grumbling. At least Authority has nothing to say.

DECEMBER 31 · I can't make Tenerife.

I've just worked out my position after a good sight, and I've been tweaking the sheets and renewing the shock cord. But I cannot make the island of Tenerife with the self-steering lash-up and this wind. I thought about hand-steering for 24 hours, but it would be foolish to exhaust myself in that way. So I hope to weather Gran Canary, and then put in to Puerto Rico on Gran Canary for repair. Then west, on to Tenerife.

It's been a good day, after a beautiful starlit night. I watched through the bright darkness, waiting on my step for the dawn, which came roseate and very beautiful, flooding the sky. Then I tried to doze but with a stiff wind the motion of the boat was violent. I have the weather bunk, and the little ship was rolling around broadside-on. I should have been deeply concerned that *Kairos* hadn't sailed well all night and that I was off course, but I regarded the whole scene with remarkable cheerfulness. As I fussed happily around the cabin, whistling softly, I noticed that the methylated spirits filler that I use to start the stove, Smoky Stover, had been dripping into my stew-pan. The meth was getting low and I was getting high. I greeted this discovery with a feeling of complete well-being and good humour.

We spent most of the day slashing through the water. Doing five knots we had covered 120 miles over 24 hours, for which I continued to be happy. But suddenly there was a lot more wind than I realized, running before it, and in a very sudden motion and a quick lop *Kairos* flew up into the wind. Standing at the foot of the companionway steps I was caught off balance and went hurtling over Smoky Stover, tearing the screws out of the galley light. I knocked it right off this time.

As I picked up the broken pieces of the globe, the only spare I had, Authority lost patience.

"Clumsy clot! Drunk on meth."

Submission showed a bit of fire.

"Not at all, sir. It's a bloody strain standing up with this kind of motion."

Then, instead of trying to balance, Submission clasped the grab rail and collapsed into the bunk.

The day was sunny, the sky cloudless. I got some very good positions and confirmed them on the RDF bearing on La Luce light. For supper I avoided the stew-pan and settled for sardines while I kept watch, and saw La Luce at eight o'clock. At 10:30 p.m. I was abeam of La Luce, going like a train. Time to slack her up a bit, I thought, and took a couple of rolls in the main. I managed to get the small jenny up, mainly to keep *Kairos*'s head down instead of blowing up all the time into the wind. I calculated I had about another 12 miles and the land would fall away.

I stood on watch in the cockpit under a panoply of stars, hand-steering because it's so difficult with my shock-cord lash-up to make *Kairos* steer properly with the wind on the quarter. It was a short little sea, quite lumpy, and I had my hood down with the wind whistling round my head when the ocean threw one at my back and down my neck. Soaked and spluttering I let out a yell toward the heavens, and suddenly, as though in reply, the sky over Gran Canary filled with fireworks, sparklers and rockets – quite a wonderful sight. It's New Year! Happy New Year! A very happy New Year to you, Margaret, and all who are with you!

JANUARY 1, 1981 · All day the wind has given us such a wild ride down the coast of Gran Canary, with such horrific motion, I haven't attempted to doze. The lash-up on the self-steering held as we flew along, really sailing on our ear. I felt sorry for *Kairos*, and a bit apprehensive about bringing her to and getting the main down. I waited for a lull. It didn't come, but I managed, and then we ran quite smoothly under the jenny toward the southeast corner of Gran Canary. Once 'round, I got under the lee, but it was still blowing hard.

Puerto Rico is not well marked on the chart. It's just a spot on Gran Canary, and I didn't know if there's a light or anything I could recognize it by. So I got into the coast fairly closely, close enough to see the buildings. Every little nook and cranny is filled with big hotels, motels and apartment blocks.

It was still blowing hard and I realized how tired I was. Tired, dirty and hungry. This coast, I decided, obviously caters to visitors. At the marina there would be welcome, hot water for a shower, a restaurant with the smell of hot coffee.

It turned out that there were two marinas, one for boats that are here permanently and one for the odds and sods like me! I blew up into the first one and my weather-beaten little ship was promptly waved away. The second one, where I have now tied up, is not completed and has no laid-on services. No water. But a man comes 'round sometimes with a hose. No electricity. No showers. No laundry. No garbage bins. At low water I am five feet below the level of the dock and must heave on my bow rope and clamber up on a dirty truck tire.

But it's still blowing very hard and I'm glad to be in. I can only think of sleep.

On the next boat is a crowd of Frenchmen, all laughing. And there's one very charming lady who kissed me on both cheeks and offered me a drink.

"Comment vous appelez-vous?"

"George."

"Georges. Attendez!"

She vanished into the cabin and came back again holding three orchids. Perhaps they were a New Year's gift. None of the men seemed to mind.

"Pour vous!"

"Thank you. Merci. Very much."

I should have put the flowers straight in water I suppose, but I was so exhausted I fell asleep on the bunk, clutching the orchids as though they were the greatest treasure.

Which, of course, they were.

I want to forget Puerto Rico.

Yes. The French welcome will be a lovely memory. And the fresh fruit, vegetables, eggs and cheeses, although at an exorbitant price, still made my heart sing after Gibraltar. But Puerto Rico seemed to be desperately striving to remain Spanish while being overwhelmed by the tourist industry.

Visitors were packed into row on row on row of concrete-block cabanas. They were crammed into hotels, motels and some quite nice studio apartments. Police, waiters, cleaners and taxi drivers are Spanish. Most signs are in German. Men and women of all sizes, shapes and ages walk about topless, giving the visitor a feeling of constant surprise.

I slept, exhausted, after arriving at the marina but woke with a start to find *Kairos* being boarded by the police. There were three men, one in uniform and two in plain clothes, one without a shirt, proving that anyone in Puerto Rico can go topless. They demanded to see my papers, which were passed to each one to examine. They clearly knew little English but pored over my documents at great length. Then they produced a map, and by pointing to a village five miles south ordered me to go there.

I pulled myself together and began to scurry 'round, finding bus information and changing money for the fare. It was late when I'd prepared to go to this village. Early next morning I lined up at the bus stop.

I tried to explain to the driver where I wished to go, and everyone on the crowded bus joined in with directions in German and Spanish. We bowled along for some time and then I was put off the bus onto a narrow street with a scattering of small shops and houses among the motels.

I asked a passerby for "Police" and she looked at me with alarm, but pointed me in the right direction. One solitary policeman sat in his office and I pushed my papers at him. He pushed them back. I gave them to him again and he looked at them blankly, smiled helpfully and then shrugged.

"You're a clot, George," observed an ex-Merchant Navy captain who had a yacht near me and who was aboard *Kairos* that night. I was saddened by this information. However I cheered up when he added, "You're too honest."

He went on: "The Spanish are passionate and a bit touchy. You know how they feel about the Brit possession of Gibraltar. You saw the closed green gate across the road from Spain. There are dozens of people here straight from Gibraltar, but they've all lied and there's been no hassle. You come into a Spanish port saying your last port of call was Gibraltar and you're punished with this runaround."

"Yes, George," I silently admitted. "You're a clot."

I longed to talk to Margaret. I tried to phone her from one of the big hotels that provide international service, and I lined up, then spent almost three hours at the desk trying to get through. It was not possible to connect me. Perhaps everyone knew I had put in to Gibraltar! My Canadian passport hadn't saved me!

I was determined to sail as early as possible for Los Cristianos, Tenerife, but first I must fix the self-steering. I did this with infinite care, threading the rope through the tiller and putting plastic right at the bottom to protect it. But for all that, two hours after leaving Puerto Rico, in rough weather that made the little ship pound, the line broke again. I was mystified to know what was wrong. If it does this on the long hop to the West Indies, that will be tiresome indeed.

In strong winds I hand-steered into the lee of the island of Tenerife, and put in here, Los Cristianos, my port for receiving mail from home. A young Spaniard, handsome in a splendid uniform, met me in a boat and pointed to where I could anchor. It's a bit rolly but very quiet. Here I have found peace to prepare myself and the boat for the long crossing to Barbados.

That evening I lit my Tilley lamp, shut myself into my little home, stretched out on the bunk, and began to dream. From here to the West Indies I will take it gently. I know *Kairos* so much better now. We understand each other and are a good team. Hopefully the trade winds will be steady and true and I must use them efficiently. It will help if I get a new bearing-out spar.

So I dreamed, rolling at anchor in the harbour of Los Cristianos as the sea became flooded with moonlight. The next day I would explore the town, and find someone who would make me a new spar. All I needed was a nine-foot pole with a hook at one end and a spike on the other. I couldn't know then that the making of such a spar would take over my life, and so in ignorance I slept a deep and beautiful sleep....

I woke the next morning with a feeling of anticipation. After breakfast I unbagged the Avon rubber dinghy and launched it to row ashore and pick up my mail from home. The swell gave me a roller-coaster ride and the sea threw me ashore like so much garbage. I secured the dinghy, found the post office and joined the lineup for letters. It was a most impressive pile of mail that I put away in a plastic bag. I felt loved and deeply missed.

I rowed back to the boat against the wind, climbed the ladder aboard with my precious pile of letters, and then realized they were all for Sally Griffiths. I rowed ashore again, returned to the post office, and with all the patience I could muster joined the lineup. At the counter I explained with signs and drawings that I am not Sally Griffiths. The drawings resembled the pictures on washroom doors that depict the difference between ladies and gentlemen. The clerks and the lineup craned eagerly to see what I had drawn.

"Are you on a boat?" asked the young Frenchman behind me.

"Yes."

"So am I."

That was enough for friendship. He understood English well, and to him I confided that I was about to explore the town to obtain a nine-foot pole with a hook at one end and a spike at the other. As I clearly knew no Spanish he marvelled at this plan and decided to stay with me. He knew the town and spoke Spanish.

I gladly put myself in his hands, and after I had glanced quickly at my still unopened letters – this time ones meant for me – and felt a pang of homesickness, he led me away toward the old part of town and I was glad of his company. There were several fish boats tied up at the wharf, and old houses clustered together, weathered by the wind and sun. Old ladies in black moved slowly, and young women sat gossiping along the warm seawall, calling to their children. Up a side street he led me to a little carpenter's shop, very basic, and to a balding man with bright dark eyes he explained that I needed a nine-foot pole.

The man nodded.

"*Mañana*," he promised. Wonderful! Now for the spike and the hook.

We went back to the main street, and there found a metal shop. It seemed to be a one-man, one-room operation, and after my friend had explained to the one man what I wanted, I drew the hook and spike to scale and gave it to him.

"*Si, mañana*," he promised. All was going well.

My new friend and I went back to his lovely yacht for lunch. He charters for eight months of the year, and sails for four, through the winter. He told me he was leaving the next day for the Paris boat show and I suddenly felt bereft. How would I manage without him?

"I miss you already and you haven't left yet," I told him, but good as his English was, this statement was beyond him. We dug into fresh fruit and cheese for lunch, and when we later said goodbye it was with handgrips that were firm and sincere. I rowed back to *Kairos* and scurried around. I had a date with a bathtub. I must read my letters more slowly later, after glancing through them.

When I had taken back Sally Griffiths's pile of mail, a lady who was working at the post office for the summer months had come over and asked where I was from.

"From a little island off the western mainland of Canada – Galiano Island," I told her.

"I'm also Canadian, from North Vancouver," she said. She offered the hospitality of her apartment and the bath was arranged. So it was that I reported for this luxury at the apartment of Kay and Bruce Gilmour.

The tub was small, and you could either stand in it and slosh water over yourself or sit with feet in it and behind on a cold step. I managed to immerse various bits of me at different times and then washed my hair. A brisk rubdown with a soft towel, clean underwear and shirt, and all my cares fell away like the pile of discarded clothes on the bathroom floor, gathered up for the laundry in the town.

Supper was pleasant indeed with such good people, and I told Kay, whose Spanish is fluent, all about my adventures to obtain a nine-foot pole with a hook on one end and a spike at the other. It was to be ready tomorrow, I told her. Kay looked at me in total disbelief. But instead of distressing me with her doubts, she picked up a local magazine and read, translating from the Spanish as she went, a description of Canada. It is, she read, a vast area of snow and ice that yields one crop in the summer. Small towns are dotted through the flatness, and there is only one holiday in the year, to celebrate the wheat harvest. We laughed, and then the power went off.

I walked with Kay and Bruce across the piazza under the stars. Then I left them, feeling grateful, clean and happy, found my dinghy, pulled on the oars against the tide with all the joy of the exercise, and arrived home to light the lamps and prepare my bunk for bed. Tomorrow I would pick up my pole from the carpenter and take it over to the metal shop to fix the spike and hook.

I lay in my bunk reading my letters. I knew I would read them over and over. I thought about home and looked at my photographs of the house in springtime with Margaret in the driveway. In a happy mood, I considered how nice it would be when I got back to get a dog. Perhaps a bulldog. I had told Margaret about this idea once and then I forgot about until now, when it was the least useful thing to have on my mind.

I have so much to do before the long sail to Barbados. I plan to arrive there the first week of March. My letters from my sons, Mark and Blair, say they will meet me there, in Barbados, and help to prepare *Kairos* for the Pacific sail to Canada. Margaret wrote that, with the boys going to meet me in the West Indies, she would wait for us to be together at a time without deadlines, when she would not delay our work on the boat and sailing plans. With a full heart she sent me good wishes for safety on the Atlantic crossing.

If I am to leave on time for Barbados there must be more work from now on and less socializing. I must take on water, get diesel, grease the engine and winches, change the oil, patch the inter-jenny where it had chafed, check all the rigging, buy batteries, take on stores and at the last minute buy fresh fruit, eggs and fish from the wharf. I plan to be away from here in three days with everything, particularly the repair of the self-steering, well done.

When I complete the Atlantic crossing and turn for home I must be out of the southeast Pacific by June at the latest to avoid the hurricanes.

With my life governed by deadlines, I counted still more jobs to do. Clean the stove and lamps. Buy bottled spring water for drinking....

I fell asleep and scarcely moved until morning flooded the sky with all the light and hope of the new day.

I breakfasted on fresh fruit, read again my letter from Margaret and rowed ashore to get my pole. I walked in the winter sunshine to the old part of town that delighted me so much with its sounds and character. We need our past, and walking here in the old fishing village of Los Cristianos I could imagine the place as it had been until late this century. I found the carpenter's shop, and my pole was ready, somewhat primitive and heavy, but serviceable as a bearing-out spar, spread like a strong arm holding out the foresail to give me an extra knot and perhaps save me a day or two on the long hop to Barbados. I was very pleased, and hoisted all nine feet of it onto my shoulder to the surprise of the populace, who gave me a wide berth.

So I walked to the metal shop.

There was a different man behind the counter. I showed him the pole. I had, I said, arranged yesterday to have a hook made to fix on one end and a spike on the other.

He looked at me levelly.

"I know nothing."

This was disconcerting, but I was also glad he spoke English. We could sort this out.

It transpired that this sentence was the only English he knew. Not understanding this, I told him the other man had promised to have the hook and spike ready for today. Look around the shop. There must be a hook and spike somewhere, all ready to attach.

"I know nothing."

I was feeling desperate. I had so much else to do. I drew again the hook and spike as I had done yesterday, and pointed to each end of the pole that leaned against the wall. He held up four fingers. Did this mean that my hook and spike would be ready by 4:00 p.m., or that siesta ends at four, and so nothing will happen until then? Or was it a rude Spanish salute?

I signed with a nod and four fingers that I would return at four, and went out miserably into the town, leaving the pole against the wall. How my day had changed! How my time was wasting. After lunch of salad in a little café I rowed back to the boat and got on with some of the chores, taking apart the stove, my friend Smoky Stover, to clean it. The stove still lay in pieces as I returned to the metal shop at four o'clock. There my pole leaned against the wall just as I had left it. There was no spike at one end and no hook at the other.

The man was working at a lathe and ignored me. Perhaps he had misunderstood my four fingers. I stared him out. He came over leisurely and inspected both ends of my nine-foot pole as though he hadn't noticed it before. Then he spread his arms and shrugged.

"*Mañana.*"

"No, *mañana* no good."

"*Mañana.*"

I had no words of Spanish to argue. Back at the boat I tackled Smoky Stover with all the energy of frustration. Unused to this treatment, the stove refused to go back together again properly.

I shrugged.

"*Mañana*," I said, and went to bed.

The next morning saw me back at the metal shop. The pole leaned against the wall. No hook. No spike. I had passed Kay and Bruce Gilmour strolling in the main street in the January warmth. I left the shop and ran back to find them, trotting them toward the metal shop, explaining as I went.

The man was at the lathe again. Kay held the pole and asked how soon it would be ready. There followed a torrent of Spanish. Kay told him that if he were to attach a spike and hook to this pole instead of talking so much it would all be done.

The man was unoffended. He went slowly to the back of the shop and produced a hook and spike. While we watched he attached them to the pole! I was beside myself with joy and relief, grateful again to the Gilmours. I carried the pole over my shoulder, spike in the air, feeling anyone who got too close behind might prefer to be hooked rather than spiked.

I lashed my pole to the dinghy, which was tied up to a wharf. Then I pushed out into the slight swell and rowed like mad. A young Spaniard sped up beside me in a rubber Zodiac with an outboard and took me in tow.

"*Gracias.*"

I was indeed grateful, and I was also soaked to the skin by the spray from his outboard.

I wrestled the pole up the ladder and lashed it on board *Kairos*. Let no one criticize this odd-looking pole. Ever. I worked hard for it. And it will always be a tribute to the fluent Spanish of Kay Gilmour.

On board I got busy. Time was fleeting. I went methodically through the list of things to do, crossing them off as I went. The dinghy went ashore often, bringing in stores and water in containers to be manoeuvred up the ship's ladder. I went over the rigging meticulously. In the evening I finished my supper, and then unshipped and stowed the table to give more room for the long voyage. After a cup of Bournvita I sat down and considered the self-steering. What am I doing wrong? Granted it's set low in the water and it will be lower still when I have all stores aboard. But did the bang in the Bay of Biscay knock it out of kilter a little bit? It looks okay. Or because the paddle is low does it need to exert a lot of extra power? Perhaps my sail combination isn't right? Am I giving her too much weather or lee helm? If it packs up on the long crossing I'll have to hand-steer as long as I can, then sleep for a stretch, then steer again. I puzzled. Then, "*Mañana,*" I said.

It was a beautiful roseate sunset, followed by a lovely soft night. The half moon was out and I lit the oil lamp to read my letters from home all over again. I had asked Margaret for the little everyday things, and now I could hear her voice on the tape she included:

> Elizabeth called to ask me to go with her to the golf course, where she heard there was a sick falcon. We found the falcon and when she picked it up it had no fight and weighed nothing. I thought it would probably die quietly that night and didn't want her to traumatize it and bring it home, especially as she wanted to pour milk down its throat. Birds don't drink that way and I was afraid she would drown it, but she wanted so much to save it and it was a magnificent bird. At home she fell on her knees and said 'Manitou, God of the birds, have mercy on your servant the falcon.' And then she poured milk down its beak and the milk oozed out through the bird's nostrils. Manitou had mercy and the falcon died. Elizabeth buried it where she will plant her next row of beans when the soil warms up.

> I met Doris in the lane. She was furious. The island gossip had been talking about her and it wasn't true, she said. She climbed the hill and confronted the I.G. 'If you want to know anything about my private life, ask me. What do you want to know?' The I.G. smiled disarmingly and said, 'Everything.' And Doris had no words and came home and was very cross.

"You will be getting ready to leave soon," Margaret went on. "My thoughts will be with you always, every day. If you are ever lonely on the long crossing, hold out your hand and I'll be there."

I lay peacefully happy over these little stories from home and Margaret's reassurance.

The morning was dark and raining. Not the best for completing my jobs. I had to change the oil in the engine. When I went on deck my own cares seemed like nothing. The big South African catamaran just inside me has a crew of four, two men and their wives. I knew they ran into trouble in the Cape Verde Islands, where they were given fuel that had water in it, bad drinking water and bad food. They all had salmonella, and one man had a heart attack. One of the women caught her foot in the engine. They went alongside a tanker while at sea to get good drinking water and fuel. This morning the boat carries a "For Sale" sign, flapping in the wind. Another broken dream. They have very little chance of selling the boat here, and I believe are short of money. My heart goes out to them. I have thought of them all day as I worked away on *Kairos*.

As night falls early, I feel satisfied with my work. The boat is ready to sail. I've thought of everything to fix the self-steering, and I'm sure it will now hold. I have quietly counted my blessings.

I have left wine and flowers for the charming Gilmours, sent a silent greeting to my French friend at the Paris boat show, and smiled toward the boat crewed by two English men, excellent people who thought I was only 54!

I leave in the morning.

It will be difficult, being single-handed, to get the anchor up with three boats very near me. I must get a bit of room, especially if the wind is blowing strongly. I'll stream *Kairos* out with the anchor just off the bottom, then I'll get the anchor up and inboard.

I have spent some time in meditative quiet. I am mentally, physically and spiritually ready for the long trip. I have read over and over the letters of good will from home

My heart is full.

Margaret, through all the miles ahead, I hold your hand.

JANUARY 22 · The land is falling away now into a soft haze. The next I will see will be the shores of Barbados at the end of February.

Kairos and I sailed this morning with a southwest breeze, red sails against the deep blue sky. Boats in the harbour sounded their horns, whistles blew. People were photographing and the Gilmours waved from their balcony.

Nine miles out the breeze died. Now we're bobbing, slatting, dibbing as we have been all day and praying no one can see us in the evening dusk.

"Not quite as spectacular as when you left, Griffiths," comments Authority.

"No, sir. But if we get a bit of wind tomorrow we can use my new bearing-out pole, and scoot along."

JANUARY 23 · I hoped the yellow sunrise would augur wind, and sure enough about 5:00 a.m. a light northeasterly sprang up. We bowled along nicely at about four knots until late afternoon. Then the jenny, with the main blanking it, began to flag and shake the mast. Now was the time my pole was needed to bear out the foresail on its strong arm to harness the wind.

I strode onto the foredeck, feeling business-like, wearing my lifeline and carrying the pole. Then began a wrestle with the pole and sail that lasted half an hour before I admitted defeat. The hook is too wide and keeps jumping out of the ring on the mast. I got the pole down and lashed it. With the jenny sheet loose the sail took on a life of its own and wrapped itself tightly around the forestay, where it hung on desperately. When I got it down it fell in the water. I hauled it out, wet and heavy, and with everything sorted out I collapsed on the bunk and drank a cup of tea. Then I laughed, a long laugh, alone on the water. What I had gone through to get that pole! And it's no good!

It's eleven o'clock at night with the wind dropping. We've only done 50 miles today. Without a pole we'll be months on this trip. The answer for tonight is to turn in and go to sleep.

JANUARY 24 · While I lay in my bunk unable to sleep last night, I decided the only thing I can do about the situation with the pole is to play blacksmith and beat the hook into a ring that I can attach to the mast ring with a shackle. I can light up my old friend Smoky Stover in the morning and hold the hook in the heat of the flame of the stove. While I do that I can beat and hammer that heated hook until it forms a ring.

When I had weighed it in my mind thoroughly and decided it was a good idea, I slept until 4:00 a.m. Then I felt the wind freshening and went up on deck to rig up a preventer to stop the boom from swinging over. As I worked, the darkness became a half-light, and then the sky began to turn clear blue with high cirrus clouds predicting fine weather. I felt it would be a good sailing day and for a while it was ideal. But under a warm mid-morning sun the wind is dropping. The jenny is flapping madly and begging for a bearing-out pole. Now is the time to light the stove and hold the hook over the heat. But the wind is still dropping and the boat is lurching from side to side. I had enough trouble with my scrambled eggs for breakfast, let alone a nine-foot pole! Anyway, here goes!

Stove lit. Hook in flame, damned hot. Trying to keep the hook over the burner. Wood charring, swelling. Hammering and bashing like mad. Can you hear it on the tape, above the sound of the boat lurching? Sweating like a pig. Trying to balance, boat and pole both moving in discord. Bashing. Damned hook is half an inch thick. Can't talk. I'll talk later.

Success! Beside me is the pole, with the end still hot. But with a nice closed eye instead of a hook! Now we'll have to see if it works. Have to eat first. Out of breath. Got to sit down. Got to let the metal cool.

JANUARY 25 · There is a time of melancholy when the day has left us and darkness not yet come. I felt its sadness. Then just after midnight the wind freshened and the night was the darkest dark. I felt lonely for the first time. Perhaps this was the "maritime wobblies" the single-handers talk about when they first set sail and something deep within still clings to land. Then the moon came up, cheerful and light, and all was well. Soon the sea was silver and I saw a ship on my starboard side and felt companioned. With the bearing-out pole in place and doing well, we moved serenely through the moonlit water with a warm light breeze. I felt some concern because I was having difficulty with my sights. They just didn't work out right and Authority was beginning to nag. But then I decided I can't hit anything for another 30 days and I told him so. However, at daybreak I did get a good shot of the sun and the moon and found I was only a few miles off my estimated position.

With this reassurance I sank into a satisfied sleep until the alarm woke me and I realized happily it's Sunday morning, the day I have hot chocolate in bed. Now we're doing one to one-and-a-half knots or so, which is very comfortable for a weekend cruise but not exactly making time across the Atlantic Ocean. The self-steering doesn't like this very light breeze and is swinging from side to side. We're steering a drunken course between 240 and 280 degrees, going generally in the right direction, toward the West Indies.

Sunday is washday. I spared some precious water for a shave, and then had a bath in seawater in the cockpit, using sea soap, which doesn't lather very well. Then I did my daily exercises, necessary because little *Kairos* doesn't offer much room for walking on deck even though I'm uncluttered and have all well clear and lashed down. Rather than fit a new tank, I carry my water in large plastic bottles secured under the starboard bunk, and I prefer this on a long voyage so that I can see exactly how much I'm using and how much is left for each day. I regularly do a little yoga among the plastic bottles before breakfast.

In Los Cristianos I took on a good supply of avocados and tomatoes. They're all ripening at once. For breakfast I had avocados and tomatoes.

Lunch will be avocados and tomatoes. For Sunday supper I shall go rash and open a tin of salmon. To eat with avocados and tomatoes.

JANUARY 26 · My world is blue, without wavetops on the blue sea. The horizon lies in a blue circle around me beneath a blue sky. Under these conditions I got an excellent sight and we're nearly 21 degrees West, about an hour and a half over Greenwich. So in an hour and a half I'll take a meridian latitude and then confirm it with a longitude. Then I'll know where we are.

As the sun gets hotter I expose my skin carefully, a little more each day, so that I shall soon be able to stand the sun without protection. To go barefoot would be a delight but I always wear sneakers in case I stub my toe, or do some other injury that would hinder quick action.

We're sailing smoothly, with the pole doing its job. We pass a Portuguese man-o'-war, a huge, bluish, jellyfish-like creature with a little sail on top.

"Hi," I call to him, wondering which part of him I should address. Now all I need is a flying fish on deck for supper. To eat with avocados and tomatoes.

JANUARY 27 · "It is better to travel hopefully than to arrive."

— Chinese proverb.

There's very little wind and we're slatting around. I would be content with a speed of just three knots but it doesn't look as though we'll make that today. We're in a great big high and the glass has moved very little.

Last night I left the pole up and only half slept. Although I pray for more wind I don't want to wrestle in a hard blow with sail, wind and pole all at once. But there was so little wind, I needn't have worried. At daylight I searched the sky for any sign of a stronger breeze to come, but dawn spread a veil of pink over a glassy sea. "It is better to travel hopefully."

Very shortly I'll be out of fresh food, except eggs, but I have plenty of dried food and tins. Breakfast was Ryvita and avocados. Lunch will be Ryvita and a tin of paté with mandarin oranges, avocados and tomatoes. And supper will be my good lentil stew, made with rather soft carrots and a precious onion. In Los Cristianos onions were rare like gold, and I was given three by a neighbouring boat as a farewell gift.

JANUARY 28 · As dawn flushed the sky, my sixth sense woke me with a start and sent me rushing up on deck. We were on a collision course with a monster bulk carrier. I didn't think she would see a little wooden sailboat in such a poor light and I let go the boom preventer, ready to scoot out of her way. But to my surprise she did see me, and altered, passing me on the starboard side. Then she circled and passed me again, blowing three long blasts of greeting that thundered and rolled away across the ocean. She was a stranger, flying no flag, ugly as hell, and I couldn't see her port of registry. But she was a ship with a great heart, and through the glasses I picked out her name, *Ephron*, and saw men waving. "Greetings to you, too, *Ephron*," I shouted in a voice they would never hear, and I waved both arms, hoping they could see me through their glasses, greeting and thanking them, in the lightening sky. *Ephron* faded away as the sun rose over the horizon in a huge pink ball. I felt the lingering glow of communion with other men and I was further blessed with a gift of northeasterlies.

Now I'm sailing right into the sun, and it's not easy to get sights with the dazzle right ahead and the foresail weaving in and out while I hang onto the rigging. Working out my afternoon longitude, I thought it was a bit out. My meridian altitude was out too, at ship's noon, but I'm happy and dry and I've played some Beethoven and changed my shirt.

We're bumbling along in a very light wind, and slow though it may be, it's a lot better than bashing into a dirty sou'wester.

Thank you, Lord, for this day.

JANUARY 29 · The wind has strengthened and we've done 100 miles in 24 hours. We're doglegging because the self-steering doesn't do well with the wind on the quarter. Nor does it like the port tack. So I'll make the most of the starboard tack.

I have learned patience.

JANUARY 30 · At dawn the wind freshened into real trade-wind weather, although I'm not really far enough south yet. I got up the mid-jenny, which I patched yesterday with difficulty through six layers at the seam. I put a couple of rolls in the main and we're practically running before the wind, in bright sunshine under a cloudless sky. The sea has fair-sized rollers and breaking crests, and there's a smooth, even motion as I stand in the cockpit with the warm wind at my back.

Today I had two precious avocados left. And I sat on them.

JANUARY 31 · I found my log-line almost severed and was lucky to save the log. I guess some curious sea creature took a snap at it. With the line renewed we're again logging the distance we travel, and my sights put us a quarter of the way across.

FEBRUARY 1 · We continue with the same easy motion without strain over a rolling sea in the same northeast wind.

To begin Sunday wash and cleanup day I made some quick porridge. The instructions were in Dutch and I didn't realize how quick it was. Good job it's cleanup day! I ate what was still left in the pan after it boiled over and added salt instead of sugar. That made me feel strong and virtuous.

When I came up on deck and noticed three slides were off the mainsail. I got the sail down and repaired without heaving to, because she's going so smoothly. But hoisting the main again while under sail took all the strength I could find from salted porridge, and I collapsed on the bunk without doing my exercises. But even while I rested Authority was at me, wanting me to list my priorities for cleaning. First the engine. It's due for checking. It's a 25-horsepower Volvo that I use mainly for entering and leaving port. I started it by hand and felt pleased that it did so fairly easily. I might need to do this when the battery is low.

Then I busied and fussed around, cleaning, sweeping, polishing, tackling the porridge mess on Smoky Stover, checking the water supply. From the luxury of my cockpit bath I watched the sea's breaking crests, then let the wind dry me while I shaved.

Working out my sights, I was happy with my position. What a beautiful world! With all chores done and a feeling of cleanliness and well-being I made lunch a surprise and opened a tin without a label.

Authority hates any kind of carelessness. "Didn't you code those tins, Griffiths? You know labels come off in the damp in small ships at sea."

Submission was too happy to be cowed. "I seem to have missed one or two. But look what we've got. Kippers!"

There was a taste of salt on my lips from the kippers and the seawater bath, and I washed down my good lunch with a mixture of water and lemon juice. Now I'm relaxing on deck in the afternoon sun. The wind has fallen to a good strong breeze that is soft and steady. I've been thinking of home in Canada, of how at this time of the year the cloud hangs in the fir trees like wafting smoke, and how the cedars will soon be standing dark among the light green, spring-budding maples. I wish Margaret could be here with me, to sit together in the sun. Lying on my back watching the clouds and the moving ocean, I have been thinking that all Creation is a dance. The West Coast Indians, whose slate knives and arrowheads we sometimes find on the beach at home, knew this well. As people of the forest and the sea they danced to nature's beat through the long, wet winter, drumming to a rhythm of animal steps, dressed in their masks depicting the creatures that share our world. The missionaries stopped the dance, in the name of salvation. But can you ever stop the dance? It's part of the music of the universe that can never be stilled. There is a dance of the sky, a rhythm from day to night, light to shadow, ebb to flow and the dance across the sea's surface above the dark depth. *Kairos* feels the music in her sails.

My little ship goes along serenely. I am bathed and shaven, warmed by the sun, supremely content, deeply grateful.

We have done 100 miles today so far.

FEBRUARY 2 · Squalls all night left me without sleep. I would shoot up on deck, then come down below listening. But the wind died as dawn flushed the sea the colour of a rose, and I stood in the cockpit wearing only the Saint Christopher medal Margaret's grandchildren gave me.

The morning brought a feeling of holiday as the ocean played, throwing sea water at me, and as the small breeze dried me. But sights showed me north of our course and the weather is breaking. I must admit I have been delaying changing tacks because I want two more good nights on the lee bunk. It becomes uncomfortable on the opposite tack, and the other bunk is piled and lashed with stores.

Looking at the blackening sky I decide I shall need nourishment before bad weather. I may not be able to cook for a day or two. Into the pressure cooker go lentils, butter beans, soybeans, herbs, miso, corned beef, rice and tinned vegetables.

As the day wears on we have squalls, calm, rain, and squalls again. A ship passes to starboard, the first sign of life I have seen for four or five days.

We must get south in the approaching storm.

FEBRUARY 3 · Sunrise was yellow and daybreak overcast and wild looking. The wind increased through the morning and the sea swell is now 15 feet. We are bouncing along in driving spray with the ocean tossing the odd one into the cockpit. I did my exercises with difficulty. I'm worried because *Kairos* is taking on a lot of water. She's been remarkably tight during the earlier gales, but now I'm pumping her out four or five times in 24 hours. I was pumping her out about an hour ago and noticed we were leaving a trail of bubbles on the ocean behind us. My washing-up soap had upset under the sink, spilling into the bilge. At least we know we have clean bilges!

Night falls and the wind blows stronger. We're surfing now. I've changed the foresail and brought her 'round onto the port tack. The self-steering is unhappy on this tack and I'm trying to help her with a shock-cord lashing but we're not going well. I just hope she doesn't jibe in the dark. I have my oilskins on, ready to dash on deck, and I'll watch her carefully through the night. There'll be no moon. It will be very dark.

I hope all goes well.

The night is pitch black now. The sea is confused and up to 20 feet with big, breaking crests. I'm well down in the cabin and outside it sounds like a sky full of banshees.

I've put another three rolls in the main and we're bouncing along through the screaming blackness, under half main and working jib. We're coping but not steering properly at all on this tack, in spite of the shock-cord rig. But as we keep flying more or less beam-to, I decide it's uncomfortable but better than jibing. The wind is growing stronger and there's a lot of water flying around. I can't steer! There are some big ones rolling along! Oh! Another! Whoosh! My poor log is completely under water. I'll haul it up onto the pulpit when I can. Hold on!

Talk later....

FEBRUARY 4 · It was just after midnight, with no moon to light my way, when I put on my lifeline and crawled forward in the gale on my hands and knees to let the boom preventer go. I had decided to heave to. I couldn't get *Kairos* to come up into the wind so I could take down the sails, and holding on – tossing around in the fury on the badly pitching foredeck – I decided to jibe her 'round. It was what my understating English friends on the boat next to me in Los Cristianos would have called a "dicey-do."

Kairos did come 'round in the anger of the night and I pinned in the main, bagged the jib and pumped out the ship. Hove-to, we're rocking badly but not taking the pounding we were.

Authority spoke to me softly, even kindly: "You've seen to the ship. Now care for the sailor." And this is wisdom.

Although not hungry, I forced myself to nibble some cheese and make a cup of Bournvita.

And now we have tossed and rocked all day. And as evening draws in and the half-light lingers I snug myself down until morning, setting the alarm for 5:00 a.m. The wind screams and then wails, like spirit voices in the growing darkness, and I listen to their tale of woe.

FEBRUARY 5 · When the alarm went we were riding well, still hove-to, and I had slept, tired of the wailing wind.

Sunrise was yellow, the sky flat and the wind 30 knots on the ventometer. Each time I wanted to get under way the wind would drop to a weary sigh after so much anger, then renew itself and scream again through the rigging.

The wind chart shows an area 100 miles ahead where the winds at this time of the year are extra strong, up to Force 12. I must avoid that at all costs. But we are drifting, still hove-to.

While we drift it's been a good opportunity to make and mend. I saw water streaming down the forehatch from one big roller we took, and so I have made the hatch a canvas cover. I've cleaned up and oiled the log and lashed it to the pulpit. And I have made yesterday's stew even more delicious by adding curry powder and a tin of sardines. I had three helpings.

As night falls it grows dark indeed. I've pumped the boat out, lit the oil lamps, and I'll keep watch 'til daybreak. I reach for a book of quotations, something I can glance at in snatches. It falls open on my lap, and I read: "Act nothing in furious passion. It's like putting to sea in a storm." Perhaps.

FEBRUARY 6 · With two rolls in the main, and working jib, we're under way again in the early morning darkness and going well. All night we had squalls and driving rain and now sunrise is yellow, a bad sign. But we're moving and a third of the way across. An inspection of the larder shows lots of Ryvita (my bread went mouldy days ago). I have one orange, one tomato and 20 eggs. I'm being most careful with water, and the supply is standing up well. I have dried legumes for my stew. The weather is steadying.

All is well.

FEBRUARY 7 · As daylight came the wind moderated and I gave myself a happy hour. I played a tape of Zorba the Greek, did a Zorba dance on deck, had a drink and sang to myself.

Morning brought a light, steady breeze and I increased the sail area, but the breeze dropped and by nightfall there was no wind at all. As I lie in my bunk the little ship is rolling abominably in the blackest darkness.

FEBRUARY 8 · I watched the dawn sky to read its promise for the day. It was low and overcast, and the wind blew hard. Then it dropped away and we bumbled along under dull skies, enveloped (as I read somewhere) "by the great grey shroud of the sea." I felt depressed and impatient because we were not making up time after being hove-to.

Then, with a suddenness that made me stand still, a brilliant rainbow, a perfect bow, was painted on the leaden sky. I sat quietly. When the Indians of the Plains (such a wise people) were shown beauty by the Great Spirit they would pray. And their prayer was silence. I prayed without words that my heart might be opened for anger and frustration to flow away, and patience, compassion and kindness to flow in. In reverent meditation I watched the rainbow shimmer on the grey water. Then a glistening flying fish flipped onto the deck in front of me. Gently I put him back in the sea. He was a little fellow.

As the rainbow faded the sun broke suddenly through, turning our watery world to quicksilver, and the wind blew stronger. We increased our speed to three knots, steady under woolly clouds. With this nice, even motion I hung myself over the stern, lashed with the mainsheet, to fix a wobble that had developed in the self-steering. I drove in three wedges to hold the steering back half an inch. This helped. And now we're going well, without strain, with the big jenny and the pole, in real trade winds weather.

A new stew is boiling in the pressure cooker and tomorrow is bath day.

FEBRUARY 9 · It was a restless night with little wind and the ship rolled badly. But then as morning came the wind blew up and Authority became pushy.

"Give her more canvas, Griffiths. An extra 15 miles a day makes such a difference over all. It could make the difference of a week."

Submission knew he'd give in, but he put up a fair resistance.

"Well, sir, it's good to be a bit conservative. The nearest land is three miles down. We don't want to lose or break anything here."

Then he allowed a moment's pause.

"Alright. We'll get more sail up and see how we go. It might save us time; after all, we are getting low on fresh food and methylated spirits for the stove. And we're being increasingly careful with water."

But I dawdled, just to show him. First I had my seawater bath in the cockpit. Then a shave. I lingered over a glass of juice. Brushed my hair very neatly. Lay a little longer in the sun.

Then I increased sail and we went well for the rest of the day.

FEBRUARY 10 · I might as well be back in the Bay of Biscay! Last night I sat on the companionway steps, keeping watch through a porthole, waiting for the dawn, watching the sky clear, then cloud over and hide the stars.

We had squalls, calm, rain, more squalls. When it blew up I climbed into my oilskins ready to reduce sail, then the wind would drop and I would go below again and take the oilskins off. Then up would come the wind.

Sunrise was at 7:00 a.m., lurid and beautiful. The wind became steady, and I decided to continue my watch, sleep a little after lunch, and anticipate more squalls by the look of the sky.

FEBRUARY 11 · A sudden fierce squall hit us just after midnight and one of the tiller lines broke. I hove to and at daylight went over the stern to fix it. While I was making repairs I made a most unwelcome discovery. The whole body of the self-steering mechanism is coming loose. I can only hope the weather is kind and the thing hangs together until we reach port.

By mid-afternoon it was blowing hard and I got under way again with the working jib. I managed to get a couple of good sights and they put us over the halfway mark. Then I worked the sights out differently and, to double-check, backward as well. It's true! We're more than halfway across.

FEBRUARY 12 · The wind dropped and the ship rolled and I lay in my bunk thinking this must be the worst night possible for the loosening self-steering, with still half the Atlantic to sail. Daybreak showed big black clouds banking to windward. The glass dropped down to 1000, quite low here, and the ocean rolled along in big dark swells. I wondered what's in store for us and thought I'd better eat while I can cook. Scrambled eggs and a cup of hot chocolate went down well, before the band began to play.

The wind moaned mournfully, and during the afternoon, swells began to curl high above our stern and slip beneath us. A couple of times I thought *Kairos* might be pooped but she rode over it well, carried forward in the uproar of wind and water. By seven in the evening we had done 100 miles since getting under way, making up time lost by heaving to. But it was a wild ride.

I managed to heat the last of my stew and was eating it while I stood keeping watch through the porthole. Suddenly I went spinning across the cabin. The starboard bunk with its stores, the locker, my navigation books – all were plastered and draped with potato, gravy, beans and lentils.

"Too bad," muttered Authority, almost kindly for him, while I opened a tin of baked beans after mopping up.

FEBRUARY 13 · I tried to sleep with *Kairos* riding a switchback in a 15-foot swell that pushes us up by the stern, down to the trough and up by the bow, down and up. By morning the wind blew south of east, backing to north of east, and the glass was down to 1003. The usual pressure at this time, according to the *Mariner's Handbook*, is 1016.

I reduced canvas to a third of the main and got the mid-jenny sheeted in tight so she's hardly pulling. *Kairos* hared along on her ear at six-and-a-half knots with the wind and sea in crashing chaos and the self-steering miraculously holding together.

Now it's dark to the north of us with black-looking clouds, and we're rolling our gunwales under, me in my oilskins ready to reduce to storm rig.

"Reduce canvas now for the night," commands Authority, but I quietly decide otherwise. As night draws in I can see the odd bit of clear sky and a bit of stars to the south of us. The depression is passing to the north, the wind is dropping away and the sea too has dropped down. We'll be alright for the night.

I've lit the oil lamps, and their golden light is reassuring. There's a new stew in the pressure cooker. Now I can see more stars, friendly, winking. I'm cozy in my little home.

FEBRUARY 14 · The glass is still very low at 1002, but the weather is more settled and we're bowling along more evenly with the main on the starboard side and the jenny on the port side with the pole. This is better for the self-steering.

Darkness closed in early tonight and I'm lying in my bunk listening to the rain on the coach-house roof, alone in the night, thinking of Margaret. I have saved a card I bought in Los Cristianos, and scribble a message without knowing when I can mail it. The hugeness of Creation all around me prompts the words.

"If love is the strongest thought force, knowing no sense of space, then mine for you might softly nudge the stars. Happy Valentine's Day, Love."

I say goodnight. Now I'll turn off the lamps and sleep. The wind seems steady. I've left the pole up after dark and hope I don't pay for it. But there's a moon until a little after midnight to give me some light if I need to wrestle both pole and sail down on the foredeck.

FEBRUARY 15 · With the moon gone and in driving rain, a squall blew up and *Kairos* jibed herself. I rushed up on deck and found the pole going clunk, clunk, clunk against the mast. In the pitch blackness I lashed my flashlight to the rail. The pole was exerting a tremendous taut on the small track foreside. I battled it down, and then, no longer worrying, I slept well. But there's something strange going on with the glass so low. We're down to 1000. At any time but winter I'd think there was a hurricane brewing. Hurricane time is June, peaking in late July and August. Time will tell what this low glass means.

At exactly 3:00 a.m. I altered course, and we're now just below the latitude of Barbados. Another 900 miles and we'll be on the Barbados chart.

As I stand on deck in a warm wind a little stormy petrel flits across the waves.

Another creature in my world.

"Hi, friend!" I call to him. But he flies on, busy with his own little business. Then a small flying fish lands on the deck with an expression of surprise and I throw him back.

Kairos is holding her course well and the self-steering is keeping together. The boat still needs pumping out often, but the problem isn't worse. The rain and squalls have passed, the sky is blue and red sails are wing to wing, with nine rolls in the main to balance the foresail.

FEBRUARY 16 · After porridge I had scrambled eggs, as it's Sunday (I'm getting quite *cordon bleu* with my little packets of herbs). I ate on deck – the last of the ginger marmalade and hot chocolate – under a blue sky with fluffy clouds. All seems well but the glass is still strangely low. Something abnormal is going on for the time of year. I ran the engine for half an hour because I like to keep it in tip-top line to be sure the exhaust isn't getting water in it. Then, all domestic, I washed up, cleaned, swept and polished up Smoky Stover before my weekly luxury of a cockpit bath. I looked in the tin mirror to shave. Who was this man looking back at me? This brown person with the week's growth of hair on his face? Well, suppose, since he's a stranger, we make him look different altogether? No one can see us, after all. Shall we leave sideburns with bell bottoms? I try it and the result is intriguing. The Mafia! I'm encouraged to go on. I have been told I should really wear a moustache because I have a long nose.

I'll shave half my lip clean, as always, and leave the other half growing a moustache, then I can see which side I like best.

But finally, even hidden from the world, I can't change myself. I must be the man that I think I know. And so I sit on the deck, clean-shaven in the warm sun, wearing my Saint Christopher medallion.

What a beautiful day!

I have checked the sails and given *Kairos* a bit more mainsail. With the wind light and very fine on the quarter, and the jenny in tight to stop flapping, we're really only doing about three knots.

"You could be doing more, Griffiths," says Authority, who thinks I am becoming slack. "Check the sails again."

He's absolutely right and I ignore him. We're going so well, I'll leave her as she is.

FEBRUARY 17 · Night does not fall at sea. The big sky holds a long-lingering light in the west, and the expanse of ocean remembers the day and holds every last glow. When night did come last night, it was full of starlight and we sailed evenly on. But in the very early morning I looked through the porthole and saw black clouds cover the moon and hide the stars. The wind was sudden and strong, and we blew up into it. I think my centre of effort must be too far aft, sailing as we are with most of the mainsail up and the smaller headsail. So I brought the main down like a trisail, with the big jenny on the other side, wing to wing. Now *Kairos* is keeping her head down and we're going well.

I wondered what to have for breakfast when a really plump flying fish landed on the deck at my feet. I apologized to him, then thanked him, then bashed him on the head and put him in the frying pan. Delicious!

People sailing the Atlantic, particularly single-handers, all seem to report being gaunt and haggard by the time they reach the other side. My problem instead is putting on weight, and I have extended my exercise time. I recommend my stew.

FEBRUARY 18 · The glass has dropped down to 996 – very strange indeed. We're losing the wind. *Kairos* is rolling her heart out, the last thing we need for the loosening self-steering.

We've only done 63 miles in 24 hours.

FEBRUARY 19 · There's hardly any wind. The sun beats down and I'm sweating profusely. I've tried different sail combinations to get moving, but we're making very little progress. The glass remains at 996.

In the fresh-food larder I still have one lemon, which I squeeze into my drinking water, half an onion the worse for wear, and some eggs. In the sprouting jar are mung beans, delicious to crunch.

FEBRUARY 20 · Happy Birthday to you. Happy Birthday to you. Happy Birthday, dear George. Happy Birthday to you! Thank you. Thank you all, I'm overwhelmed! Margaret, you shouldn't have! Sixty-seven today!

My gift from the weather is the slightest breeze, very fine on the quarter, and we move slowly indeed toward Barbados.

FEBRUARY 21 · I was reading in my bunk when there was a quick almighty bang. *Kairos* shuddered up into wind and. I shot up on deck. Everything looked fine. Shrouds alright. All seems in order. Then I looked aft. The paddle had broken off the self-steerer. It's made to do this if it's hit or shoved from beneath. I suspect a shark under the boat. I do have a spare paddle. But to get it shackled up at sea I would have to get right down into the water to unscrew a little T screw at the waterline while holding the paddle vertically. I don't think I can do this. Especially if there are sharks around....

So what now? Hand-steer these last few days? We're getting close to the island but there would still be weary hours at the tiller. And the difficulty of leaving the cockpit to cook and to get sights.

I'll tie the tiller in the position I want it with shock cord. This should get her to steer by herself after a fashion. Having a long keel, the boat is fairly directional and I should be getting a 12-mile push from the Ecuadorean current.

I'll just plod along like that and hope for wind.

FEBRUARY 22 · After going slowly through the night, with *Kairos* holding a course with the tied tiller, the wind died right away. The glass remains down at 996. Morning was overcast, oppressive and sultry, and the sweat just poured out of me.

Here I sit. There must be some way to catch a breeze, get moving and steer better. I'll try the jenny and pole on the starboard side and the main on the port side. I'll let you know how I get on.

I couldn't do it! It's hard enough when you're sailing alone to be in the right place at the right time. But with the steering tied, the minute I altered the sail plan the lashed-up tiller wasn't right and we came up into wind, with the wind behind the foresail.

I feel defeated. To keep my spirits up I've eaten some dried apricots soaked and stewed in honey.

FEBRUARY 23 · Everything about the weather is unusual. With the glass still abnormally low, the wind is very light south of east. I wish it would back round a little. As daylight came and I could see, I brought *Kairos* around on the other tack and reduced the mainsail so the jenny can pull a bit more. Now, after fiddling with the cord that holds the tiller, we're moving just a little in what breeze we can catch.

FEBRUARY 24 · The glass is even lower and there's no wind at all. The ship is rolling. My supplies are getting low. I'm running out of methylated spirits for the stove, haven't much dried milk left, down to four eggs. But plenty of dried food.

About 200 miles to go.

FEBRUARY 25 · I am the Ancient Mariner, in his painted ship upon a painted sea. There is no wind, no movement of air, the sun beats down, and everywhere I sit becomes a pool of sweat. Although being careful with water, I must make myself drink to avoid dehydration.

Last night I threw a cocoa tin overboard to see how much we would move before morning. Today the tin still sits beside us on the still ocean.

But at last the sun becomes hidden, the day suddenly darkens, black clouds bank to windward. The sea is flattened, the glass down to 990. On the radio I picked up "winds northeasterly" before it was drowned out by static. A small shark keeps us company, about four feet long, swimming beside us under the boat.

There must be wind tomorrow.

FEBRUARY 26 · There is no wind, no movement in the sea or sky, no noise in our silent world, no bird cry nor lapping of water. The dark sky has cleared. The cocoa tin sits motionless beside us. I try to rest my eyes from the dazzle of the sun. The shark is still there.

The heat is heavy down here in the cabin as I lie in my bunk on cushions stained by spray and sweat. I have all the ports and hatches open but the air doesn't move and I feel slow and lethargic. Our world is a circle, with *Kairos* at the centre, on a smooth oily-looking ocean.

Margaret gave me some music tapes in a canvas bag, and I have played some Grieg that floated across the silent sea. I see Margaret clearly, but I cannot see her face. I have read a little, short poems needing no concentration, light, skipping words. I try to crystallize my thoughts but they fly away!

The sun rose pale this morning, climbed the sky and has drowned in a crimson sea. Darkness brings no respite from the heat.

Still 200 miles to go.

FEBRUARY 27 · I find myself talking to the cocoa tin, telling it in frustration about the waste of time and how I must drink but be careful with the water supply. I must think and focus on something other than the present. What about the years ahead? My mind considers them lazily as I lie in my bunk, wet with sweat. With the years left to us Margaret and I should decide what we want to do. Set priorities.

I'd like to go to a World Cup football match. And a foreign film festival. And Margaret wants to see the Arctic spring, when fragile blossoms push up from beneath the melting snow and unfold briefly across the tundra. We could store up the Volkswagen, two tires on the roof. See how far the Alaska Highway will take us. How wonderfully cool it will be on the Alaska Highway! I try to imagine the sting of cold on the skin.

When I get home I'll be seeing friends again, of course, from this journey. Several have said they'll come to see us in Canada. I'll give them some of my stew. That'll fix them up! I've run out of visiting cards and written to Margaret to send some more but she hasn't sent any.

And what about my now close friend the cocoa tin? Should I take it home as a souvenir? A reminder of torturing heat and wasted time while Mark and Blair wait for me in an expensive Barbados hotel? I feel quite down, thinking of the boys, Mark without much money and Blair on two weeks' holiday from the CBC, wondering what has happened to me while I sit and sweat and wait for wind.

But then my spirits rise! A bird of great beauty hovers above us for several minutes, the first sign of life I have seen since I called to the stormy petrel 12 days ago. The nearness of another creature stirs my heart.

FEBRUARY 28 · I don't feel well, but better when I drink. I am watching the water but must not forget to drink. I have been reading a little, snatches of things from my book of quotations. Something I wrote down awhile ago is tucked in there, copied from somewhere onto lined paper after I had walked through an aspen forest in the fall. I remember the dry, cool crispness of that forest and I live it again in this broiling heat.

"Sunlight through the aspens,
Golden leaves in the wind,
Morning mists of silver mystery.
I have seen the glory of all these."

I wish I knew where that quotation came from. I remember walking under the aspen trees. I remember they were glorious. I see them again, whispering and golden. I see them as a trembling grove, painted on a shaking curtain, and I am standing looking at them with my back to the tired, heavy person on the bunk who is me. How strange it feels to be two people! The aspens are light in the wind and they bend. The blessed wind, blowing, and the leaves are falling, falling, twisting, falling. This is no good! I must stop my mind from spinning, go on deck and give myself a seawater shower.

A shark swims around us and under the boat, staying with us for about 15 minutes. I wait under the hot sun until he leaves, and then throw my bucket over and haul it up again, pouring the sea water over me, and go over the side again with the bucket. Splash! The warm water falls on my shoulders and trickles down, cooler than my burning skin. Splash again as I feel the joy of it, and again. Carefully I wipe my lips in case I lick the salt and become more thirsty and use more water than I need.

Soon I feel cheerful enough to fret again over wasted time, and throw a few sharp words at the cocoa tin. More seawater showers and another drink, and all is well this hot day under the sun, alone and enclosed by the ocean.

MARCH 1 · The sun rose pale yellow and I got a good shot of Jupiter to fix my position. As the sky lightened, little cat's-paw waves ruffled the flat surface of the sea and the cocoa tin made an occasional curtsy. I flew into action to get ready to sail. But the breeze died away again.

A huge tanker passed on my starboard side and then steered back toward Africa. I wondered: what was her story, and did anyone on board know there was another man just a mile away?

A breeze ruffled the sea again, and then a puff pushed us along as I hoisted the jenny. The sudden rocking of the cocoa tin in the little wind was, I thought, a message of Godspeed as I said farewell.

Late afternoon and we are moving along slowly, the heat made bearable by the light breeze. I think we may be doing half a knot, vaguely in the direction of the West Indies. I sit in the cockpit unclothed with my feet up beside the tiller, which with its cord lash-up needs just a touch every two minutes or so to keep her on course. Barbados radio now comes in clearly: "This weather forecast is brought to you with the compliments of Manning Wilkinson, hardware, lumber and appliance dealer, conveniently located in Bridgetown. Wind northeast, 8 to 15 kilometres an hour, sea slight to moderate in open water. Take some time to relax and put your feet up. But oh, my dear! Your footwear! You need Benson and Company."

As night falls we've done 15 miles in 15 hours. And they tell me the winter is the time to sail the Atlantic, when the trade winds are strongest and truest!

MARCH 2 · The early morning darkness brought soft, cool air on my face, and a huge bird hovered about five feet above us, his dark outline against the darker sky showing a wide wingspread and square-cut tail. A land bird, tired, looking for a perch?

"Wait there, my friend," I told him, "and I'll bring you a light on the rail to encourage you down to rest."

While I went below he left us, but like my other bird visitor two days ago, the warmth of his presence stayed.

It was a beautiful dawn, good to be alive in the early morning light. When the breeze shifted a little I was concerned that we were sailing slightly off course. But when I picked up the RDF station in Barbados I knew all was well this lovely Sunday morning.

The church service comes swinging in loud and clear: "Oh Jees-us, come to me today-ay. "Oh Jees-us, keep old devil away, clap clap."

Now we have a good strong wind at last and we're running straight for Barbados. The tiller remains tied with cord and I'm using the pole to boom out the jenny on one side with the main on the other. But she's not steering herself even with the cord because the wind is practically dead aft. She's sheered off twice while I've been talking. So I must stay at the tiller just to give her a touch every few minutes. This is really bothering Authority.

"For God's sake, Griffiths! You're getting close to the island. Can't you put the boat on a tack so she'll steer herself after a fashion with the shock-cord lash-up? Then you can leave the cockpit to square up, ready to come into port. Have a shave, you've got a bit of water. And you must get a meal, work out your position, put on a clean shirt."

Submission didn't want to listen. We're going beautifully, straight for Barbados. He was exhilarated and didn't want the excitement to stop for the sake of a few chores. "On a tack, sir, we won't be headed for Barbados, and we'll have to come back on course. But I suppose that's what we'll have to do."

On a tack she steered herself, more or less, while I cleaned the stove, kettle and pressure cooker. I laid clean canvas over the stained and water-marked cushions on the bunks. All looked neat. Then I raised four flags, the pennant of the Royal Naval Sailing Association, the Barbados flag and the Canadian flag and ensign. They streamed and snapped in the wind.

Forty miles to go. I've altered course now and returned to the tiller for the run-in.

Now it's 9:30 at night. It's dark.

In the blackness I can see a light! Just a pinprick.

I haven't identified it yet. But that's the island alright. My navigation was spot-on. Forty days alone.

A light!
I can't talk.

MARCH 3 · It's after midnight and I'm on watch in the cockpit under the stars. Now I can identify the navigation lights, and I can see the shore lights winking and the loom over Barbados.

There's a bad patch of turbulent seas and currents ahead and I need to get in toward the coast a little more. So I'll change tacks to start the run-in to the South Point and round the corner.

I've been alone with *Kairos* for so long. The only sounds I've heard have been the boat working, the wind and the sea. They have all given me their messages. Now I'm feeling ambivalent about arriving. If only I could enter civilization gradually. The noise, the forms. The bustle. If only I could slowly lose the timelessness of the sea for the hurry of the land....

Now we're coming in. It was a wild ride down the northeast coast. There's a reef to watch out for and I was about a half mile outside it, practically planing. After I rounded the South Point, with six miles to go, I got the main down. And now we're sailing into Carlisle Bay underneath the jenny. I can anchor at the yacht club.

It's a very blue sky with soft clouds and the sea deepest blue. We sail, a battered little boat with flags flying almost defiantly, past white beaches, hotels, houses. The pier on the point where yachtsmen used to land is now part of the property of the Barbados Hilton. Civilization! Restaurants! Hot coffee! I suddenly realize I haven't eaten for 16 hours. I can't leave the tiller now.

I entered Carlisle Bay under motor. Suddenly something went wrong with the engine. The red light was on and, tired, I assumed it was telling me it needed oil. But the oil spurted back violently, spattering the clean cabin. My heart sank. There were some beautiful well-kept yachts at the anchorage. Little *Kairos*, smelling of oil, came in alongside them.

It was a remarkably strong wind for the shelter of the bay, and we blew around a couple of times. I was backing and filling when we were hailed by a swimmer coming toward us. "*Kairos*!" I peered to see who it was.

"Congratulations, Dad!"

"Mark!" I wanted so much to see if I could touch his hand. But *Kairos* needed all my attention.

"You go over there, Dad, to the careenage – you see where I'm pointing – to report to Customs. I'll join you over there."

He swam away. I still feel delight that he saw me. Yet I sit here, head in hands, in the cockpit. I need just a few more still moments. I should have remembered to go to Customs first. But I've been so free of bureaucracy and filling out papers, out there on the water.

Let's be quiet together for a little while longer, *Kairos*, just the two of us. The way we've been. Alone with the sea and the sky.

Thank you for your courage, little ship. And now it's done. An old man's dream.

I have a card in the "odds and ends" plastic bag and I'll get it out now while all is quiet and write my message, ready for mailing along with the earlier Valentine card.

This card I got in Gibraltar. It has a basket of roses on the front. A blank page inside waits for my message.

"To my Margaret,

In mid-winter you looked inside my heart and found the lingering glow of summer,

And now I'm coming home to you.

Keep a light in the window, Love."

MARCH 3 · I started the engine after Mark directed me where to go, and with a spurt of oil around the galley we came alongside the Customs wharf. A tall man with beautiful white teeth against his dark skin greeted me and asked my last port of call.

"Los Cristianos," I told him. I couldn't understand his reply but I realized from his gesture that he was offering to keep the boat tied up at the Customs wharf until the morning. Then I could clear and anchor outside Carlisle Bay.

I was grateful.

Mark was there and had brought me fresh milk and fruit. After we had gone below to be quiet in the cabin together, and I drank some cool milk and nibbled the fruit, he took me back to the hotel, about 20 minutes away, where Blair greeted me. He had stayed inside, nursing an eye infection.

I felt such joy to see both my sons. Tired, tired joy.

I had a shower at the hotel, blessed sweet water splashing over the salt on my dry skin. At a turn of the tap out it rushed, a soothing, comforting miracle, fresh water running through my stiff, salty hair.

"When did you last eat, Dad?"

"Hours ago."

"When you've rested we'll take you out to dinner. We'll walk slowly while you get your land legs." I needed to phone Margaret to tell her I had made it. "We'll find a phone."

I would tell them later how I had stayed awake at the tiller since coming into shipping lanes, about 36 hours, then let the boat steer herself on a tack so I could tidy everything up. And then the engine acted up and sprayed oil all over the place, over the chart table, over me, over the galley.

But I wouldn't talk of that. Just now it was all smiles. I had wanted to sail a little boat by the winds and the currents across the Atlantic with only the very basics in equipment, and it was done. My dream that I waited until old age to fulfill. So why, in my rejoicing with my sons, was there this feeling of anticlimax? Is it really better to travel hopefully than to arrive?

No, I was just tired.

There was joy and celebration in a restaurant with a good menu and a tablecloth. From a telephone in the lobby I phoned Margaret. I heard her voice.

"You're safe! You've done it! You've lived your dream. Who shall I tell? I'll tell the whole world!"

I laughed. "I don't think the world will be very interested!"

All my anxiety anticipating the complication of land after the simplicity of the sea was gone now. It was done! Such happiness! Such weariness! Such lashings of hot coffee!

When I was clearly fading the boys put me in a taxi to go back to the boat. Low with exhaustion and high with celebration I trundled across the Customs wharf to board *Kairos*, so glad not to have to paddle out to the anchorage and climb aboard in the dark. And so glad to have water and light that had been provided by a new man on duty who was expecting me.

I lay in my bunk on a hot velvet night with the moon in the quarter showing through the hatch. I picked up the tape recorder to talk to Margaret but woke in the first light to find it nestled in my arms. I began to record in the half-light.

MARCH 4 · "Margaret," I told the instrument,

> I'll leave here and come home as fast as I can. The boys will help me
> to get the boat ready for the Pacific, and for that I must be out of the
> southeast of this ocean by the end of June. I have a long list of jobs to do
> before I leave Panama and I must hurry, but for Blair and Mark on
> holiday we'll sail around the islands and overhaul the boat as we go.

I'm very tired.

I'll still be the same when I come back to you. But you may think I'm different. No one can be alone for 40 days and nights and still be exactly the same. With only the dome of the sky above, and the rhythm of the sea under the boat, sailing toward the horizon, I have learned silence. This isn't natural to us. If only the world could learn it, we would all be at peace. But it takes effort to stop the chatter in our heads, and when we do we can get rid of all the unproductive darkness and let in the light. This is what has happened to me and I'm sharing with you my heaped-up heart. You will so readily know what I am saying.

It's almost April now, and you will see from the kitchen window on the island the heron on the point by the beach, and he will be squawking his coarse cry to let the world know that he has found a girl heron, and they will stand together, side by side, on their long spindly legs, looking for a ruffling of the sea that might mean breakfast. Do you remember the seagull who offered a girl gull a gift of evergreen as they stood on the point? And she ignored it. He just said 'To hell with it,' and flew away.

Born on a Thursday, I still have far to go. There will be many, many more miles under my keel before we come storm-weathered into Montague Harbour, back to you and the house and the fireside.

So I prattled on, dreaming, until I was suddenly boarded by Customs, given a quick look over, and released with kind smiles to anchor off Carlisle Bay.

The boys went off exploring Barbados in a hired car, to give me space to sort myself out. At anchor I was of interest as the new arrival, the new boy. People rowed over from a nearby yacht to ask about the voyage and give me a coconut.

"Was it a good crossing?"

"Mixed weather. Some rough bits. I lost the wind for a few days." That seemed to sum it up.

"Weather's been funny all around this year."

"Would you like to come aboard? I'm clearing up after an oil spurt from the engine. Mind where you sit."

"Where are you from?"

"British Columbia. From an island off the west coast of Canada."

"Is that your house – that picture propped up against the sink? You must be wanting to get back. I've often wanted to visit Canada."

"Come and see us. Margaret will be delighted. I haven't a card to give you. I ran out and asked her to send some more but it seems to slip her mind. Here's our telephone number."

I went ashore with my new friends for a celebration and toasts for the success of the Pacific journey ahead. Then, very early to bed, homesick but content, and tense thinking of the engine to repair and everything else I have to do before I start the next long haul across the ocean for Canada.

MARCH 5–23 · In the morning Mark and Blair came aboard. They had snorkels and fins, baggage and cooking utensils in case I give them my pressure-cooker stew. Looking like a tinker's stall, we got under way with stores reduced to a minimum for space and spare sails lashed on deck to make room below so three of us could sleep. Before we left Barbados a young Dane came aboard to look at the engine. He prescribed parts that might be obtainable in Martinique....

The boys and I are working on the boat. Intending to visit St. Lucia and St. Vincent, we came here first, to Bequia harbour, without using the engine. In the dark, using eyeball navigation and with the rain coming down like a curtain, we anchored under sail. From here we have put in to different islands, becoming used to seeking harbour without the engine.

I have become old-maidish, knowing where I can reach out my hand in the cabin and find what I need in a hurry. Under fins and snorkels and pans this has become a challenge. A few nights ago the boys took the dinghy over to another yacht to join a party of young people drinking the local rum. At two in the morning voices carried this way. Laughter. Splash. More laughter. Who fell in? Bump against the boat. Coming aboard. Two wet giggling bodies framed against the night in the companionway.

"We didn't wake you, did we, Dad?"

The next morning they went over the stern to fix the self-steering. They didn't look well. Blair was wildly wielding a chisel and Mark said they couldn't get the sleeve off the disconnected paddle. To mend and secure it took days of work from all three of us. But it was done and well done.

Mark wears a bandana because his hair is receding and he has sensitive skin. He also wears dark mountaineering glasses, and with a huge glob of zinc ointment on his nose he looked fierce enough to ward off any thieves. But the next day we woke to find the dinghy missing. Our three perspiring bodies were marooned below decks in pouring rain. If I had tried in vain to get a new valve in the West Indies for the leaking dinghy, I was hardly likely to be able to purchase a complete new dinghy here.

Two kids came by in a rowboat, soaked to the skin, selling limes.

"Lost your dinghy, sir?" asked one politely.

"Yes. Do you know where it is?"

"Oh no, sir! But I know where you can get another one. For three hundred EC dollars."

He was looking most helpful.

I felt cornered. I handed over the money and got back my inflatable dinghy with a leaky valve. There was not much air left in it.

That was the day we met Anton, a young German with excellent English who came over from a nearby yacht, the *Anton V*. Anton was furious. He had taken the inter-island ferry, an old schooner called the

Mary Rose, to sail to St. Vincent to shop. A young man neatly dressed and wearing a smart peaked cap stopped him just before he boarded.

"Going on the *Mary Rose*, sir? Ten dollars, please."

Anton paid, boarded the schooner and settled down with a book. After a while he felt a tap on the shoulder.

"Fares, please. Five dollars."

"I've paid," said Anton.

"No you haven't. Where's your ticket?"

"I paid a man in a peaked cap in Bequia."

"Oh, you don't want to take any notice of him. Five dollars, please."

Anton could only fume and pay.

"They're bandits," he told me.

"No they're not," I said, because I thought I should be cheerful. "They've just got the cheek of old Nick."

"Who is old Nick?"

I changed the subject.

"You must be a very experienced yachtsman," I tried. "This is your fifth boat."

"It isn't and I'm not."

"But it's the *Anton V.*"

"I had it registered like that so everyone would think I'm an experienced yachtsman. I've sailed for only two years. I'm going 'round the world. I live with my mother and she said she could manage without me if I went 'round the world."

I wanted to do something to make Anton happy.

"If you care to relax here a little while I can play you some Wagner. *Die Valkyrie*. My wife gave me some tapes. Do you like Wagner?"

"O ja!" And as the music played he stood up. About five feet three inches, he suddenly seemed to grow as he opened his arms and took charge of the orchestra. A long pointing hand would bring in the strings. A sweep would raise the music to a crescendo. Then he personally decided to introduce a trombone, "room-room-room."

Suddenly he said, with his German sense of order, "I must return to my ship, set the alarm, sleep, and sail at three o'clock for Martinique."

I turned off the tape and he sank back to five-foot-three. As he got in his dinghy and rowed away I was sorry to see him go. God bless you, Anton, going 'round the world by the clock.

Then there was the couple, Jeff and Lulu, on a catamaran. They had spent so much money repairing a mizzenmast broken in a storm that they couldn't afford to slip the boat. They decided to careen her native-style, pulling her onto the beach to inspect and paint the hull while she rested above the tide. There had been an outpouring of sympathy in the harbour over the broken mizzenmast and the cost of repair, and on the strength of that Lulu enlisted every young, able-bodied man she could find, including Mark and Blair, to pull the catamaran up onto the beach. Fortified with the local rum, they were to heave the boat out of the water on a rope. Straining and sweating in the heat, they could only pull her so far and then she stuck.

Lulu dished out more rum punch and everyone pulled and sang and pulled. The boat didn't budge. Stronger rope and bigger blocks made no difference. The catamaran remained half in and half out of the water and Jeff seemed very low in spirits.

I looked at the scene, and thinking aloud, said, "A Land Rover would help." The next thing I knew Jeff was renting a taxi. It was a scantily equipped Land Rover and he engaged it for a couple of hours. Horsepower added to human power hauled the boat up.

While Jeff and Lulu worked on their hull we left Bequia and sailed to St. Lucia and then on to St. Vincent for Blair to fly back to Vancouver via Barbados to return to work. Mark went to Martinique to see if he could get the engine parts recommended by the Dane in Barbados, and I promised both my sons that I would let them know how Jeff and Lulu got the catamaran back in the water.

MARCH 24 · With so much going on around me I'm no longer talking regularly into the tape recorder. That was part of my solitude. But now, after time with my sons I am alone again in the harbour of the island of Bequia. I have told Mark that if he finds a glamorous boat going to romantic places from Martinique, he should go where adventure takes him, and if engine parts are available there, and he lets me know, I can scoot up to get them. So I wait to hear from him, aware of deadlines to get out of the southeast Pacific before the hurricane season.

The rain is teeming down, drumming on the coach-house roof, the air heavy and hot in the cabin with the ports and hatches closed against the downpour. Lying in my bunk, perspiring and thinking of home, where the cool mist hangs in the fir trees and the wind blows from the sea, I have been listening to the tapes that Margaret sent with Mark, hearing the everyday happenings and sounds of our place in the bay while she and our friends wait to hear where I am, and if I made it safely across the Atlantic. She has been building rock walls in the garden at different heights according to her level of anxiety. One of them, she says, is seven feet.

The neighbours send good wishes, and I hear on the tape Cynthia's lovely laugh and Gordon's repertoire of funny stories in the life of a doctor. Ragna, the Swedish lady up on the hill who will never use one syllable if three will do, sent advice, believing I am surrounded by topless ladies in grass skirts. They all toasted me at a party, wished me safe return, and sang in wonderful discord:

> *Red sails in the sunset,*
> *Way out on the sea,*
> *O carry my loved one*
> *Home safely to me.*

Then Margaret chatted with the news from home that I waited for.

> *Today it was cold and snow piled up among the daffodils. The*
> *first hyacinths are beaten down by the rain and I've gathered*

*them and brought them in. They scent the house. Blair has
pruned the maple tree by the deck.*

*I think of you coming in to Barbados, tired and wanting rest. I
wish I could be waiting for you with the boys as you come into
harbour. I sat on the stairs and thought about it. But you and the
boys need to get the boat ready for the long sail home. That's the
most important thing, for you to come safely back. My thought is
always with you and we'll have our own quiet reunion without
deadlines, sometime, somewhere."*

I won't mention to Margaret my hope that we can meet in Hawaii
for a few quiet, magical days, not until I see how the time goes, but
cherishing that hope, I shall get harbour charts for Honolulu. I
should have brought them with me. I should have done a lot of things,
like knowing to clear Customs when I came in to Barbados, but I had
gotten so far away from bureaucracy. Now I am lying in my bunk remembering it all, that day when I came in, exhausted in my battered,
oil-stained little craft.... and the weeks that followed.

After I said goodbye to the boys, I got back to Bequia in time to
see Jeff and Lulu's problem solved. This is where the *Tor Helga* came
in, a charter boat operated by a young Canadian called George Harris.
She was a funny ex-steamer kind of ship. As her brochure explained:
"A yacht she ain't." She was a popular boat with charterers who wanted
to stand upright instead of over on one ear with the wind. Jeff went
to talk to George Harris and a deal was struck to tow the catamaran
back into the ocean. The success of this feat was celebrated with a
party on board the *Tor Helga*.

Seeing my Canadian flag, George Harris asked me where I was from.

"From a little island off the Canadian west coast."

"I've just bought land in BC, on a beautiful island called Galiano,"
said George, and we had a bond. I was asked to the celebration.

Alone now, with more room on board to attend to my toiletries, I decided to make the best of myself for the party. I shaved, washed my hair, scrubbed myself in the cockpit and then applied an expensive and tasteful aftershave with matching deodorant that Margaret had given me in a little blue box. I put on a new shirt, purchased in St. Vincent, and climbed into the dinghy, which had been newly inflated. Then I rowed over to the *Tor Helga*.

People were coming aboard from an old Baltic trader from England, and the French crew members of a magnificent schooner called *Scaramouche* were waiting to go up the ladder with dishes of food. There seemed to be at least 30 people on the deck of the *Tor Helga* when I got there and they were still coming. Recipes from around the world had gone into the making of the spread on the table. To ravioli, made by George's pretty wife, Vera, were added a dish of fried conch from the *Scaramouche* and a highly seasoned fish dish from the Baltic trader. Curries and pastas came up the ladder, and rum punch flowed. The boat rocked with music, to the delight of the Harrises' baby, Adam.

My inside has been treated to some very nice fancy cooking since the boys joined me – stuffed peppers and poached things floating in a pan – but it's happiest with my pressure-cooker stew. My digestion understands it. When my stomach began to expand and contract on the *Tor Helga* and I remembered I hadn't brought the dinghy pump, I thought I'd better get back quickly to *Kairos* before I vomited or the dinghy deflated, whichever happened first.

Back on *Kairos* I lay in my bunk feeling worried inside. Giving my stomach a peace offering of Bournvita made with powdered milk settled it enough for sleep. Alone the day after the party, I made a soothing and delicious supper. Into the pressure cooker I emptied a tin of butter beans, a tin of baked beans, a tin of mackerel, garlic and curry powder, and stirred it all 'round in oxtail soup. Such a gourmet recipe really called for onions but there are none on the island. No bread is baked here and fruit is of poor quality. But the markets at St. Lucia and

St. Vincent are excellent. I decided while trying to cook without onions that it's time to catch the *Mary Rose* to get in some stores.

The next morning I took a sailbag for groceries and lined up to board the schooner for St. Vincent.

"Going on the *Mary Rose*, sir?" asked a polite man in a peaked cap. "Ten dollars, please."

I walked past him, like a man of the world who is hardly likely to be taken in. The old ship hoisted sail and we were away, helped by an ancient engine. Then, as I stood on deck I began to have doubts. I only had Anton's word that the man in the peaked cap was not the one with the tickets. Suppose I should be arrested for avoiding payment. Probably hauled off to Jamaica, to Kingston Jail. The shame!

We ran into a squall, and everyone on deck sheltered under an awning, blocking the view of the steersman, who continued by instinct. Then, thankfully, a dripping wet gentleman came round selling tickets.

"Five dollars, please."

"But I've paid," protested the man standing next to me in the deluge.

"No you haven't. Where's your ticket?"

"I've paid a man in a peaked cap."

"Ah, you don't take any notice of him."

"They're rogues," the man informed me, as he forked out five dollars, but I was busy watching one of the crew under the awning putting a long splice and whipping into an old piece of rope anyone else would throw away. I used to be good at that as a boy. It felt right, now, standing on the deck of the old schooner, in the rain.

When we left the *Mary Rose* for a quick shop in St. Vincent, the next rainstorm began to come down in a noisy, solid sheet that flooded over the gutters. I found shelter in a little store that sold bales of cloth, rat traps, chamber pots with roses on, Tilley lamp mantles and globes that just fit the galley light on *Kairos*. When I found a fruit and vegetable shop next door I was in clover, and poured stuff into my sailbag.

We all rushed back to the boat in the rain, carrying various prizes home. Stores were being loaded aboard for Bequia. Potatoes, cement and washing soap were stacked under the awning on deck. There was limited space below and a crowd squeezed under the awning, in front of the steersman's window, with the wet cartons of cement and washing soap. The crew hoisted the mainsail and the foresail and we headed for Bequia through the downpour. Once there, I pumped up the dinghy with a car pump I carry, rowed my stuff over to *Kairos*, struggled the sailbag up the ladder, and home, sweet home.

There was some of my good mackerel stew left to be warmed up. I read a little of Tillich under the Tilley lamp, knowing I had a good supply of mantles. The globe for the galley light fits exactly. What a thoroughly satisfactory day!

APRIL 1981 · The rain has been holding up many of the things I should be doing on deck. Still waiting to hear from Mark, I am not certain whether to take time slipping the boat here or wait until we get to Union Island. I keep reminding myself that I should be well out of the southeast Pacific by June and time is going quickly. But once in the trade winds we can scoot along under a boomed-out mainsail and foresail with a bearing-out pole. Yesterday I decided I really need a different, lighter pole for the Pacific than the one I got with such effort in Los Cristianos for the Atlantic. The ideal would be bamboo. But I wasn't sure as I got dressed whether I wanted to climb around looking for bamboo. The day had started unfortunately.

The heat in Bequia is too much to layer clothing with underwear. Most men just wear brief bathing trunks. With my old limbs I wear knee-length shorts. Those I managed to purchase locally were all in the wash bag, so I raked out a pair I bought in England but found the zipper had rusted. I rubbed it hard with WD-40, put the shorts on, and gave the zip a very sharp pull up. It shot up very quickly and inflicted on me great pain. My short scream was picked up by the terns and echoed by the bosun birds. Heads popped up in boats. A dinghy put out from the *Scaramouche*.

"Are you alright, George?"

"Just a little accident."

I thought I must be getting edgy, with the deadlines. I needed action. I needed to go and look for bamboo for a pole. I should also get some bits of bamboo to cover the outside shrouds where the wooden covers I have now are chafing and rotting away. At the local pub they had told me Alfred James is the man to contact. He looks after the cattle and the bamboo fields.

I started off to where the bamboo grows, along a road with scrawled notices saying the revolution is coming. Striding in giant steps over the fields was a man I thought might be Alfred James. I caught up with him.

"Excuse me, are you Mr. James, sir?" I added the "sir" because he was about six-and-a-half feet tall, four feet broad and carried a machete.

He walked on as though I hadn't spoken. I ran after him.

"Are you Mr. James?"

He stopped and looked at me in silence, weighing me up.

"Yes, I'm Alfred James. Are you the man wanting bamboo? You can have some. Here's a cutlass. Cross the road and follow the path up the hill. There you will find bamboo."

He strode away and I wandered across the road and followed a path for about 150 yards. Then the path vanished into bush. I walked around among the trees, hot and sweating, with the sun beating down on the hillside, until I found some bamboo.

I felt fine taking the brown bits because the new green shoots were already growing. I put my cutlass down and walked around looking for the best sticks. If I could find good ones 10 feet long I could trim them down to nine feet very neatly and have a foot left over to make a new ship's ladder.

I found some good bits, but then couldn't find the cutlass. I looked for it desperately because I could see Alfred coming up from the road below. My shirt was wringing wet with sweat. I took it off and spread it on the ground to dry while I scanned the hillside for the cutlass. Then I couldn't find my shirt.

Alfred was coming up fast, in huge steps.

"How ya' doing?"

"I've lost my shirt and your cutlass."

He said nothing at all. He just turned, and we both looked carefully over the ground, walking it one way and then the other under the beating sun. I found his cutlass and he found my shirt.

Alfred looked rather doubtfully at the bamboo sticks I had picked out. In fact, by now, he was looking doubtfully at me altogether.

"There are better ones higher up." He started up the hill with me scrambling after him, perspiring, carrying my shirt and the cutlass. Up a ravine, over rocks that loosened when I grasped them, up higher we went, finding at last a sheltering of trees. There, in a small clearing, the good bamboo grew.

I chose two sticks that lay on the ground and cut off 10 feet. Then I found thinner bits I could split for the shrouds. As Alfred and I lugged them back to the road his shiny black skin began to pour with perspiration.

"Would you like a beer, Alfred?"

He would. We headed for a rather grand hotel that seemed to be having a lean season in the rain and might admit us. I put on my wet shirt and Alfred mopped his brow. We left our weapons, the machete and the cutlass, in the hall. In the bar Alfred perched on a stool, doubtful that it would support him, but it was stronger than it looked. The barroom was cool and the barman brought two long glasses of cold ale. We lingered over it, side by side, balancing on our high stools, speaking few words, tired and satisfied. We parted with a handshake, Alfred proudly refusing payment. Then he gathered up his weapons from the hall and was gone.

I had already learned in Los Cristianos that the way to meet people with a genuine interest in you is to walk along the waterfront carrying a very long pole. I received several inquiries about the bamboo sticks I carried, and a young German boy on a nearby boat dashed over in a dinghy to help me to row them out to *Kairos* and struggle them up the ladder. When we got aboard he showed me how to split the thinner bamboo and then make eyes and toggles to secure them around the shrouds. He brought news of Henri.

"Have you heard?"

Henri made his living helping on boats and painting very good watercolour pictures of yachts for 10 EC dollars. He had made a picture of *Kairos* and I had mailed it to Margaret. He was a sensitive and unworldly Frenchman. His pleasures were simple. Klaus, the young German, told me Henri had been arrested for smoking marijuana. He had been sitting by the seashore puffing on his cigarette, in the quiet of the evening, in harmony with the world, watching the sun go down, when a policeman in plain clothes took him to Kingston Jail. They put him in a cell for a year unless he can pay a fine of 1,500 EC dollars.

I thought of Henri sweating in that hot prison in Kingston as I prepared my supper of scrambled eggs. I had suddenly lost all appetite. The eggs were beaten but I didn't put them in the pan. I didn't want them. Henri would rot in prison. He wasn't physically strong. He had delicate hands that loved to paint. Would he be given hard labour? Perhaps, if everyone at anchor in the harbour gave a few EC dollars, we could get him out.

"Georges! Georges!" I heard a cry from a swimmer. I couldn't believe it. It was Henri! "Georges! I'm free!" He was swimming around the harbour and calling to each boat.

"That good American lady who rents a house on the shore, she paid my fine! She got me out! But I'm leaving the islands. They're no good now. All is changed. It's all prison and fines and come the revolution." He had met some French-speaking people from Luxembourg who were going down to Venezuela, and he was going with them.

Now I felt hungry. I poured my eggs into the pan, scrambled them up and thoroughly enjoyed them.

As evening came a fierce squall blew up. My flags flapped madly and boats in the harbour began to swing at anchor. The rain suddenly beat down on the coach-house roof again. Yes, the locals must be right and the rainy season is starting early. In fact the weather pattern is very odd, with one or two days of westerly winds, which is most unusual for the season.

But as suddenly as it started, the rain stopped. Now all is quiet and the sea is calm. I have lit the Tilley lamp and it makes the cabin hot, but when this downpour is over I can open the ports and hatches and let in the air, hot air though it may be. As darkness falls the moon comes out and the still sea is full of phosphorescence....

I am lying in my bunk thinking of my family and the long voyage home to where the rain is gentle. It was quite wonderful to have Blair and Mark with me these past weeks. Mark has been an Outward Bound instructor for six months. The boys recently went off together to climb Mount McKinley, and a few months ago Blair made a spectacular film of mountaineering in Peru. He hopes this will earn him a place as photographer with the planned Canadian ascent of Mount Everest this fall. Through a new satellite technology it will be possible to beam a video of the climb as it happens into people's living rooms on the CBC news broadcast. Blair, as a CBC cameraman specializing in the evening news, wants the job. It would be the film of his life. I am fearful for him, just as, I suppose, Margaret is fearful for me. I thank her for her patience and anxious waiting. I now know a little of how it feels. Until I get home the highest mountain in the world will haunt my thoughts. As I plan to sail on I have a strange feeling of foreboding and I don't know what it's about.

It's beginning to rain again but I shall leave the ports open.

I am thinking very much tonight of those I love – of my sister Eileen, who died just as she and her Jack were planning to leave Alberta and live in a house not far from us. Of my niece Sue. And of Margaret's children, Michael and Corinna. I love Michael's sudden smile. And I love it when his two little boys put their hands in mine and we go down to the beach below the house to find all the wonders in the pools, the little crabs under the rocks, the funny sight of a seagull eating a starfish, only able to eat half and leaving the other half outside his beak until his stomach has digested enough to swallow the whole thing. The youngsters run around, watching the spit rise from hidden clams.

Corinna knitted me a woolly hat for the voyage and I blessed her for it over and over, especially in the Bay of Biscay. Her children gave me my Saint Christopher medallion to wear on this voyage and bring me safely home. But in some wrenching movement I broke the chain and lost the medallion. I can't find it. It must be in the bilge. It was important to me. Wherever it is on the boat, it sails on with me as a talisman....

A little while ago I went through my tapes and chose something Viennese. I imagined Margaret sitting on the bunk beside me and in fantasy I asked her formally: "May I have this waltz?" Then slowly in my half-dream we circled the cabin, then upward, faster, above the mast, circling, in step together, light as feathers, up, up, 'round and 'round, into the sky, until we were dancing on the clouds.

Our music will always play, I told myself.

Now a tune is floating this way from a ship somewhere in the harbour. It drifts across the water. Someone else is full of longing in the never-ending rain. I recognize Nancy Sinatra singing "alone on the water and turning for home."

This morning I had a telegram from Mark. He said it has proved impossible to get the engine parts in the Caribbean.

So we must sail to Canada without an engine, little ship. It's just you and me, the wind and the sky.

8 PANAMA

MAY 1981 · We shall be two on the voyage home. And my diary on tape is written rather sporadically.

I waited on Bequia to hear Mark's plans, because from Martinique the opportunity opens up to crew on fine vessels to so many exotic places. When he came back to me I was delighted to see him looking so well, and even more pleased when he climbed aboard *Kairos* and said, "Dad, let's go home together."

But if we are to be a crew of two, there are plans to be made and quickly. With the extra food, water and baggage we shall be heavier than before and the boat will ride deeper in the water. So we decided to slip *Kairos* at Union Island, and while hauled high and dry, to raise the waterline.

As a solitary sailor I had used the starboard bunk for stores. With two of us on the long haul home with extra food and water, and the bunk needed for sleeping, we would have to revise the storage plan.

Sailing without the use of an engine needn't be a problem until we reach the Panama Canal, which is traversed under power. And then in the Pacific, crossing the area of chaos known as the doldrums – propelled by unpredictable winds without the occasional push of an engine – will be a challenge.

With all planned, stored, repaired and ready except for slipping, we left Bequia for Union Island on May 10. The wind was steady all the way, and we dropped anchor under sail. Planes were landing, bringing people in from Martinique to many French-run charter businesses for fishing and exploring the clear water and coral of the Tobago caves.

We pumped up the old leaky dinghy and rowed ashore to make arrangements to slip. The next morning I ran the engine for three minutes to position *Kairos* on the cradle, and an alarming plume of black smoke came from the exhaust. Once she was hauled up it became a "do-it-yourself" project.

For four days on Union, Mark and I gave the hull a good going-over, raising the waterline and applying antifouling paint to the ship's bottom. All the oil I poured into the hull in Mashford's yard has paid off and she is standing up well in the tropics. We gave her another coat of oil. Alongside us was a very large schooner. One of her crew called to us: "You're not sailing the Pacific in *that* wee boat?" If *Kairos* could hear I hoped her stout heart was not saddened by such an insensitive comment.

It was good working with Mark. In the hotel at the yard we got morning coffee and toast and then started a full workday. We lived and ate aboard. One morning we found a conch shell, covered in little shells, and decided to praise the Great Architect and commend the fishy inmate and builder rather than drag him out and have him for lunch.

Finally, with a feeling of work well done, we slipped down and anchored under sail off a reef, an unavoidable adventure in such a jagged underwater landscape.

There was no one at the yard to advise us about the engine. We were anxious to leave for a better anchorage.

"It's the beginning of the rainy season, alright," called one of our neighbours in the harbour, in a voice almost lost to the rising wind. There were fierce squalls that night, and in the morning we left in a strong, steady wind that brought us under the lee of Grenada. There we sailed into a rectangular harbour in the middle of town and anchored in an area for seagoing vessels. No one from Immigration came to visit us, so in the morning we rowed ashore. At the office we were told we were not seagoing, and to leave the harbour and go to the lagoon with the small pleasure craft. I said that if we had come from England and were going to Canada, we must be seagoing. A reluctant customs officer looked disdainfully at our rubber dinghy, allowed himself to be rowed over to *Kairos*, boarded her, gave her a cursory look, refused to stamp our clearance papers and said we were mad to take a boat that size into the Pacific. He told us to go to the lagoon, as we had been told before. There, another customs officer stamped our papers and apologized for treatment that may have left us insulted. He felt that a little storm-battered vessel should not have to lose respect.

We topped up the lamps and the fuel in the stove, filled the water containers and took on more stores.

We had two more ports of call to make before reaching the Panama Canal. Mark wanted to see the flamingos on the island of Bonaire. And our friends in Vancouver, the den Oudens, have a nephew on the island of Curaçao, and he had promised us showers and the use of a washing machine. In the stifling heat a shower is a real luxury, and we decided to hurry.

On May 24 we sailed for Bonaire.

We beat into an anchorage and rowed ashore. The island was still and eerie. Mark wanted to change some money. The bank was closed. I wondered if we could get some milk. The grocery was closed. The streets were empty. It was as though some disease had wiped out the population. A man walked alone along the sidewalk. We caught up. "Why is the town closed down?" Mark hoped he spoke English.

The man smiled at him and flapped his arms. "Today we fly to Heaven."

It was Ascension Day.

Mark was sure something must be moving on the island.

"Where are the flamingos?" he asked and flapped his wings too.

The man laughed, then indicated to the north.

We thanked him. There was no traffic. No taxis. No means of getting to the north end of the island. Everything had flown to Heaven, even, perhaps, the flamingos.

In the early hours of May 30, just after midnight, we had a good sail to Curaçao in a hot tropical wind, thinking of a cool shower. Through a narrow passage that widened into Spanish Bay we found an anchorage and went to sleep. Both bunks in the cabin have flaps that can be lashed to the grab rail above, forming a kind of hammock. We were gently rocked, listening to the soft slap of water against the wooden hull.

In the morning we were boarded by immigration officers, who illegally took away our passports. We objected and they explained that people on small yachts like ours are likely to run up bills at the local stores and then sail with the wind. By now we had found nothing was an insult. We and the boat are indeed weatherworn and probably look disreputable.

We explored Williamsburg, a sophisticated, expensive and prosperous place on this island made rich from oil. We phoned Alex den Ouden, and the next day he and his gracious lady took us to their apartment in a wide, cool alley and invited us to shower in cold water, there being no need for running hot water in the tropics. In freshly laundered clothes we ate in the shade at a local club. Clean, fed and grateful, we returned to our small storm-battered vessel bobbing at anchor among the luxury yachts. Most boats here fly the flag of Venezuela and have come for the sport-fishing.

On June 4 we sailed for the Panama Canal. As we left, the wind was 16 to 20 knots, gusting to 35, and we were under a reefed main and mid-jenny. For three days there was a shrill and following wind, sometimes gusting to gale force. Big rollers came up astern and sometimes broke into the cockpit. We flew on under reduced sail with old *Kairos* really kicking up her heels. In three days we had covered 350 miles and were halfway to Panama.

Then everything changed.

Mark said the seabird overhead was an omen.

It was a bird I call a shag, blackish-brown, and against the roaring wind it hovered above us with its legs tied with twine that blew out about four feet. It dipped into the rolling sea to try to free itself. Weary, it may have tried to rest on top of the mast but slipped and caught in the topping lift, hanging upside-down. As we dashed forward to lower the topping lift and release the flapping bird the blowing twine wrapped itself round its wings. It fell into the sea and sank, and we had a deep feeling of helpless sadness.

The sky blackened. We lost the wind. As we crawled along toward Panama the sea and sky were lit by lightning and the night filled with the roar of thunder. It was nine more days before we sighted land.

Mark and I organized ourselves into watches. Nearing Panama I was on watch from midnight till six in the morning, with Mark supposedly sleeping below. Because of the shipping around us, I sat at the tiller, hand-steering under a solid sheet of rain. Lightning was arcing all around, striking the water within half a mile. Mark came up on deck as a flash lit the sky as bright as day, then all was crashing chaos.

"Lucky we're in a wooden boat, Dad."

With the wind constantly changing we began to drift slowly round in circles. Within sight of land and anxious to set the best course possible, I would reduce down, thinking we must be in the forefront of the wind, but it would change and die away, the sound of the weakening blow lost in the roll of the thunder. Under black clouds we drifted closer, toward a breakwater, entering the Port of Cristobal on June 17. With such fluky winds I ran the troubled engine for three minutes, time enough to find an anchorage.

The port had five designations: big boats, small boats, transient boats, yachts and small craft. We had learned not to be uppity, and steered toward "small craft." Then wearily, we became lost children in the hands of immigration officials. We had no idea that a direct route to get our passports stamped was to slip someone 10 dollars. Otherwise a labyrinth of complexities would lie ahead, at greater cost in the end.

The Canal is administered by Americans who live in a fenced compound at Colon, and Panamanians, who boarded us at Cristobal and ordered us ashore. After filling in countless forms we protested against the removal of our passports but lost the battle. Vaguely we were directed to another immigration office. After walking about half a mile, past the university, we found a small shed marked "Immigration." The people there called a taxi that took us to a building at the other end of town. There, a man fumbled uselessly in some files and addressed us in Spanish. We waited and waited, with the taxi ticking outside.

Eventually a van drew up. It appeared to have brought our passports from the shed we had just left. A woman solemnly stamped them at a cost of 10 dollars and passed them to another woman. She also solemnly stamped them at a cost of 10 dollars. Then we were directed back to the taxi, which followed the van that was to take our passports back to the shed. There the passports were stamped for another 10 dollars and delivered to us. We were handed our property as though it were some generous gift, ours to keep. We were told to tie up at Number Two Dock. Arriving wearily back at the boat, we pressed the protesting engine into service long enough to squeeze ourselves between a French boat and an American one. I secured *Kairos* by the bow line and put out a stern anchor.

Then I began, with little hope, to examine the engine once more, groping underneath the cockpit floorboards, unable to face the mess and delay of taking them all up.

Someone peered at us from the French boat.

"Oi," he said, looking at our Canadian flag.

Thinking this was a French greeting I smiled.

"Oi," I replied politely.

"Where are you from?"

The man spoke English! I didn't expect anyone to know about Galiano so I said "Vancouver."

"We're going the same way. I'm Rand, and I come from Sidney. The Sidney on Vancouver Island."

"Then why are you flying a French flag?"

"The boat was registered in France. This is my friend Michel. He builds boats in Sidney."

Michel had just come up on deck and gave a warm smile.

I sat down heavily, glaring at the engine, wiping the sweat off my forehead in the noon heat.

"Will you tow us through the Canal?" I asked, encouraged by Michel's smile. "Our engine needs new parts and I doubt that I can get them anywhere here."

"You might have to wait for us," Michel warned. "I'm expecting money by registered mail and I can't leave until it arrives."

With winter drawing in soon, bringing gale-force winds off the American coast, we had no time to wait. But our options were few.

"I'm sure my mail will be here by next week," Michel was saying. "If it is, we'll tow you through."

My heart sank. I had found mail arrival to be a real uncertainty. I could see my quietly cherished plans for a reunion with Margaret in Hawaii withering on the vine. It was a good job I hadn't told her of my hopes. But perhaps Michel's mail would come soon.

"Thank you. We'll wait for you if you'll take us," I told Rand and Michel, seeing this as the only certain way to get through the Canal into the Pacific. We all decided to close the deal with a drink ashore.

As we climbed into our dinghies a woman on a small Contessa that had a motorbike in the cabin gave us a wave. It was apparently known on the dock that she had butterflies tattooed on various parts of her anatomy. We all waved back.

We made our way to the bar of a restaurant inside the yacht club that looked to be a popular meeting place. It was full and we shared a table with two Americans.

"Where are you from?"

"All of us from British Columbia, Canada."

Both of our new friends were familiar with BC. One, from Alaska, was working in Alberta but living in BC, travelling back and forth. He had registered his 42-foot boat in Vancouver and the provincial government had notified him that the sales tax due on his arrival in port would be $6,000. He was despondent.

I said, but not seriously: "Why don't you register her in Alberta? The sales tax is next to nothing there." Our friend was a huge man with a big black beard. He roared with laughter and slapped his leg. The idea of registering his boat in land-girt Alberta, in the shadow of the Rocky Mountains, appealed to him enormously.

"I'll register her in Calgary. I'll call her *Foothills Princess.*" He laughed again.

The other American was more solemn. He came from Port Townsend, in Washington State, and had often been to BC.

"We have a land of plenty," he said, "but you have a land of abundance. Your rivers! We in the States are becoming so water-short we shall have to come to Canada to buy yours."

"Can't have our rivers." Mark was appalled. They were for canoeing, for the salmon and tourist industries, for wildlife, for generating electricity in some cases.

Our friend persisted. "One day it will be inevitable that water from your rivers will be piped down to the States. What will you do?"

Mark said, "We'll pee in the pipe."

I said, "It's time for supper."

Back on *Kairos* I examined the soybeans I had left soaking. It was my turn to cook. These beans are so full of protein, and so light and compact to stow, unlike tins, that they're just the kind of food to see us through when *Kairos* commits herself to the winds and currents of the Pacific Ocean and we need our strength to do our part.

I made a good stew of beans, peas and sardines. Mark didn't like it much.

One late-June evening we lit the lamps and talked. We were finding the inequality of Port Cristobal hard to take. All the luxury, the expensive boats, the yacht club, protected by guards and fences, while a quarter of a mile away was grinding poverty, crime, police with guns and billy clubs, and the constant admonition not to walk alone in the town. We will be glad to be away, through the Canal, through its heat and fumes from running engines, out into the open sea.

Mark and I have gone over the boat, the newly greased winches, the sails, the rigging, and all is ready. Unfortunately I have lost the bearing-out pole that I went to such lengths to get in Los Cristianos, but we'll see how the bamboo will serve us. It tends to score the mast, but I'll see what I can do. I have also lost the log rotator but we can sail without one. It's just a matter of getting the boat home now by the easiest and quickest way possible.

We have been advised to take on all stores here, where the tide is only two feet and the shops are less expensive. At the other end of the Canal the tide is 16 feet, shops are 10 miles from the anchorage and everything is very dear. We'll get all we need here in the way of food and stove fuel to get us home. Water at this wharf is on tap, which saves us lugging it over to an anchorage. More water cans can be lashed on deck, and I've also made a canvas rain-catcher.

And now we're waiting, waiting, for Michel's money to arrive. We have waited, kicking our heels, for a week. Then another day, then another. Now the idea of spending time in luxury with Margaret in Honolulu seems just a fond dream that flew away.

And still we wait.

Mark has fallen asleep. He and I are getting along well in spite of such a small cramped space below. He's a tower of strength and will make it much easier for me on the homeward stretch. He's interesting, reads, and is studying an anthology of poetry, which we quote from together. He has shaved off his beard. We have worked on the hull of *Kairos*, but the hot sun has beaten down on the less-oiled cockpit and the brass portholes are sea-encrusted.

"Look as scruffy as you can entering home port," advises the man sailing with the motorbike and the butterfly-tattooed woman. "Customs will put their own value on the boat as you come in."

I lie in my bunk and think of home as a warm wind pipes up and the boat rocks.

Kairos will need work each spring. Then you and I, Margaret, will sail together to Blackfish Sound. And we'll go to the Charlottes, to wild, untouched country, just the two of us. Life will be wonderful.

I hold out my hand to you. You are there in my half-sleep but I cannot reach you.

You are so far away.

JULY 25 · We waited and waited for Michel's money to come, and finally it arrived.

Our friends fixed a tow rope to *Kairos* and began to pull her through the Panama Canal in the scorching heat. It took about eight hours, all ships under motor, to negotiate locks that lifted us high above sea level and down to discharge us at last into the Pacific Ocean. We gratefully said goodbye and wished Rand and Michel a safe sail home.

After looking longingly northward toward Canada and home we turned to sail southerly toward the equator, into the equatorial area of tropical current convergence known as the doldrums, so that we can arc around the hurricane tracks.

Under sail we seem to be taking forever to pass through this tropical area of low pressure, confused winds or none at all, and converging currents. It's a place where the ocean seems to have lost its mind. We are lucky to make 50 miles a day, not always in the right direction. When we reach 3 degrees North, or perhaps a little lower, we shall be able to pick up the southeast trades and they will carry us westerly for about 1,500 miles, still skirting the hurricane tracks. Then we shall angle north, back again through the doldrums, to pick up the northeast trades. They will take us, beating, home to those we love.

In a light wind the self-steering doesn't work; the current is adverse, the wind will freshen and die right away, the rain is incessant and the sky dark with lightning flashes. The sound of thunder rolls almost constantly over the ocean. The little boat is heavy with stores stowed fore and aft, and in a confused sea she is apt to hobbyhorse as well as roll.

We are finding the space below decks cramped for two on a long voyage. The table is up in the cabin, with crates and three water cans lashed on the cabin sole. Under these conditions tensions aboard could snap, but there is harmony, an appreciation of each other's efforts and a sharing of them. Sometimes there is a sharing of despondency over so little progress for so much work and the constant sail changes as the wind blows up only to die again.

JULY 26 · It is impossible to get good sights under the low, sullen sky but I estimate our position at 4 degrees North and 84 degrees West.

This dark, brooding area of the ocean has its own beauty. Today in the morning light, the sun sends one bright shining shaft through a break in the dark, banking cloud and a big black bird hovers with the sun on its wings.

JULY 27 · The pilot charts show the risk of gales increasing remarkably each month as we sail farther north, and time is of the essence now. The delay in Port Cristobal waiting for Michel's money to come through was hard on us all and I am afraid that my dream of meeting Margaret in Honolulu is definitely now just a fantasy. But delay is often the reality of sailing and we are grateful to be on our way, although in a chaotic sea.

I'm standing in the rain under a sky that is always overcast, with *Kairos* flopping around but doing her best. Beyond the dark clouds overhead the distant sky to the south is clear blue. It's all ahead of us, *Kairos*. When we get through this band of bewilderment we shall meet the steady winds and the warm sun. You're like the little red engine that said "I think I can, I think I can." When we pick up the trade winds you'll scoot along, singing "I knew I could, I knew I could."

JULY 28 · I have got good sights. We are 60 miles north and quite a distance east of our estimated position and I feel dejected. We have quite a way to go to that distant blue sky.

JULY 29 · We have closed the cockpit drain to collect the rain. After we have bailed out enough for our domestic needs, particularly for washing dishes that don't get clean in seawater, we leave the rest in the cockpit for a bath to clean off the tropical sweat. I miss my Saint Christopher medal. Wearing no clothes, I feel undressed without it.

I have just looked around for my mate. Mark is standing, sloshing around in the cockpit bath covered in suds. By the look of the sky there will be a shower in a minute to hose him down.

JULY 30 · We continue in the uneven tenor of our ways, but today was exciting. We saw another ship. We sent telepathic messages of good will to other souls on our ocean.

And then a little bird flitted around us, over the water. We wondered where he relaxes, has a home life, meets his mate.

"I suppose he has to wait until he gets home," I said.

"Just like us, Dad. Flitting over the ocean, thinking of a nest so many miles away."

JULY 31 · In conditions of such uncertainty we keep constant watch and hand-steer a lot of the time. If we leave *Kairos* to self-steer she will almost certainly fall astern, and we will have to bring her round and get her on course again.

Tuna and corned beef are getting monotonous and I trail a fishing line over the stern. But not a bite! A gannet flew overhead this morning, then dropped like a stone into the sea, pulling out of his dive with a fish, flying away low with his catch.

"Show-off!" I shouted, and tweaked my empty line.

The sky is still overcast and I haven't been able to get sights since July 28th. Not that we can hit anything. But with the need to save time we must plot the best course we can.

AUGUST 1 · I estimate we're fast approaching 3 degrees North and should soon turn, picking up the steady winds. Meanwhile, with hope, we make the most of every unpredictable puff in the rain and thunder, for beyond is that beckoning blue sky of the trade winds.

AUGUST 2 · We have caught nothing on the fishing line and long for fresh food. Today a fish landed on the deck: a beautiful creation, a wonderful gift. He shone, glittering with translucent spots. Judging him too perfectly made for the stewpot, we threw him back into the ocean.

AUGUST 3 · On the edge at last of a wind that blows up and pushes us along, we begin to angle westward. We are making three-and-a-half to four knots. Here we go! The southeast trades!

AUGUST 4 · The wind has been strengthening, and on a sunny morning, under that blue sky with white wool clouds that once seemed so distant, we have turned to be blown on a steady southeasterly and are abeam of the Galapagos Islands. Mark and I decided that when we pass the Galapagos – and they are now about 200 miles south of us – we will celebrate. As if invited to our party, about 50 dolphins appeared astern of us and danced around the boat. They leapt in the air, some a good six feet, and laughed like kids out of school. They jumped with wagging tails, wriggled, flopped back into the water in a wonderful dolphin game, and we were all laughing on this lovely morning. Dancing still, they fell back to play in the ship's wake. Goodbye. Take care. Thank you for coming to our celebration.

In the evening I made a bean stew that redeemed my stew-making abilities, which have been so derided by others. Onions, beans that had soaked, very flavourful Japanese tuna bought in the West Indies, herbs. It was so good I felt vindicated.

Now I am on the night watch and we are dashing along in spray under the moon.

AUGUST 5 · Sunday is washday. We wash the cockpit and the galley, we wash ourselves, and not wearing clothes saves laundry. I shave, but

Mark, having grown a fierce red beard since he shaved in Panama, doesn't need to.

We have picked up the favourable current. Soon the wind should swing around further to the southeast. We are listing at 15 degrees. The one on night watch has the weather bunk and checks the boat at least every hour. The one sleeping has the lee bunk.

AUGUST 6 · Our perpetually blue sky is darkening, and two bosun birds hover against the cloud. The wind is hot and the sea is full of whitecaps sending spray that hits the skin sharp and warm. In weeks to come, as we approach the Strait of Juan de Fuca in the cold, almost home, the sea temperature will have dropped 20 degrees and we shall remember these warm waters as we shiver in our oilskins!

AUGUST 8 · My fishing line went taut! I wound in another beautiful translucent fish, another work of art beyond any human creation. We admired his magnificence. Then, at the thought of more tuna and bully-beef, we apologized to him, banged him on the head and ate him. Then we thanked him.

The sky is overcast and we sail on under reduced canvas, averaging four-and-a-half knots.

AUGUST 9 · Running out of onions is something of a crisis. We are nearly out of fresh food and as I came off watch today I used the last eggs for breakfast. We've almost finished the fresh vegetables and have been out of bread for some time. We shall have to become very creative.

AUGUST 10 · We made a chowder of the leftover fish and Mark added dumplings made of Bisquick. It was excellent. We ended the meal with a toast to Prince Charles and Lady Diana and hope they will be very happy.

AUGUST 11 · We're down to a little below 2 degrees North under blue sky and white clouds. *Kairos* is running, heading westerly, with the current well behind her. We are embraced by the wind, blessed by the sun, alone on our ocean. We average 130 miles a day.

AUGUST 13 · We seem to be keeping the daily average of 130 miles. As I said, we have no log rotator now. A barracuda may have taken a liking to it and it was my last one. It seems to happen in these waters. We know so little of the busy marine world beneath us.

AUGUST 14 · We have a fair wind of Force 3 to 4 on the port quarter. With the big jenny up and full main we're rolling along at four-and-a-half knots.

I'm getting good sights in the clear blue sky. In two days we may begin to shape north and have to break again through the chaos of the adverse current. Then we will steer between the mainland and Hawaii.

AUGUST 15 · I'm looking at the stores and the possibility of a need for repair. I think we should keep our plans open to change, to put briefly in to the Hawaiian Islands if need be. But in my eagerness to meet Margaret there, in the days it seemed we would have time, I only got harbour charts for Honolulu. We are now being practical and saving time, and so we should put in to Hilo rather than go further up the chain. But it's not seaman-like to enter port without detailed charts of the harbour, and I don't like doing this at all. However, we're coming now to the point where we must decide whether we will alter course, to sacrifice a few days in order to check the boat before we face more severe weather as we approach the American mainland.

AUGUST 16 · Today was housekeeping day and I tackled the galley while Mark scrubbed out the cockpit. Then we scrubbed ourselves.

I still have my fishing line out, hoping to catch something small and tasty. A huge fish swam by, ugly as hell, and we were glad he gave our line a miss. Mark made a very good macaroni and sauce in the pressure cooker.

It's 20 days since we last saw a ship. I look up at the stars at night and wonder if we are companioned by other life in the universe, or do we on our planet sail through the cosmos as alone as Mark and I are, on *Kairos*, on our huge ocean?

AUGUST 17 · This evening there was a loud bang as the wind increased. The port after-shroud that helps to support the mast was blowing in the wind, snapped off at the eye. We jibed around quickly and got to work making a temporary eye with bulldog grips, and lashed it up with tackle. There's a strain on the shroud with three big jerry cans of water lashed to the bottom, and there must be pressure when the seas hit it. I have a spare if this repair doesn't hold. Now I've reduced canvas. We're only making two-and-a-half knots although there's a lot of wind tonight. But we're getting another 40 or 50 miles a day out of a freaky current.

AUGUST 18 · We're angling north now and we've decided definitely to go into Hilo to repair the shroud and take on stores. It blew hard all night and there was a wild-looking dawn. As we turn we still need the steady southeast wind we've been enjoying, but it's suddenly shifted 'round to blow from the east and we can't quite steer the course we need to take us straight for Hilo. I want to be a little high to allow for the westerly-going current. The northeast trades, when we pick them up, will also push us west.

AUGUST 19 · We're sailing with the mainsail and foresail extended like arms spread to the wind. With the twins up we have no steadying sail and we're rolling abominably. In all this motion Mark made bread in the pressure cooker. He amazes me! I made a curry and we followed it with tinned peaches as we literally roll along.

AUGUST 20 · I'm happy now about putting into Hilo. Without large-scale charts, I won't go in at night. When I'm there in harbour I want to go over the boat and be in the best shape possible to approach the North

American shoreline, especially as there's one particular patch at the head of the hurricane tracks that shows Force 9 winds on the pilot charts.

AUGUST 21 · Happy Anniversary, Love. Thank you for the wonderful years. You did say once you would like a single pearl on a gold chain. When I get back to Galiano we'll go to Victoria on the ferry, and we'll go to Birks and someone behind the counter will smile and lay out a piece of black velvet cloth and put a choice of pearls on it. And when you have chosen, it will be laid in a little box lined with silk.

With the wind and the current we're making 100 miles a day, coming home to you.

AUGUST 22 · The strong southeasterlies are still with us, pushing us along, but we begin to roll so abominably it's clear we are entering the low-pressure trough of the doldrums again. We spend time lashed in our bunks.

AUGUST 23 · There is a lot of uneven motion and the port after-shroud almost went again last night. An inspection in the dark found it hanging on with half the strands gone, and we began repairs at first light. I am at fault. The working of a wooden mast puts strain on the splice, and the bottle screws are too rigid. I should have put toggles on to give movement. All this rolling around in the adverse current is too much.

Another disaster was the rice pudding I made in the pressure cooker. It went wrong after I added powdered orange juice.

Before anything else goes wrong I'm going to bed.

AUGUST 24 · I officially came on watch at midnight, but with all this rolling I spent most of the time lashed to the bunk. I had a fantasy. We tied the boat up in Victoria and went to dinner at the Empress Hotel. The menu was lavish. There was music. The maître d'hôtel was so pleased to see us.

The reality! If we were to go into the Bengal Dining Room in our sea boots and anoraks, would the portraits on the walls frown down on us? Would the maître d' tell us to come back properly dressed? Would *Kairos*, sea-weary, with the dodgers stained with oil from a misbehaving engine, get a notice to move on while we were dining, and would we be hauled outside?

Oh well! It was just fantasy!

AUGUST 25 · We're now really breaking through the countercurrent and rolling our guts out in a troubled sea. But last night was beautiful with a brilliant moon bright on the crazy movement of the water, and all our friends the stars shone down on us. Daybreak seemed slow across a sky grown dark with tropical cloud, and then the rains came. Water spilled from the sky in a sheet and battered the little boat, filling the cockpit that still has the drain closed. On watch in the early light I rushed to get a bar of soap.

I swished around happily in the cockpit, thoroughly soaping myself while the sun came slowly up. The downpour rinsed me off. Then the rain stopped as though the hand of the keeper of these things in Heaven turned off the tap. A strong blast of warm wind caught *Kairos* by surprise, and dripping, I rushed to reduce sail, snapping on my harness. Looking at the black threat of the sky I put up the storm jib and well reefed the main. Just as we were all snugged down the wind died and we were left bobbing in a sea of current madness.

Mark woke in the badly broken rhythm of the boat and we prepared breakfast in the dips and jerks made by little peaks of waves running in all directions like frantic, frightened creatures. This kept up all day while we attended to our light chores of inspecting the rigging, bailing out the cockpit and retarding the clocks.

While heavy cloud hid the moon, Mark took the night watch. The sea surface remained darting and anxious.

AUGUST 27 · Ahead of us is blue sky. The northeast trade winds. The steady winds. The predictable current. I feel like a pilgrim looking toward the Promised Land.

But overhead it is dark and the sea flow beneath us still pushes and pulls. Earlier the skies opened and the rain poured down. We hung a bucket on the end of the boom. In no time we had about five gallons, and washed our hair and Mark's beard and our towels and sponged the sweat of the tropics from our bodies.

Then suddenly, about 30 yards off the port beam came toward us the beginnings of a water spout. It came on like a giant garden hose, twisting within a circle of about 80 yards, advancing on us like some huge sea monster. I shouted, "Let go the sheets!" Mark scurried for the foresheet and I for the main.

As the spout gathered energy and passed us astern the boat was spun around twice with frantic sails flying unsecured. Then all was still, a windless vacuum, with *Kairos* sitting on the water like something stunned. We watched to see if the spout would form itself into a pillar, but as quickly as it had appeared it dissipated into the blackness all around. We looked longingly at the distant blue sky.

Supper was macaroni, tuna and tinned peas. We carefully marked off the tins from ship's stores as we used them. The curry powder is going mouldy. We should have brought a fruitcake.

I'd like a piece of fruitcake. Not too dark and lots of cherries.

AUGUST 28 · I'm standing in the cockpit under a full moon that looks like a big fruitcake in the sky. We're rolling, clattering, with the boom slatting on a preventer. The sea seems to be acquiring some rhythm and less confusion, but barely.

Dawn will soon be breaking, and today is Mark's birthday. I've saved a tin of chicken for dinner and want this to be a birthday to remember.

AUGUST 29 · Mark says yesterday will indeed be a birthday he will never forget. First, the port shroud went again and we put shackles on. But then Mark decided to go up the mast and rig the spare shroud, which is not as thick as we shall need when we run into severe weather as we approach the mainland. The Oregon Coast particularly is notorious for its gales in August and September. But we can make repair in Hilo, and rig a new shroud there.

At breakfast we reviewed our lack of progress. Three hundred and fifty miles in six days, an average of 50 miles a day, and so far to go before winter. And it's not just the fault of the confused winds, or lack of wind, and the converging current. We have known for some time that a growth on the hull is holding us back. It's very bad on the starboard side, which has been deep in the water while we heeled over.

While I was considering this, Mark suddenly appeared wielding a scraper, wearing flippers and mask, and leaped overboard. With *Kairos* hardly moving he worked along the starboard side, taking off long, thick strands and throwing up on deck anything of special interest. I received gifts of a long tuber, a streamer of weed with a shell on the end and a crab living in the greenery, and a sea slug like a seven-inch centipede.

When he had worked along the starboard side he started on the stern. Suddenly he surfaced and flew through the air on the port side in a superb fluid movement, landing on deck with one hand on the gunwale. As I watched this feat with total admiration he pulled off his mask and sputtered, "Bloody shark!"

We peered over the stern and there he was, deep and shadowy, not huge, about six feet, hardly visible in the dark water, waiting. I give thanks that my son is safe.

After lunch Mark earned my admiration even more by announcing he would go down into the water again and finish the job. In mask and flippers he plunged over the port side and worked, looking over his shoulder every minute or two while I stood ready, holding a pole, determined to give any shark a sharp shove on the nose. When it was done, and well done, we declared a happy hour as the boat began to glide, slipping slowly and easily through the water.

For dinner the chicken went into the pressure cooker with some tinned asparagus, the juices making a gravy with marmite. With some dehydrated mashed potato, it was a celebration and we toasted ourselves, toasted each other separately and toasted everyone we know generally....

On deck in the hot night we looked up at the stars and considered the immensity of it all. We in our boat are such a tiny speck in the universe, living alone in our own small circle of horizon, with no other life but the creatures of the sea. Not a bird. No human voices but our own, here on the edge of the trade winds. We are at 127 W and 11 N.

AUGUST 30 · With the clean hull we slide through the water easily in a light breeze. On night watch I have been reading Ogden Nash's poems by flashlight while hand-steering, and as the new day breaks full of promise with a streak of turquoise across the dark sky, I have company. A seabird I can't identify tried twice to land on the mast and finally gave it up. He sits on the sea beside the boat, and we have chatted, about the weather, about his children, his mate, and has she laid any eggs lately?

"Do you like poems?" I asked him, and he bobbed up and down beside me.

"Here's one for you – Ogden Nash:

Hark to the whimper of the sea-gull,
He cries because he's not an ea-gull,
Suppose you were, you silly sea-gull
Could you explain it to your she-gull?

The bird had heard enough. He flew away in disgust. Alright. Your life is serious. All to do with survival. But so is ours, and laughter is part of survival. If only you could try it instead of crying.

The sun has risen warm and bright. As we glide on to harness the trade winds the sky is the colour of a robin's egg.

AUGUST 31 · The wind is still hanging in the south, on the port quarter. Under a clear sky I worked on the cockpit and transom, sanding, applying protective oil, trying to make my beautiful wooden boat look less of a tramp. One cloud crept across the sky, rained on all my work and moved on. I shouted, "And the same to you!" But I cheered up when my fishing line went taut.

"Mark, we've got supper!" But it was a case of the fish that got away. Perhaps I need a larger hook, but I don't want to catch anything too big.

Getting through the doldrums, or as the meteorological boys have it, the "intertropical convergence zone," has delayed us more than I anticipated, and stores are getting low. Introducing some variety into our meals is beginning to tax our ingenuity, and tomorrow we plan to sort out the tins of food stored in the bilge in double plastic bags.

SEPTEMBER 1 · Breaking into the northeast trades, we're sailing in ideal conditions now, with the wind NNE, Force 3 to 4. I put us at 13 degrees North, but I'm having difficulty with star sights because the silvering has almost gone from my sextant mirror, and the standby I brought along in case of accident is proving not good at night, though it's alright for sun shots. It's just as well that we've set course for Hilo. Also, the guard rail needs repair and I must renew the problem shroud. Smoky Stover needs a checkup. One burner is giving us trouble, and although we've tried to address the problem, it's not easy to disassemble a stove on a moving boat.

We examined the cans of food in the bilge and found that the metal on the tins bought in the West Indies is thinner than we use in North America, and didn't stand up to the rolling in the doldrums. Many of the cans of fruit have small holes. So our food supply is getting low and boring. We have some pulses, sardines and tuna, and eight packets of mashed potato. We still have two-and-a-half pounds of rice that I tend to avoid using. The black specks in it look to me suspiciously like droppings.

We'll store up in Hawaii before beating on the long home stretch. I want to check everything and make sure it holds together before we sail through the equinox into the long dark nights and shorter days.

SEPTEMBER 2 · At dawn I thought I saw a ship's lights, other humans in our world after 40 days at sea, but it was a very low star. The ocean is quiet, the wind steady at Force 4. Sailing under the mid-jenny is as perfect as I can ever imagine it.

SEPTEMBER 3 · I'm still using my standby sextant, and approaching an area where the hurricane track can reach. It's essential to have an exact position, so I'll begin using my old sextant with what is left of the horizon mirror.

We are bowling along under jib and well-reefed main at Force 6 to 7, making four knots toward Hilo.

Mark is stirring a pot of beans, muttering about crusty bread and fresh cheese.

SEPTEMBER 4 · We're averaging 100 miles a day. Using what mirror I have left in my sextant I took Sirius and an old moon that is nearly gone.

SEPTEMBER 5 · A good star shot put us within 500 miles of Hawaii, and I suggested we celebrate by adding a tin of ham, saved for such an occasion, to our pot of beans. Another excitement was a ship's light, probably on a vessel bound for Japan.

I asked Mark if he will come to the party I am beginning to plan for my 68th birthday in February. There will be people, and voices and laughter and a table piled high with every kind of food. Mark graciously accepted.

There is harmony on board, just the two of us, and I stretch out my hand to you, Margaret. That makes three of us.

SEPTEMBER 6 · I am anxious for a weather forecast. We are in an area where we need to know if there are any tropical storms around. I have tried to get the station that broadcasts from Colorado out of Hawaii with long-distance weather reports.

I also need to know exactly where we are. With so little silvering left on my sextant mirror, I missed the Pole Star, but just as day broke I got a good horizon and Capella, Sirius and the moon, which is just a departing sliver. I have difficulty getting a good cut. We roll along at Force 3 to 4.

SEPTEMBER 7 · It's overcast and raining and I've been nagging at myself for not getting more large-scale harbour charts for Hawaii. If we arrive at Hilo in the dark we'll wait outside the harbour for the light.

As I chafed uselessly at myself, a Hilo radio station came in loud and clear, with a good weather report, some commercials, and music that makes the feet tap. I told Mark there are no tropical storms in the offing but his mind is very focused just now on crusty bread, and his answer was unrelated to my important piece of information.

We began to work on making the boat shipshape and finding some clothes to wear to come into harbour. Clothing will feel strange.

I scrubbed the galley, around the stove and the white-painted bulkhead beside it. Then the boat lurched and I spilled the last of the Irish stew in the pressure cooker all over the cleaned counter.

SEPTEMBER 8 · The wind has changed, off the land, and we are tacking in. As we were changing tacks Mark shouted "Land ho!" and we passed the glasses back and forth to each other searching the far grey shadow. I looked at Mark and said, "Crusty bread." He slapped my raised hand and shouted, "Fruitcake, oranges, pineapple!" And I yelled "Salad bar!"

Aloha!

SEPTEMBER 9 · The wind was light and we crept closer, standing close-hauled offshore as darkness came. Now, in a gentle night full of the perfume from the land and with friendly lights about two miles inside us, we wait for daybreak to approach the shore.

SEPTEMBER 10 · Dawn streaked the sky in rose and saffron streamers and the sweet-smelling breeze blew us, tacking, toward the shore and inside the breakwater. We drifted slowly around a large hotel and looked for the marina. A man on a pier shouted through a bullhorn and directed us away from the marina to a commercial area. We got the protesting engine going for two minutes to moor where there was a Coast Guard office and a toilet. No matter what the scenery, it was good to stretch our legs on land after 60 days on *Kairos*. But thank you from us both, little ship.

Mark saw a sign saying "Store" and ran over, coming back with a bag of oranges.

We're moored beside a couple who retired, sold their house and bought a 40-foot boat. The lady spends some of her time weeping. They told us the town is four miles away and that we are not allowed to use the head, and the toilet onshore has no light. We thanked them for that information and walked toward town, turning into a promising-looking building that advertised a salad bar. Mark filled his plate lightly, intending to go back. When the waitress said this was not permitted he was deeply saddened.

The cedar beam construction of the building was like our house and I felt an ache inside. From a very public telephone I called Margaret. When I heard her voice I suddenly found it hard to talk. With so much to say I said almost nothing. My head told me: "When I come home we'll make our own little world and I'll never go away again," and all I seemed to be saying was that my American Express card has run out. And I was longing, and soon Margaret was gone. Tomorrow I would mail a letter.

Mark and I walked to the supermarket. We walked and we walked and we walked, past Japanese faces, under cherry trees, past beautiful gardens. There is a Japanese influence everywhere. In a strip like most North American towns was the supermarket. It was Aladdin's cave. A huge place spread before us every kind of food, arranged to tantalize the senses and please the eye. We couldn't carry much. We would have to rent a taxi another day to bring all our prizes back to the boat. But we bought two huge avocados. I got some fruitcake and Mark got éclairs and doughnuts.

Then, walking the street of commerce, we found a McDonald's and went in for a hamburger. It began to rain. We took a bus back, and the driver was a smiling lady with a flower in her hair.

On board again we put the leeboards up and shut out the world, lying on our bunks chewing doughnuts and cake until we fell asleep in the quiet, with a gentle movement of the boat. We slept until eight o'clock in the morning.

SEPTEMBER 11 · It wasn't quite the luxury I had dreamed of with Margaret in Honolulu. We woke beside the toilet. But it was good to sleep late and we found a shed with a shower. For breakfast we waded into the avocados, and then Mark went into town to look around. I found a mechanic to look at the engine and give me a diagnosis. But he said a diagnosis would involve taking up the cockpit floorboards and then probably waiting for parts. It would take time. I thanked him. Time, I explained, is something we don't have, with the weather closing in as we sail toward the mainland. He said he was sorry he couldn't help.

So I'll concentrate on the repairs we can make, and cross them off as they are done. We have to rig the new shroud, repair the guard rail, overhaul Smoky Stover and put a patch on the mainsail where it's developing a split. And go over the boat with every care, all in two days.

I wrapped the mildewed ship's papers in plastic after Customs inspected them. Last thing we shall rent a taxi and store up with food, water and stove fuel. Then I can wrap up my mildewed wallet. Rummaging in the plastic bags I have found warm clothing and oilskins, and have spread them out to air in the sweet scented breeze that blows through the cabin.

The day after tomorrow we sail into winter.

10 THURSDAY'S CHILD

SEPTEMBER 22 · Six days ago we set the alarm clock for 4:30 in the morning and were under way by six o'clock from Hilo.

In a confused sea with big swells and very little wind we later found some measure of comfort in a new warm southerly breeze which has pushed us along steadily and put us in holiday mood. In fact, on board there seems to be a feeling of tense happiness. Happy to be on the last leg of our long journey. And tense in case anything should go wrong when we are so close to arriving home. This ending should be memorable, but for the right reasons!

We left Hilo as we had left Panama, low in the water. Already heavy with stores, we had gone mad in Safeway. We bought a whole lot of dehydrated stuff that needs water to make it look like what it is, and we have extra water. We have fresh vegetables, eggs, bags of rice, pasta, tins of cookies, cans of corned beef, sardines and chicken, and at the last minute it seemed to me to be a good idea to wrestle a whole crate of canned tuna on board. The box contains 48 tins.

"Dad, when are we going to eat 48 cans of tuna?"

"Well, you never know."

The stove has been overhauled and works well, but Smoky Stover's past performance shows him to be such a moody thing that we need reassurance we won't starve if he packs up on the way. We should be ready for anything.

We have some delicious fresh bread, avocados, tomatoes and onions, and the cookies are the ones with holes and jam in a big red, sugary blob at the centre. All this should keep our morale high. We may also have been influenced by a book Mark has been reading about the early explorers of these waters, who were sometimes reduced to gnawing on bones and dried deerhide.

SEPTEMBER 23 · We had a cockpit picnic of avocado and cream cheese on flaxseed bread.

Hardly had we finished our leisurely meal when the wind backed to the northeast and freshened, and we reduced to mid-jenny. Now the wind is strong and we're taking seas over the bow. When I went forward I was drenched, and realized how cold the water is getting, and we have another 1,500 miles to go northward!

At night the wind died right away. We sat on the ocean with darkness creeping over the sky and sea. I lit the hurricane lamp and hung it in the rigging. The flame didn't even flicker.

SEPTEMBER 24 · Sunrise was yellow and red, and banking clouds indicated strong winds to come. Although we were practically still in the water, I reduced canvas. When the wind picked up, it seemed the northeast trades have set in. It's blowing east of northeast, which is good. East of north would be better.

In all the motion on board, Mark produced a delicious lunch of cold meat and coleslaw.

"What about all our cans of tuna?"

"We'll get around to those," he said.

Mark seems to be less keen on tuna than he once was. Perhaps it's the sheer quantity he finds a bit daunting.

At nightfall the wind is still strong and steady, and we are bouncing around with seas over the bow. Under mid-jenny with two-and-a-half rolls in the main she's at the maximum she can take and we're averaging about three-and-a-half knots. If the wind strengthens we'll have to reduce sail.

I'm hoping we can get on the other side of this high in eight days. Then the wind should swing 'round and we can alter course for the Strait of Juan de Fuca, and home.

A backstay that helps to support the mast is beginning to vibrate very badly, and gives concern. Remembering all too well the calamity in the Bay of Biscay, I've put a lashing between the twin backstays and that seems to ease the vibration. I can replace the backstay if we meet calm weather.

We went over the boat very carefully in Hilo. I'm hoping everything will stay together on this long home stretch.

SEPTEMBER 25 · We still maintain a watch system, and at the turnover at midnight we make hot chocolate. Last night when we lit the stove it flared up on the right-hand burner and leaked fuel in the left. I had thought Smoky Stover would last the journey but already his performance is beginning to get a very low grade. We still have time to turn back and get a more reliable piece of cooking equipment that fits our small galley Although one with that measurement won't be easy to find, it might be worth a try.

The decision whether to turn back or keep going has to be a joint one. We are approaching really cold weather, and if we should have to eat 48 cans of cold tuna, Mark's input into the decision is important.

After a short discussion we have decided to continue, even if we may have to face only cold food as the temperature falls. Our spirits rise as we hear a voice from Canada. The CBC radio time signal came through loud and clear and spurred us on into a perfect afternoon.

Now, under a bright blue sky with the odd fluffy cloud we are the centre of a perfect circle. I reflect that the Plains Indians of North America regarded the circle of the horizon resting on the flat prairie as sacred, having neither beginning nor end, laid down by the Great Spirit when he spread his perfect blanket over all the earth. Like an open umbrella, he placed above the circle the hoop of the sky. He made smaller circles and blessed them – the nest that shelters the young bird, the round pebble in the stream, the flower in the grass. He blessed the round tipis, pitched in a sacred circle. When he'd made the earth he made the roundness of the sun, and the moon that often shyly hides her circle. He made the stars also.

We sailed in our silent blue world with hardly any sea or swell and with a gentle breeze in our red sails. It was a holy moment that I thought demanded an Indian prayer, such as the one I once learned and always remember:

O Great Spirit
Whose voice I hear in the wind,
Hear me now.
I come before you,
One of your many children,
Asking your strength and wisdom.
May I walk toward the red and purple sunset,
May my hands respect the things you made,
And not wound the earth,
And may I always hear your voice.
I see you in every rock and leaf,
I need strength, not to fight my brother,
But to find myself.
I need clean hands and straight eyes.

A gentle rain fell and we sailed softly through silver phosphorescence and a flowing sea with just an occasional wave.

SEPTEMBER 26 · Happy 61st Birthday, Love. Thank you for your support and belief in me on this long sail. We have such wonderful years ahead, with our books and music, and rain on the window when we're warm inside, and butter tarts.

Smoky Stover celebrated your birthday by lighting both burners brightly at breakfast time. Then he refused to be extinguished, which was overdoing it. We had to turn off the main switch, which stopped the pressure. When we turned it on again he celebrated further with fireworks. We had to take him apart and deal with him.

In a gentle evening Mark went up the mast and replaced the troublesome backstay. We watched the sky cloud over in the stillness of the night.

SEPTEMBER. 27 · There was a red sunrise, perhaps a sailors' warning. A swell came up from the east and black clouds banked to windward. We had better know our position while we can. There was still a sliver of a low moon just before the dawn. With Sirius I got a good sight and I've been looking at the chart. We are west of our course. But we are making about 100 miles a day and that's alright. When we reach 40 degrees North we'll turn eastward for home.

We have a strong wind and breaking crests.

SEPTEMBER 28 · We are not alone in our big ocean. A ship passed us as we prepared breakfast. It was an occasion that brought us both on deck.

I hung my fishing line over the side as I do each morning, to Mark's amusement. I never get a nibble. Although I'm trying a larger hook, the line never twitches. But it's a routine and I think routines are good at sea.

SEPTEMBER 29 · Heeled over, we're going well in the trade winds. Before a pale, watery dawn I got a good shot of Sirius and we're now holding our course, a little east of north, in a Force 6 to 7 wind. The glass is high. There's about a 10-foot swell, with a few dollops in the cockpit.

SEPTEMBER 30 · The wind remains steady but it's tiring sailing on our ear. The strong winds have eased a little and I shook the rolls out of the main a while ago. Going forward to do so I got some water over me, and it's cold, cold, cold! The temperature is now dropping dramatically. Mark is reading Captain Cook's diary and the captain was cold, too!

A huge dollop of ocean splashed down the companionway. I keep my charts and navigation papers under plastic. The galley got some water but not on Smoky Stover. However he still acted up and the evening meal was cold bully beef and spaghetti. We have a crate of tuna unopened.

OCTOBER 1 · A family of whales swam with us for a while. The parents stayed about 50 feet away, blowing, submerging, breaking the sea's surface and blowing again, while their baby swam close to our bow in curiosity, a small study in strength and majesty.

A ship passed only about a quarter of a mile away, so we feel truly companioned.

When I came off the night watch I put some guck on the leaking burner of Smoky Stover. It hardened and at breakfast the stove lit well. Mark suggested we hard-boil the remaining eggs in case the band-aid arrangement on the stove doesn't last. As I went forward I found a flying fish lying on the forehatch. So we had fish and devilled eggs for breakfast. My larger hook on the fishing line has so far caught nothing.

We sailed all day on a steady breeze.

OCTOBER 2 · On a beautiful morning our red sails catch the light wind under a cloudless sky of deepest blue. If there were singing it would be Pippa's song:

God's in His Heaven –
All's right with the world!

Mark is concerned about growth we may be collecting again on the hull below the waterline and as he leaned over to peer down into the depths he called me. A fish with a huge bull head and small body was swimming by, surrounded by a swarm of little hangers-on. Neither of us had ever seen a fish like it. We know so little about the world of water that stretches over our planet.

Toward evening all was still, with not a ripple on the sea, and the sun went down in a flood of red. I took in my fishing line.

A black-footed albatross flew low. A bosun bird hovered over our stern with the sunset pink on his wings.

I hung the hurricane lamp in the rigging; we lit one oil lamp in the cabin and fell asleep to the gentle rocking of the sea until the alarm called for the night watch.

OCTOBER 3 · While I was on deck at dawn the sun rose over the horizon in a wild sky. The wind is strengthening and has icy fingers. We're doing three knots and I don't want to push the little ship. I may not be able to get sights today unless the heavy cloud lifts.

We're still in shorts and sweaters but it will be oilskins very soon to keep the wind out.

OCTOBER 7 · I have missed three days talking to you. They have been days of steady wind, and now it's early morning and very dark. We are heeled over under working jib and rolled main and the sea has white horses. We are making eastward but should be more northerly. I trail my fishing line as a joke now.

Twelve hundred miles still to go!

OCTOBER 8 · Early this morning Mark had the deck, and I defiantly hung my fishing line over the side before seeing to my chores. Suddenly he shouted that the line was taut.

I wound it in against the motion of the boat and the panic of something large fighting for its life. We hauled it in and manhandled it into the cockpit, where it thrashed and threatened to break something. I wanted to remove the hook from its mouth and heave it back into the ocean, but occupying practically the whole of the small cockpit it fought valiantly. Finally I had to hit it on the head before it did damage, but I did so with respect for its courage.

"I'm so sorry," I told the creature lying suddenly still. "I wanted to throw you back in the sea, but you would have had a long painful death with the hook still in your mouth. And you wouldn't give up. I don't blame you. I would have done the same."

We looked at the huge corpse.

"It's a tuna," said Mark. "What are we going to do with it? It must weigh 40 pounds. We've still got 48 tins of it."

"We could poach it with potatoes."

I think the hook I was using was too large.

I cut off about a quarter of the fish. Between us we hauled what was left over the side, to feed some denizen of the dark deep world beneath us.

Mark cut up carrots and onions and put them in a pot with oregano, garlic, curry powder and butter. He's a good cook, and the tuna stew was excellent.

When the wind died we began to roll our guts out on a large swell. The slatting of the sails as we violently rocked became so noisy that we took both of them down, and in the evening we were lying still on the water with the tiller lashed.

I use a smaller hook now on my fishing line.

OCTOBER 9 · We have made only a few miles north against a northerly wind after making sail during the night. This lack of wind in the Pacific is incredible for this time of year. It blew up fitfully during the day and by afternoon we managed two-and-a-half knots. Now it's evening and we're down to one knot under an overcast sky in light rain.

At dark a huge Japanese car carrier came straight for us and I prepared to tack. But he saw us and altered. We must be in shipping lanes.

OCTOBER 10 · Wind at last! Right on the nose! We've been beating all day. It's colder, and I appeared on deck in a pair of striped cotton dungarees of Margaret's. Mark made a rude remark about calling the cows home. Then he announced that, as we are at the 40th parallel, we would celebrate with scrambled eggs for breakfast. He whipped up a mixture of powdered egg and garlic and made me a heaping serving, which I tucked into. While he was mixing his own the stove died. He had cold cereal.

I took Smoky Stover apart, cleaned him thoroughly and put in a new jet. Both jets lit! They burned brightly and we boiled a kettle for tea and I had enough hot water for a weekly shave. As Mark missed out on scrambled eggs at breakfast, I put them on the lunch menu.

I beat up the egg mixture, cooked it just right and gave Mark his. Then the stove went out and I had cold cereal.

To one isolated at sea, inanimate things can seem animate. I became convinced Smoky was doing this on purpose. He was not going to win. Bouncing around on a sea that had lost its rhythm, with spray flying all around, I got the stove to show a light in one burner, and made a Thermos of hot chocolate for the turnover watch at midnight.

Then Smoky Stover died and didn't come back. We did everything we could for him but it seemed he was mortally injured with rust in a vital part of his anatomy.

He had given all he could.

OCTOBER 11 · On watch in the cold, at six o'clock in the morning, I unaccountably attacked Smoky. It had turned bitterly cold and I felt there must be some small breath of life left in him to make a hot drink. Mark got up and treated him more gently. With his Outward Bound knowledge of troublesome pieces of equipment, he gave the stove further inspection. But Smoky needed professional help. More than resuscitation, he needed a transplant.

"Rust. I'm afraid he needs new parts," Mark confirmed.

Breakfast was cold beans.

Continuing to beat, with the wind still on our nose, we have made only 85 miles in three days, with a position of 41 degrees North and 131 degrees West.

After a supper of cold tuna, I lit the hurricane lamp. The wind continued against us, and then died in the night.

OCTOBER 14 · We have made such small progress I have had little to record for the last two days. Mark wakened me to take the watch at four o'clock this morning, and I went on deck as dawn was pointing a pale finger across a calm grey sky. After a still night there was no wind.

We are on a course for the Strait of Juan de Fuca and home! As the sun came up a gentle zephyr caught our sails and we made one knot. We continued at one knot all day on our huge ocean, blown by a small cold wind from the northeast.

OCTOBER 15 · Even yesterday's breeze has died. As we ate a lunch of cold chili and spinach there was not a breath of wind to ruffle the sea. We sit, drifting, in the middle of an expanse of cold, flat ocean, reading, going nowhere. I'm worried that this delay will bring us into storms as we enter Juan de Fuca on the edge of winter. And there are strong winds off the American coast, particularly Oregon, at this time of year.

Mark is wondering why we are trying to get to Canada instead of Tahiti.

While it's so calm I tried to take a very quick bath in the cockpit, but it was a shock to the system I wouldn't repeat. It was Ogden Nash who discovered with wonderment that water that is alright to the thumb is icy on the fundament.

After a supper of cold sardines following my cold sponge-down I hung the lamp in the rigging and there was not the smallest movement of the flame in the stillness. We put up the washboards, lit the oil lamps, looked through our collection of books and played some music on the tape recorder until I took it to talk on the night watch.

OCTOBER 16 · There has been no wind all day. Since October 3 we have made only 300 miles. Bobbing around in the moonlight under a starlit sky we pray for a strong breeze to blow us home to all we love.

Now that our course is set toward the Strait, it feels psychologically more like coming home. I never sleep deeply, listening to the boat. I dream in my half-sleep. In my dream I stretch out my hand to Margaret. But we cannot touch.

She is so far away.

OCTOBER 24 · No nearer! We have been becalmed and frustrated for a week now. Sitting, drifting on the Pacific Ocean, reading our books.

Just before sunrise there was a splendid show of Northern Lights, like darting angels in a crackling sky. At dawn a dark sun came over the horizon and spilled its blood on the sea.

Then came the wind! Lots of it! I celebrated by playing some Wagner on the tape recorder. *The Valkyries* were shrill on the screaming wind!

We are bouncing, close-hauled, making a little north of east. If the wind will move around just a bit more we shall make Cape Flattery.

Now it's evening and it's raining – drowning rain. I'm standing, moving with the motion of the boat, reading under the spray hood. Earlier I browsed through a collection of poems, favourites of General Wavell's, which he called *Other Men's Flowers*. Now I'm flicking over some short essays put together by William F. Buckley, and one in particular, written by a retired newspaper man called Kilpatrick, carries me away from winter at sea to the gentle spring budding of the land. Of the early profusion of flowers, he claims "the trillium is the loveliest of them all, which kneels as modestly as a bride in white beside the altar of an old oak stump. If you are not familiar with the trillium, imagine the flower that would come from a flute, if the music from the flute could make a flower. That is the trillium, the work of God from a theme by Mozart."

Night comes and a sickle moon shows shyly in a cold, cloudless sky. The rain has stopped. In a strong wind we blow toward land, and home, as fast as we can.

OCTOBER 27 · It's exhilarating to be moving at last and we're on the port tack, with the lee rail under. Constantly heeling at an angle of 20 degrees, we shall have one leg shorter than the other when we get home. We are close-hauled under mid-jenny, with four rolls in the main. The wind is Force 6 to 7, and each time I think I should reduce to the working jib, the wind dies, then blows up again a little to the northeast. We're actually sailing north of east, heading for the coast of Washington State. During the days we lost the wind we drifted south and now we're trying to make up for it. When we can see the coastline we'll tack out and back, to pick up Cape Flattery.

OCTOBER 28 · Still on the port tack under an overcast sky we are, by dead reckoning, not far from Flattery. But I would like to know exactly where we are. I hope for just a few days of fair weather to get sights.

OCTOBER 29 · On we go, under banking cloud that darkens the sky. We had friends today to greet us as we neared land. A killer whale, about a cable away, blew several times and then went about his business. In a lull of the wind a shark about seven feet long circled us for about half an hour, rubbing his back on the boat.

As the wind began to blow up again and then give us another lull, a dove-grey gull plopped down on the sea beside me, riding on a wave, flying to keep up, plopping down again. I gave him a graham cracker. He ignored it but still kept me company and came closer while Mark dozed in his bunk below.

I inquired about the bird's health and asked after his family. Just as we were really getting to know each other he suddenly flew off as though he had just remembered something.

It's been a day of minor calamity. After I spilled washing soap all over the deck I lurched with the boat and broke the last surviving light bulb. Not able to run the engine to top up the batteries, we don't use electricity, but it was our last light bulb and I was keeping it as a memento. Then Mark threw a tin with the wind to see how far it would go and broke the hurricane lamp. We blame Smoky Stover for deserting us in our hour of need.

With a slight wind shift we could make straight for the Strait and be on our way to Victoria and hot coffee.

OCTOBER 30 · I still hope the wind will veer to blow us into the Strait. We're on the port tack, sailing south of east under full main and jenny, with the wind shrill but easing a little under a dark sky. We're hoping to go northward to make Flattery without tacking. I pray for good sights for a position.

Then in a strong, cold wind, as I came on the midnight watch, the whole canopy of the Heavens opened up. Orion's belt, Sirius, the

Plough, all my friends! At that moment I knew I wouldn't be anywhere else. But the sights I took show us west of our course.

OCTOBER 31 · The winter wind is blowing up to gale force from NNW, with a breaking sea. If only we could make a hot drink! The mast has begun to judder. With four rolls in the main and the working jib this may be a lot of canvas for the strength of the wind, but I've been hoping we'd weather Cape Flattery. Now I don't think we will. We'll have to tack out to sea and lose a day.

Looking at the mast, I see the forestay may be a little slack. I can't tighten the back stays. They're both down to the bottle screws. We're pushing on, hoping everything holds together on our little ship. There is no moon.

NOVEMBER 1 · In a wild dawn, after a wild night, we are sailing on our ear. As the sky clears we're getting good sights and find we're further west than we hoped, still a full 50 miles off Cape Flattery. But it looks as though we shall weather the Cape and go straight into the Strait of Juan de Fuca....

Now there's little wind and the sky holds no promise. We're crawling along at night, into a lighted circle of fish boats. We have a smaller hurricane lamp in the rigging.

This must be a good place to fish. But even if I were to put a line out and catch something, Smoky couldn't cook it for us!

NOVEMBER 2 · Yesterday Cape Flattery light was aft and we entered the mouth of the Strait without having to make the tack out to sea that I feared might be needed. Today the wind died. It began to rain. But toward evening a breeze blew up from the east, right on our nose, and we are beating inside the Canadian side of the Strait. In the last 18 hours we have made 10 miles! In our oilskins, wet and cold, practically opposite the lights of Port Renfrew, we debated whether we should go in and anchor and get a night's rest.

But we have so much against us now – a stove that isn't working, an engine that will only run fitfully for a minute or two if started by hand, a compass light that doesn't work, a mast that still judders, it's very cold, and the sky looks like rain tomorrow. Do we really want to face all this again in the morning? We decided to push on, both of us on deck through the night, with visibility low and some fog around. So, on we go. In the darkness. Margaret, I stretch out my hand to you. Soon you will take it in your own.

We look toward the friendly lights of Port Renfrew and the sound of the foghorn, then go about into the darkness across the Canadian side of the Strait. Then we go about again at the American border toward the lights of the home shore, a mile on each tack....

Now Port Renfrew is well aft, and the lights along the shore are going out, as folks go to bed with the sound of the rain on their windowpanes.

We take turns standing at the tiller in oilskins in the rain.

It seems a very long night. The wind picks up from Race Rocks and then dies. We crawl on. The few flickering lights of traffic along the shore gradually stop. An inner voice says "Stay alert. Stay awake." Ahead, in the sky, the friendly glow over Victoria is like a constant twilight.

On the chart under the spray hood I can identify navigation lights that seem to say "Welcome home, travellers. You've been away a long time."

NOVEMBER 3 · Pinpricks of light began to show along the shoreline in the early morning dark. Folks were waking, no doubt still sleepy and looking out at the beating rain that would slash against their windshields as they drove to work, rain that ran down our oilskins and drummed on our spray hood. Then it eased, and a gentle breeze took us onward, still tacking, and a soft morning glow shone on the sea. There were lights now all along the shore, and flickering car lights. We passed familiar landmarks as daylight signalled it was time for hot coffee before the rush of the day. Hot coffee! If only we had some. I could almost smell it.

We came into Victoria under a sputtering, smoking engine that, protesting, took us past the breakwater and into the Inner Harbour. There we nonchalantly secured *Kairos* at the steps below the grand Empress Hotel. Our boat's hull is bare of protective oil and discoloured. Her portholes are green. We didn't care. She has scars of battle.

The city was waking and the street lights were still on. The noise of traffic grew. In the distance was a siren. Sounds bombarded us. For so long we had heard only the wind and the sea.

Now we used what was left of the water freely. We squared up the cabin. Then we squared up ourselves, washing, scrubbing our nails, brushing our salt-caked hair. Mark brushed his salt-caked beard. I scraped my unshaven face with a razor, and then found a pair of slacks in the plastic clothes bag. I had bought them in Gibraltar and they were a bit flashy but I put them on. They were damp. We both put on clean damp shirts, and covered them against the cold with oilskin jackets.

Then we dodged our way through unaccustomed traffic across the road to the Empress Hotel. To the side was a little café, less imposing than the rest of the building, and we went in. Shown to a table with a white-patterned tablecloth, we gloried in the aroma of hot coffee! Bliss!

We looked at the menu. Yes. We would have the hot breakfast. The whole hot meal. Yes. Eggs sunny side up. Yes, we would have the bacon. Sausage? Yes, all on the same plate, please. Hot pancakes with maple syrup? Yes. Will it all fit on the plate? Toast and marmalade on the side.

The waitress seemed puzzled as she filled our coffee cups over and over, but then, people have different capacities.

Back on board we had a visit from Customs. Then a man came down with a camera from a TV station, and someone else from a local newspaper. Remembering how long it was since we had a shower, we debated how to present ourselves to a Galiano homecoming without giving offence as soon as we removed our oilskin jackets.

Mark went home on the ferry to Vancouver for a bath and clean clothes, to return tomorrow to sail on with me. I phoned Margaret from a phone booth. It's hard, on long distance, to pour out your heart into a mouthpiece. All choked up I told her I would be in Montague Harbour the day after to-morrow. All choked up she said she would look for my red sails coming home.

When I thought that Margaret's daughter, Corinna, would be back from the office that afternoon, I took a taxi to her apartment.

There was warmth, a hot shower, dinner and a sofa bed if I wished, but I was unwilling to leave *Kairos* alone tied up in the harbour, decrepit though she may be. I slept deeply aboard, giving thanks from a full heart which embraces all my extended family.

NOVEMBER 4 · By noon Mark and I were together again on board *Kairos*. We sailed for the Gulf Islands, satisfied we looked clean and rested no matter the appearance of the boat. But she looked proud.

The rain beat down, and in the early darkness a very strong, cold wind blew up. We sought shelter for the night and anchored in Browning Harbour, Pender Island.

The wind continued shrill even in the harbour, and we were glad there was no call for the night watch. That was over.

NOVEMBER 5 · In the morning there was sun after storm. A soft breeze blew as we got under way and sailed for Galiano Island. We passed places we knew so well on a day when some of the maple trees were still golden, and the sun was smiling. In fact, I believe he was laughing.

Approaching Montague Harbour we took down the sails, bagged the jenny and neatly rolled the main under a sail cover. Then we risked the fitful engine to round the point and come into harbour.

A neighbour, Tom Hennessy, met us in his catamaran to escort us in. Two eagles flew low and I saluted them. The engine spluttered. A cheer went up from a group of friends who had gathered above the marina. The battered little boat, coming into her new home, graciously acknowledged the applause and bobbed and curtsied on the ripples.

Margaret and Blair were on the wharf. As we came alongside, gliding in on that golden day, with Mark in the bow ready to leap ashore with the bow line, Margaret stretched out her hand. Still careful at the tiller, watching the boat, I stretched out mine, and touched her fingers.

It was done. I was home.

The Island

"...We shall not cease from exploration
And the end of all our exploring
Will be to arrive where we started
And know the place for the first time."

— *T.S. Eliot,* Four Quartets

NOVEMBER 1981 · T.S. Eliot must have written those lines when he came home from a voyage. Perhaps he was sitting by the fire as I am now, looking at a familiar scene outside the window but seeing it with new eyes.

I am listening to the wind. Black shreds of cloud are blown across a pale moon. There is no light on the sea. No noise but the sound of the waves in the wind. I am home. I shall never go away again.

This place is dearer to me than when I left, so many months ago. My heart didn't break then, when I said goodbye. But as I neared home my longing became a pain, a deep ache.

It's six weeks now since *Kairos* came into Montague Harbour to the cheers of neighbours as I jumped onto the wharf and took Margaret in my arms. We hadn't visualized embracing so publicly after so long. But just for a moment no one else existed.

It was when I left my yellow deck boots outside the front door that I felt truly home at last. It turned out that the boots were really Margaret's. She was fond of them and had looked for them for two years. But it was a time of reunion, when she forgot to be indignant.

The house seemed smaller. It also needed me. The trim around the windows could use some paint and the grandfather clock didn't chime.

Everyone who had come to the wharf was invited back to lunch. There were toasts and speeches and Blair took photographs. Mark and I were hugged. We had been on an adventure together, however humble. There was so much inside us that others couldn't share. And so we said little.

Only to Margaret had I opened my heart to speak of love and fear. It was to Margaret that I wrote that in the wide dark sky, the morning stars really did sing together. Then the dawn would trumpet the day's arrival, perhaps with streaming banners of rose and purple.

Alone with Creation, I had learned from my voyage that I am never solitary. When there are problems the answers come in quietness. I had learned so many things sitting in the dark on the companionway steps, looking through the porthole, keeping watch, waiting for the new day. And what I had learned will support me always. I feel very deeply that however long the night, we all carry the morning light within us. Dawn will come at the end of the dark, perhaps as the first bar of pale light after a storm. Perhaps as a song of joy that needs no choir.

"Glad to be home, George? Does it all look the same?" I snapped back from dreaming. In my own world, I could still feel the motion of the boat.

"Yes. Few changes. Glad to be home."

So glad to see everyone, more people than I had been with for a long time. But I still had to get myself sorted out. In a crowd I felt strange. I wondered, does Mark feel the same? When we were sailing together he taught me patience, and sharing in cramped quarters. I cherish the memory of him standing brown and bare in the boat with dolphins dancing all around him. I felt blessed to be at such a celebration of the sea. And here I am at the end of it all, knowing that this bay I left with such preoccupation to live my dreams is my true place, my last harbour.

People drifted slowly away after the welcome-home party. Mark went back to Vancouver. Margaret and I felt as though the long months had simply melted away. We went down to the beach to be quiet together, and then Margaret told me she had received a phone call from Michel, who towed us through the Canal. He and Rand were safely home but the boat had been caught in a storm and ship-wrecked on the Oregon coast. I was relieved they were safe but deeply saddened, in fact torn apart, over the loss of the boat. Two kind people dealing with a loss that only those who build and sail boats will truly know.

Now I am finding this island world anew. I watch the colour of the sky. On a day of winter wind, *Kairos* dances, still full of spirit, and strains at her lines in the marina. "Wait 'til spring, little ship," I tell her.

Life is slower. I am suddenly free of deadlines. I am seeing little things. I have lived with so few birds. Now I am companioned by all manner of wild creatures and Nature's smile.

DECEMBER 1981 · On the point the heron stands each morning, like a statue, waiting for a sign of breakfast in the sea's shallows. His flight is beautiful, his cry coarse and unhappy.

Last week it snowed in mean little flakes slanting down on an east wind. A thin white carpet lay over the black rock. Creatures and old folk stayed home if they could. Then came the thaw, with ice breaking in little lumps from the point and sailing away on the current in a flotilla of miniature icebergs. Rain lashed the windows. Winter birds came to the feeders. A dish left absent-mindedly on the deck filled with water.

A bird came and perched gingerly on the edge of the dish. He stuck a toe in the cold water. Then he considered the matter with care. Having made his decision he plunged in; hopped out, in again, jumping, flapping wings. Another bird came, and another, pushing, splashing. I thought of Edward Lear's nonsense rhyme:

> *"Ploffskin, Pluffskin, Pelican jee!*
> *We think no Birds so happy as we!"*

The stream in the wood is in full spate, flowing over the beach pebbles to the sea. Morning brings a flight of gulls to the little estuary, all in a frantic hurry, skidding on the water as they put on the brakes, forgetting why they came. They paddle around. "Who called this meeting?" Then, as they feel the fresh water flow underneath them over the salt they begin to dance with the dancing sea, splashing, sloshing, generally messing about. Perhaps fresh water removes parasites. "Ploffskin, Pluffskin, Pelican jee!"

Cormorants offer a sail-past by the kitchen window. Standing on pieces of driftwood, wings held out to dry acting as sails, catching the wind, gathering speed on the current, whoopee!

But Nature has its cruelties as well as its joys. I saluted the courage of the gull that swooped and manoeuvred to escape attacking eagles. Then, exhausted, it faltered and fell to its fate on the beach.

A seal chased a salmon until the fish beached itself, lying helpless on the pebbles with the seal lying waiting in the incoming tide. Then the ravens pecked the eyes out of the gasping fish.

Two days ago it snowed again, this time in large, generous flakes that settled in a soft carpet. The fir trees were dazzling white beside the grey sea, like sprayed Christmas trees, casting long shadows under a weak sun.

A family of otters arrived at the point where the heron stands. Under maternal supervision the cubs climbed up the rocks, rolled down in the snow to splash into the sea, up again, roll down and splash. "Ploffskin, Pluffskin, Pelican jee! Did you ever see otters as happy as we!"

Tonight the wind is rising. The sea beats on the rocks below the house. Inside all is content. Margaret is making Christmas cakes.

Warmth and comfort made me doze until I felt a fly on my forehead, and I batted it uselessly. Now I am awake but deeply at peace. After putting another log on the fire I can lie back in my chair and listen to the wind. How our grandest dreams count for so little beside the smallest things of love and comfort.

On an empty envelope on the table beside me I try a haiku.

"George sleeps in his chair;
He has sailed many seas.
Fly buzzes 'round lamp."

JANUARY 1982 · This Christmas was the first we have ever spent completely alone together. This was our choice. The wind blew in from the east, and it was warm by the fireside listening to winter.

We celebrated the New Year watching the arrival of the snow geese. They were late this year; no one knew why. People began to speculate. Perhaps they wouldn't come. Perhaps, as they multiply, there is too little food for them in the places where they have always grazed and rested on their flight south from the Alaskan lakes where they raise their young. Perhaps the rapidly developing mainland confuses them at night with so many new lights that could send them off course. But when we heard there are hundreds this year heading as usual for the mud flats in the Fraser River estuary, we wrapped up well and caught the ferry for the mainland. They had been reported not far away, further north, a huge white cloud against the threatening sky.

The marshes by the river are at the edge of a wildlife refuge, beyond a lake where mallards, grebes, harlequin ducks and buffleheads in their winter plumage swim in safety. Beyond this, hunters hide waiting with their guns ready for the geese to come in.

We arrived at the refuge and joined a little crowd on a hill, looking down at the mud flats. The geese were coming in, they said. We heard them overhead but couldn't see them for cloud. They flew on and were gone. It was cold and some people left. The geese flew over again! They must be making a wide circle in their descent. Then they were landing eagerly, hungry at the end of this stage of a long flight. The noise was deafening even over the sound of the guns. Breaking through the dark cloud, a white wave rolled in like surf. It surged over the marsh, rising, falling, birds half running, half flying, with legs unsteady from long flight. They came in a never-ending wave. Perhaps there would be enough marsh grass to sustain them, as it had before in a miracle of feeding so many, down by the river.

We ran along the muddy path, still watching. Now it was snowing in large flakes, settling on the marshes but thawing quickly. The noise subsided as the birds began to feed.

We caught the ferry home to the fireside As evening came it still snowed. I looked up from my book, full of content after a wonderful day, and said: "What we really need is a dog." Margaret just said, "Perhaps."

The chairs on the deck stand under their white covers like ghosts of summer. Herbs are dried and in jars, and the apples of autumn are made into applesauce and frozen in pies. Geraniums brought inside make bright splashes of colour on the window ledges.

The night is still and the snow lies gently on the fir trees. The snow geese will be resting in the grass by the river.

All would be perfect with a dog stretched out by the fire!

FEBRUARY 1982 · It is my birthday. Sixty-eight years, if counting is important.

Last year at this time I was alone on *Kairos* in the great blue bowl of the Atlantic.

This year Margaret and I have run away together to the Pacific. We drove over rough roads to where the ocean explodes against rock on the west shore of Vancouver Island.

Here, in a delightful inn that has a tree seeming to grow through the floor of the hall by the reception desk, we are happy. Hand in hand along the beach we laugh at the sandpipers tiptoeing to the edge of the outgoing tide and running backward as the sea races in again. "Ploffskin, Pluffskin!"

Giant cedars hold such silence that we tread quietly. They drip moss and are festooned with lichen. This is the rainforest! We are dressed in storm gear and Margaret has on her yellow boots, slightly the worse for wear.

In the evening we sit quietly together, reading. Or we walk as darkness falls and feel part of the chorus of the stars.

Two old people sharing a solitude, walking into a mellow future with all travelling done.

MARCH 1982 · The month came in like a lamb and went out like a lion. The eagles, mated for life, are refurbishing their nest in a fir tree across the bay and will have brought to it a new piece of evergreen to awaken spring's courtship. Otters end their solitary winter and swim by in pairs. A sea lion near the rock announces unmusically to the world that his harem has left him to go north to calve, after keeping people awake at night with sounds of passion in the freezing cold water. Yellow crocuses that smiled to the sun early in the month bow to the wind off the sea, and *Kairos* dances under her winter tarpaulin....

After much discussion we decided to buy two bulldog pups and I brought them home in a shoebox from the kennel where they were born. They are the old English bulldog, before the breed became snuffly and salivating. Margaret has called them Kate and Mavis, which she says are good bulldog names.

APRIL 1982 · The March winds have blown away the daffodils and April is nearly ending. The old boy sea lion still remains, snorting rudely beyond the kitchen window.

The bulldog pups are confined by a gate to the kitchen, which makes cooking more of a challenge. We went out one night and they destroyed their dog basket and were found lying innocently in the ruins. We tried going out again and Katie, the bigger one, broke out of the gate and devoured my hiking boots. We don't go out much now.

Margaret, beachcombing in the late spring sunshine, found a slate knife and put it on the mantel with other relics cast up by the sea. We both held it, so beautifully smoothed and bevelled by some native man who walked in these parts long, long ago. He and I held the same knife.

I find myself thinking a great deal about a past people. I have read of the Coast Salish, who came here seasonally for clams and berries and to gather nettle roots for rope. In a softer climate than some eastern peoples of North America, they told their history with humour. How Crow created the world, painted the little birds, and painted Eagle with his head of white. But his own head remained black as a result of treading on a herring rake through not looking! Living was not hard; the sea was so full of herring that it was simply raked inside the boats, to the distress of missionaries who nobly fought the devil in their search for anyone enjoying spare time, with idle hands.

My thoughts turn easily from the people who came to our bay for the herring spawning to the people of the Great Plains. For them life and its creation were a more serious affair. They knew the harsh winds of the flat prairie. There, land meets the Big Sky in the circle of the horizon much as I knew it at sea, and perhaps that's why I feel more akin to these ancient people of the Plains. They were a people of poetry who told how, at this time of year, the Great Spirit would take his winter garment from the hoop of the sky as the sun climbed higher, to let its rays warm the land. Then the soft winds could caress the earth after the beating of the winter winds of endurance.

Now, I think to myself as I feel the soft breeze, it's time to ask Power of the World to send good winds as we take the winter tarpaulin from *Kairos* and let her go free, to sail to a boatyard to be made into a beautiful lady.

MAY 1982 · Tonight the house is full of preparation – groceries, water, sleeping bags – for us to live aboard *Kairos* when she is propped "up on the hard" at the yard on Vancouver Island. Margaret has packed the striped overalls that went on the long sail with me, along with her yellow boots. She is glad to be reunited with them both. The pups are to be looked after by kind, masochistic friends.

All is ready. A light rain is falling and there is little wind. We sail tomorrow. But it's a huge job that lies ahead, restoring a sea-weary *Kairos*. The cabin is darkened from stove oil and lamp fumes; the hull, cockpit and mast are ready to drink up oil after prior sanding and scraping. I am both pleased and anxious about how it may turn out.

Blair has news. He has a very good chance of joining, as cameraman, the team planning to climb Mount Everest for Canada this fall. He is supremely happy and I am proud of him. Twelve national teams have reached the summit, the roof of the world, and Canada hopes to be lucky 13, with Blair shooting the documentary as they climb. His film of mountaineering in Peru has received praise for showing vividly the challenge of the climb, the early start in the dark, the hard ascent, the thrill when the sun hits the summit, and the threat this brings of avalanche. He knows what he faces now, and is ready to marry his

148

two loves of climbing and photography. Both offer self-reliance and a sense of wonder.

But I am concerned for him. It was Blake who wrote: "Great things are done when men and mountains meet; this is not done by jostling in the street." But it was also Mallory who said: "We expect no mercy from Everest," and he received none. Frostbite, hardship and death in the screaming wind was all the mountain gave him at the end.

Things are better now, I tell myself as I lie in bed trying to sleep. The equipment. The leadership. Each climb draws on the experience of others, like Sir Edmund Hillary, who came to Vancouver some time ago and who was interviewed by Blair for a CBC newscast. They talked of the Khumbu Icefall, with its deep crevasses and teetering pillars of moving ice, the infamous gateway to an Everest climb. Some have died there. On first coming home to the island after my long sail, I wrote in my diary: "I am in love with this world. I have climbed its mountains, roamed its forests, sailed its seas." Now here was Blair, more alive than I had ever seen him, in love with the world, too, full of activity after dreaming. His own *Kairos*.

The night seemed long as we waited to take the boat to the shipyard at Canoe Cove. With my mind racing, but with the assurance of Margaret's presence beside me, I listened to the grandfather clock chime the hours as I waited for the dawn.

With early shafts of light came a bird's first note of inquiry. Then the answer. Now the garden is full of singing.

Outside the bedroom window are boxes of yellow pansies. Beyond is the sea, and beacons that guide the sailor safely through the rock-strewn channel to Victoria.

All is ready. *Kairos* is waiting in the harbour. The rain is lessening and there is a weak sun but no wind for our sails. Power of the World, just a zephyr or two, if you please. Just a puff!

Or a fair wind would be better.

13 SUMMER

JUNE · We have been here, up on the hard at the boatyard, for two weeks and *Kairos* is becoming less of a sorry sight – but Margaret and I are beginning to need a bit of restoration.

The boat's hull, so beautifully splined, built of mahogany, was bare except for the odd patch of oil. The brass inside and out was turquoise. The cabin was badly weather-stained around the galley and chart table.

Our days living aboard are work, sand, oil, clean, then rush to the shower room before the lineup. When the light fades in the sky, and lingers awhile on the sea, we fall exhausted into our sleeping bags.

Today I look rather hopelessly at the mess around us. The boat is propped up on oil barrels with planks for staging, which have to be rerigged as we move around. Margaret, my lodestar, is sitting in the cockpit with grimy face and broken fingernails, devouring an enormous bun. I thought she was elegant when I married her. What have I done?

Our meals are sketchy, but each evening we have a treat. Supper is Olde English Fish & Chips at a shop in town. The proprietors are used to serving disreputable-looking characters restoring boats. In fact there is a camaraderie around the table of dishevelled sailors smelling of oil and paint in spite of hygiene facilities provided by the yard. The topic of conversation is always when we shall "splash," or put the boat back in the water. Most of us look as if we should be thrown in along with the vessel.

Ravenously each evening we tuck into our fish, Margaret smothering her chips in ketchup in a kind of desperate comfort-seeking return to childhood. She wonders if the garden is alright, and the dogs, and the bad-tempered squirrel that comes to the bird feeders.

Each day, *Kairos* responds to our care.

The mast and boom are cleaned and oiled. The encrusted rudder needs help with mechanical cleaning. The deck will be steam-cleaned. I have scraped the hull and planed the dark marks. After 20 coats of oil, including two finishing coats, I shall wash her down with a little bleach in the water. Scrape, scrape, scrape. I remind myself that it's Murphy's Law that a list of jobs stuck on the bulkhead will grow longer rather than shorter as the work progresses. And it does.

Oil the shrouds, check shackles for rewiring, check the hurricane lamp, fix the navigation lights. Margaret has repainted the white above the mahogany panelling in the cabin and around the galley. The stove has been checked but I'm afraid to light it. I'm sure it's fine but if it blows up and blackens the new paint around the galley, we shall both burst into tears. Perhaps I should have bought a new stove. But I've grown fond of Smoky Stover. For so long we have both tried to get the better of each other, and I'm not ready to admit defeat.

Margaret and I nearly went home for a few days when the engine was checked and the pistons replaced. The floor boards came up, the after-end of the cabin was filthy, the engine disemboweled. But we pushed on and everything we do now lifts our spirits, as I give the rudder, tiller and name-boards more coats of oil and Margaret tackles the forehatch.

As I climb up and down from the staging I feel muscles that I don't remember feeling before. But as *Kairos* looks more and more beautiful while we grow increasingly dilapidated, we have decided to enter her in the Classic Boat Show in Victoria in September. We will be a few more weeks putting the finishing touches to our little ship.

So, although our hands are sore from scraping, our legs are tired from hopping up and down the stagings and our arms are weary from sanding, our hearts are singing because *Kairos* is almost restored to pristine glory.

Soon all will be fit and ready for the homeward trip.

JULY · *Kairos* fairly flew home with the wind to her berth in Montague Harbour. She is rejuvenated.

The summer is hot. Our well is low and we are careful with water. The sun has dried to brown the thin grass on the rocky point where the heron stands.

In the fresh morning after a mercifully heavy dewfall the deer in the woods come to the dried-up stream looking for puddles. Hungry, they are breaking into gardens. Some people shoot them out of season. Some love to see them and feed them apples. The maples are changing colour early. Gusts of wind blow the dried leaves.

We are due at the Classic Boat Show in the first week of September and *Kairos* is ready, with all the love we can give her. Although she is not quite the 25 years of age that would make her a classic, she has a story and they let us in.

And in our own estimation she looks quite splendid. The fine construction of her hull shows through the gleam of layers of Norwegian oil. Her brass portholes are dazzling. Her teak deck is clean. Her cabin cushions are new. But I haven't dealt satisfactorily with the salt marks on the washboards.

In places she's still storm-scarred.

Blair came for a last visit. I didn't say goodbye and neither did he. He has definitely been accepted for the Everest climb, and almost immediately joins an awesome expedition of the country's best climbers. His primary role will be shooting videotape for TV, but he hopes to be of use on the climbing team.

He looked confident and happy and told Margaret he had never been so content. This expedition is altogether the most he could ever hope for.

It is to Debbie, who shares his life in their North Vancouver apartment, that he opens his heart and shows his sombre respect for the mountain. Like the sea, Everest can take the aware and the unwary at any time. Blair does not take her for granted.

In the middle of July Blair left for the 150-mile trek to Base Camp. We have had three postcards, fretting over the non-arrival of his broadcasting equipment and the low priority it seems to have after the transporting of goods necessary for the climb. Customs has impounded the team's radio transmitters without giving a reason. The rains have brought leeches. But in the heat there are welcome plunges into rivers in the foothills.

To us Blair appears casual, even offhand, but not to Debbie. She sent us a copy of a quotation he had left on his desk. It moved me greatly. Written by James Segerstrom in 1976 for the magazine *Summit*, it seemed to make clear that Blair knows only too well the realities of climbing:

> *I've discovered the capabilities and limitations of my body.*
> *I'll try not to abuse it needlessly. I need it here.*
> *I've learned satisfaction.*
> *It's a personal thing.*
> *No one ever again has to praise me.*
> *I don't search for happiness anymore.*
> *Happiness is an occasional reward for my efforts.*
> *I now know patience.*
> *I understand discomfort and pain.*
> *They serve to put comfort and pleasure in perspective. I fear but*
> *I handle its massiveness.*
> *I appreciate your hospitality. Your manners are faultless. But I*
> *won't underestimate your cleverness or your frustrations.*
> *I climb. My body is past exhaustion and my mind is moving*
> *upward, hand in hand with my soul.*
> *My bivouac is my home.*
> *Any food here is a feast.*
> *I'll be frightened if you take my life.*
> *I'll understand though.*
> *You are not my servant. I am yours.*
> *I am also a simple person. You made that of me.*
> *I'm no longer occupied with theories. I know a few truths instead.*

What I see was no accident. It was intended. Whoever you are
is inconsequential.
It is beyond my comprehension.
I am a guest in your house and it's more than I deserve.
Thank you.

AUGUST · The late afternoons brings the croak of tree-frogs and the harsh cry of the raven. Tomorrow *Kairos* will feel the breeze in her red sails and show us how well she will go with a clean hull as we circle her round the island.

The latest postcard from Blair shows the team is almost at Base Camp, where Sherpas have gone on ahead with the tents. While to me his messages are all enthusiastic and rather irritated at things that fail to go smoothly, it is still to Debbie he opens his heart.

She phoned yesterday to say Blair had written her a letter in which he gave careful directions showing the exact position on the map of a place of wonder above the rest of the world. He had found it when he wandered off alone near a hamlet called Lobuche. He had stood in a panorama in the sky, a place of ice and snow and glaciated rock. To her he wrote, "If the pale horse should come I can think of no better place to rest than in such a cathedral."

The CBC evening news is to show footage from the climb, but no date is set.

In the bay the cycles of the seasons know nothing of such excitement. The wind rustles the dry maple leaves. Against a blue sky four eagles returning to Galiano from their river feast of spawning salmon ride the breezes, touch briefly, fall and sail upward, silhouetted against the sun....

* * *

The Everest climb is gathering interest in the media. A New Zealand team is following close behind the Canadians. There will be national flags all over the mountain!

A long letter came from Blair, and I went down to the beach to read it. It was mailed when he was still trekking. "We've been walking for two weeks now. Another week to go to Base Camp. The countryside has been marvellous." He tells of rugged ridges, streams in torrent, rice paddies, forests of rhododendrons, magnolias and firs in a beautiful world. There are several hours of dry weather in the morning and the leeches are not so bad. Everywhere, there are flowers. Most homes have chrysanthemums and roses.

His big news was saved until the end. He's been put on the climbing team and will go at least up to Camp 2. Then perhaps higher.

And finally he asks, "Is the boat sailable yet?"

Yes! If only you could see her, Blair. She's almost totally restored, though the storms have left some marks. And we are away tomorrow to Victoria to tie up in the harbour next to the BC Parliament Buildings, with all the bustle of the city.

A little blue butterfly has just landed on the beach pebbles. Then it flitted onto my hand and gazed at me. I've never been stared at by a butterfly before. What a golden day this is.

A red-golden leaf twirls and twists in the breeze as it falls from the maple tree behind me. I pray for a strong wind for tomorrow to get us to the harbour for the boat festival. We hope to arrive early for a place at the wharf instead of rafting up. But the breezes around the islands are fitful compared with the steady winds of the open ocean. I must be patient.

SEPTEMBER 1 · Early this morning there was mist on the water and no wind. By the time I had made a pot of tea the mist was clearing and the sun breaking through. Then a few ripples on the sea and a promising breeze in the falling leaves.

A pod of killer whales went through the pass between Mayne and Galiano islands, following in the wake of a ferry with obvious enjoyment. We accepted it as an omen for good without knowing quite why.

We motored out of Montague Harbour, but soon the breeze strengthened and we were under sail, past tree-cloaked islands where children played on pebble beaches in the freedom of the last day before school. Some waved as we passed, running in and out of the water in what must seem to them to be endless summer.

I sat at the tiller while we had our lunch. Margaret has hung curtains, made new cushions and polished the portholes again. How *Kairos* has taken all this homemaking I'm not sure, but the curtains will give us privacy tonight when we're crowded in with other vessels and we light the oil lamps in the cabin.

Entering Victoria Harbour we saw many boats arriving earlier than we expected. All sizes. Old and treasured. Power and sail. All old-timers with new paint and varnish.

We tied up beside some steps opposite the Empress Hotel where Mark and I had pulled in almost a year ago. It's in a tourist-attraction horseshoe of the harbour where people were already gathering to watch the boats. The ages and histories of the vessels were displayed. Flags fluttered and snapped in the breeze. People boarded one another's boats and talked of their sailing experiences.

As evening came some began to sing. Now we crawl into our bunks for the night after supper downtown, and they are still singing as the stars come out.

SEPTEMBER 2 · We woke early, unused to the noise of the city. Then gradually the hum of on-board housekeeping and breakfast-making rose over the water.

Across the harbour a lone piper played. Margaret said, "The pipes sound sad."

I said, "The pipes are always sad."

On the other side of the world Blair worked on the ladders over the crevasses on the Khumbu Icefall. There was a sky-splitting report as the entire glacier seemed to descend in enormous lumps of ice.

Blair was crushed to death.

The pale horse had come.

14 A FALL OF LEAVES

OCTOBER 1982 · The ocean is one colour with the sky. This morning
the orange of the maples round the bay was mirrored in the sea until
a ruffling breeze came up and sent them twisting, dancing and sailing
away. My mind is closed. It cannot join the dance of the leaves.

It's getting colder. Last night was very clear, a sky of stars and the
first frost.

I have tried collecting all the photographs I can of Blair, from an
infant carried in a knapsack on my back to a confident adult. But they
are like fallen leaves blowing in winter against a door that has closed.

I hadn't said goodbye.

News came slowly from the mountain to Canada. Blair had previ-
ously mentioned that the radios were impounded by the Nepalese and
that any updates were brought by runners to Kathmandu. The media
seized on everything they could learn without waiting to know if
next of kin had first been informed.

One morning his poor mother Emily turned on the radio for the
early news and heard her son's death crisply announced with no details. She sat in numbing shock while friends did what they could.

Mark was working at Outward Bound when a colleague, who had
heard the news, casually remarked that the CBC had lost its cameraman in deaths on Everest. Shaken, he left his job to go to his mother.

Kairos was still in Victoria Harbour at the boat show. She was
decorated overall with bright little flags flapping in the breeze of an
Indian summer. I got up to make tea and automatically switched on
the radio to hear the news. When the radio didn't work I was puzzled.
All through the long voyage it had never let me down, and now

that we were plugged into electricity at the wharf and we had been getting good reception, it was suddenly refusing to make a sound. I tried it on battery with no response. I gave up. There was probably nothing important happening.

Corinna, Margaret's daughter, had been calling in at the boat on her way to work at the BC Parliament Buildings, a step away from the boat show. But that morning she was early, and she was weeping. She held me in a hug, and then, as I obviously didn't know, she whispered, "There's been an accident on Everest." I knew it was Blair.

"Is it?" I asked her. "Is it Blair? Is he dead?" Still holding me, she said through her tears, "Yes, I'm so sorry."

Naval formality took over. I became very correct and felt suddenly alone. I went on deck and took down the dancing flags. I folded them meticulously. Then I suddenly felt the sharpness of a fall. I was helped to the cabin by the man working on the boat beside us. On the bunk Margaret, Corinna and I sat in a forlorn row until news time when we tried the radio once more to see if anything further was known. The radio worked perfectly. Some things are without explanation.

Corinna went to work and I walked with her until I reached a public phone to talk to Emily. I felt guilty because I had heard the news more gently than the others.

People on nearby boats helped us to unraft and *Kairos* took us home.

In life's shadows we reach, like most fellow plants and creatures, for the light. I found it for a moment, thinking of a child.

Before Blair gave his heart to Debbie and shared his life with her, in an earlier relationship he had a son. The boy's Norwegian mother called him Erik. I would continue to watch Erik grow, playing on the beach below the house, laughing, finding crabs and starfish. He would climb the trees in the wood.

But that light wavered, and I stay waiting in my own darkness for daybreak to come in its own appointed time. Margaret has had to go to town on the ferry and I am sitting listening to the silence.

No sound but the ticking of the clock. And the pups tiptoe solemnly across the oak floor, rattling their toenails on the wood.

A letter came from Bill March, leader of the Canadian Everest expedition. I appreciated his writing. He has his troubles. Blair's was the fourth death on the mountain. Three Sherpas perished in an avalanche two days before Blair died. The expedition seems to be falling apart. The media are suggesting the whole project be scrapped. Some climbers have left.

Bill March's letter was a comfort. I am grateful to him:

"It is with a heavy heart ... Base Camp a cold, bleak place ... The team feels the loss ... Blair gentle, helpful, yet strong on the mountain ... one of the finest on the team ... six climbers have returned to Canada, for the price of the climb is too high. Those who stay hope to carry Blair's memory to the summit ... The team recovered his body in a feat of endurance ... Simple cremation on a cool, misty day ... will erect a chorten in memory ... will bring you a small casket of ashes when I return to Canada.

Yours sincerely..."

Parents do sometimes become bereaved of their children. And after the coughs and colds and infections, after the prodding to do homework, after the battles to make them eat their vegetables, after the school play, the Beatles or whatever band was filling the house with music, the birthday parties, the school report cards, the graduation ... it all ends in a box of ashes.

Debbie has left for Blair's cathedral of ice above the world. She feels the meticulous directions he gave her were for a reason. She must go. A true friend, Steve Rendall, will go with the blessing of his wife to support Debbie's trek to Base Camp to pick up Blair's ashes. Then on a glaciated ledge where Blair stood in awe above time and space, a place where tears freeze on the face, she will leave them for the mountain wind to gather and take to itself.

She has had a plaque made to mark the place and she brought it to show us. I photographed it, propped up on the kitchen table. Through the window behind I watched the maple leaves falling, twisting on the breeze. Engraved on the plaque were words from the prayer Blair left on his desk:

I CLIMB MY BODY IS PAST EXHAUSTION

AND MY MIND IS MOVING UPWARD,

HAND IN HAND WITH MY SOUL.

I'LL BE FRIGHTENED IF YOU TAKE MY LIFE.

I'LL UNDERSTAND THOUGH,

YOU ARE NOT MY SERVANT, I AM YOURS.

I AM A GUEST IN YOUR HOUSE

AND IT'S MORE THAN I DESERVE.

— J.F.S.

G. BLAIR GRIFFITHS

1949–1982

KILLED ON MOUNT EVEREST

Debbie phoned us before she left. "I know when I get to Base Camp, Blair will meet me," she said, "and he'll laugh and say of course it's not true. To pretend to be dead is the only way to get me to walk. He always said I don't exercise enough." She has begun the long trek.

And now, from diaries and publications, I am trying to piece together what happened on the mountain. I have to see clearly through the dark shadows of my imagination.

I have to know what overwhelmed this expedition.

I have to know Blair's story.

Debbie will bring me his diary. And others will help me to understand.

The Mountain

"Make sure they know ill luck, not fear, was cause of failure
And silently then explore the last white day."

— Richard Selig

15 MYSTERY AND BUREAUCRACY

JULY 17, 1982 · Blair looked through the window of the Air Canada plane on its descent into Kathmandu. To the north were mountain peaks, austere above the clouds, mysterious, magnificent. Then the plane was circling above bright green fields, vivid from the monsoon rains. Mountain ranges stretched into the blue distance where lay the path to Chomolungma, known to the stranger as Mount Everest.

In the crowd on the plane Blair felt alone. Would he ever be accepted by this team of men, the best climbers in the country, who had trained together in preparation for the ascent of Mount Everest? Plans had been five years in the making, and here was he, Johnny-come-lately, working under contract to the Canadian Broadcasting Corporation, not sponsored by the Canadian Mount Everest Society like the rest of the team.

At a reception in Toronto two nights before, the climbers had received a grand send-off, with media well in attendance, but Blair had joined the flight later in Vancouver, to take his seat on the plane among strangers. He wished he weren't so quiet.

"If only I were more outgoing," he wrote in his diary. Sir Edmund Hillary's success in reaching the summit in 1953 was thought at the time to be a victory that was complete. No need to repeat it. But Chomolungma now drew climbers under many national flags to challenge her again and again, and by different routes. Twelve national teams had reached the summit since Hillary, and Nepal had become a place that beckoned the tourist and the trekker as well as the mountaineer.

With tourism in mind, the chief sponsor of the Canadian climb was Air Canada, with 1 per cent of its advertising budget invested in publicizing the wonders of Nepal, emphasizing the courage and integrity of a young Canadian team off to climb to the roof of the world. The public would follow the climb through a video that would take the armchair adventurer up above the clouds. The person to shoot the footage was Blair, and he resolved to do his best to make it a success while contributing whatever he could to the climb.

Blair loved the myth and mysticism of it all. The Sherpa people, sturdy immigrants from Tibet, would tell you Chomolungma, Goddess Mother of the World, ruled the mountain. She rode a snarling, roaring white lion, and her anger and her smiles were unpredictable. The Sherpas who accompanied climbers prayed for safety on the mountain. Success lay with the gods alone.

While he steeped himself in the romance of Everest, Blair was also very worried. He knew exactly what he needed to be able to supply footage for the CBC, which was negotiating for television rights. But the focus seemed to be on the large vision, and not enough on the small details. Top brass was talking to top brass but no one seemed to be talking to Blair. Teleglobe Canada had spent $1.8-million at the Sheraton Hotel in Kathmandu to build an earth station that could beam images of the expedition into space, to be relayed by satellites into Canadian homes. But in the smaller picture Blair was not certain he would have enough solar-chargeable batteries, or even warm clothing.

On the mountain Blair would rely on this new employer, Advertel, for all his clothing and equipment. The other climbers, chosen from about 100 applicants, were well equipped and looked after by the Canadian Everest Society. Blair hoped Advertel had thought of all the less spectacular things he needed and could have listed if given the chance. Then he felt the thrill and joined the laughter and high spirits as they landed. After the long preparation, this was it!

Kathmandu Airport was not a gentle blending of East and West. It was a place of sharp collision. There were suits mingling with tribal dress. Bright colours with muted. Gesticulations and reserve. The baring of skin, and modesty.

The air stank in the stifling heat.

Blair discovered that a necessary case of video equipment was not on the plane. And no warm clothing for him. At customs he hung back with two large radios that he would need to broadcast from the mountain to the operations room at the Sheraton Hotel

He watched Bill March, the 40-year-old team leader, go through the customs barrier easily, his baggage getting chalk-marked. Then Rusty Baillie, a red-bearded university professor from Alberta. He too got a chalk mark. Tim Auger, a climber and public safety warden with Parks Canada, went through easily. Gordon "Speedy" Smith, so named for his rapid mountain ascents and descents, and Dave Read, originally from Yorkshire and always ready with dry north-of-England humour, both got immediate chalk marks.

Blair arrived at the barrier with his radios and permits. Both radios were impounded. He was astounded, and appealed to a man on the staff of the Canadian Embassy in Delhi who was there to facilitate the arrival of the Canadian team. In the face of adamant Nepalese bureaucracy, the man from Delhi tried to be hopeful. The radios, he felt sure, would be released soon.

Blair never saw those two important pieces of equipment again.

He went with the team to the Sheraton Hotel, with its cool marble floors and scent of flowers. He sat on his bed and stared blankly at the pictures on the wall. He had been selected with some care by Advertel for this job on the basis of his filming at altitude in Peru. His cinematography was careful and artistic in its composition. More than once it had been edited to the rhythm of classical music and the result much praised. He knew himself fairly well. An avid reader, outdoorsman, lover of poetry, strong climber, about to make the film of his life. And he had no equipment. He had checked the roster and he was not on the climbing team. What sort of video could he make, cooling his heels at Base Camp? Without the tools he needed?

In another room Bill March reviewed his situation as the leader of a team not of his own selection. It was Roger Marshall, now trekking by his own choice separately from the rest of the team, who first conceived the idea of a small, light, alpine-style Canadian climb to the summit of Everest. When he stepped down from the leadership and handed his permit to George Kinnear, the idea expanded, and the technical climbing arm led by Kinnear was split away from the promotional arm headed by John Amatt. John had responsibilities to sponsors and public relations, and this arm also had grown tentacles, broadcasting via both Teleglobe Canada and Advertel.

When George Kinnear suffered a detached retina earlier in the year, Bill March inherited the leadership of this group of strong, determined men with varying points of focus.

The team was not even of one mind with regard to planning. Some climbers wanted to keep the purity of the endeavour and disliked the idea of sponsors. While the promotional arm made sure that few people in Canada would be unaware of the ascent, other climbers didn't want to be a spectacle. Were they being sold? Still others asked, reasonably, how the team would have managed without the sponsorship it had attracted. Could they have afforded to trek to Base Camp in the comfort arranged by Mountain Travel Nepal, paid for the fares and cargo costs covered by Air Canada, paid for porters to haul tons of equipment up the mountain, for special tents with telescopic legs that would stand at a steep angle, for one-piece synthetic climbing suits and expensive sleeping bags, jackets and underwear?

The team had two doctors: Dave Jones, who was to oversee climbers' health at Base Camp, and Stephen Bezruchka, an altitude specialist. The expedition would be documented by Blair and by Bruce Patterson, a reporter with Southam News.

Climbers are self-confident people who withdraw from the safety of society to rely on their own judgment. Bill March's task was to mould these very different individuals into a single unit, dependent on one another, caring for one another and accepting his leadership. He hoped very much that the trek to Base Camp would accomplish this. Later on, when the climbers' concern for one another would prove stronger than ruthless loyalty to the climb itself, Bill would find this difficult to accept....

Blair, staring at his hotel room wall, decided not to present himself as the desolate cameraman. Hiding his inner anxiety, he cheerfully joined the group, and he and Tim Auger took a look at the city of Kathmandu from rented Chinese-made bicycles. They went to the Monkey Temple for the view, and down to Durbar Square, crowded with people. The monsoon rain came and suddenly there was no one in the square. Water poured from the sky in a solid sheet. Then, just as suddenly, the rain stopped, and the square filled again with people. Blair and Tim cycled and sloshed to a small café for a beer. Blair ordered a ham sandwich too. He knew that anxiety was making him eat too much. He hoped he could work it off.

He talked to Tim about his commitment to make a film worthy of the climb. But with what? Even the light, high-altitude camera hadn't arrived. The video equipment was incomplete. The Nepalese government held the radios. Still, there was more cargo to follow on the next plane.

Tim was supportive. He was to become a loyal part of Blair's life. And his death.

On returning to the hotel to dry off they joined a group just leaving for dinner. After meat, dumplings, spiced potatoes, saffron rice, cucumber, yogurt and honey, all washed down with Star beer, Blair didn't sleep very well. He was not sure whether he could work off all this food.

The next morning, after helping sort the cargo from the plane into loads the porters could carry, he presented himself at the office of the Ministry of Tourism to plead for the release of the confiscated radios. A thin man with glasses, who shuffled papers the entire time he talked, said someone had left a decimal point out of the radios' frequency numbers. Blair put in the missing point. Now were the radios free to go? The man said he was afraid not. The documentation must pass through two more ministries. This could take days. Weeks, perhaps.

Now Blair had to make a decision. He could stay behind to receive his video equipment, tapes and batteries, hopefully from the next plane, and continue to try to win the losing battle for the radios. This would mean trekking independently of the rest of the team, arranging his own porters. Or he could go with the others across the rugged grain of 150 miles of mountain ranges to Base Camp, hoping his equipment would be sent with porters later on. In truth, the government's grip on the radios seemed firm, with little to be gained from further argument.

That night there was a meeting. Eleven of the climbers who would trek together to Base Camp attended for a review of the game plan. Roger Marshall had chosen to join Al Burgess, who was trekking separately to supervise the transport of dangerous cargo. Jim Elzinga – who had torn a ligament falling over baggage at the airport but was still determined to climb – would follow by helicopter and later, to acclimatize slowly, by yak.

The bulk of the equipment for the climb had been flown to Lukla in the Khumbu Valley to be stored before the monsoon. It was now being carried to Base Camp by Sherpa porters and yaks. The dangerous cargo, including oxygen cylinders and propane, had been flown there separately. Other loads just off the plane from Canada were being sorted and would be taken by lowland porters as far as the trading town of Namche Bazaar. From there, Sherpas and their yaks would carry them higher, into the thinner atmosphere of Base Camp. Twenty-nine Sherpas with climbing experience had signed on for the ascent. Their welfare was entrusted to the expedition.

The Sherpas' religion must be respected, Bill March reminded the meeting, and their fears understood. In the hands of Chomolungma were the mountain winds that could scour the snow from blue ice and rock, forbidding mere humans from attaining the angular summit. She could also use the hot sun to melt the snow and kick down the crashing avalanche. The Sherpas could often read her moods. They aimed to please her. Their daily sacrifices of food and drink and sweet smoke from burning incense were important to them. Every flap of the wind in a prayer flag would send up a plea for safety from the anger of the gods.

A plan was before the team to climb Everest by the South Spur, which would be a new route and would show rock- and ice-climbing technique at its best for the camera. But to arrive at the South Spur from Base Camp the climbers would first follow the Hillary Route across the infamous Khumbu Icefall, a frozen river that dropped slowly but precipitously to the Khumbu Glacier. In the icefall, séracs, or frozen ice pillars – some the height of buildings – teetered and often fell; enormous crevasses would open up in the creaking, groaning, moving mess. It was after Hillary had fallen into one of these chasms and been rescued by the skill of Tenzing Norgay that their partnership became close, continuing up to the summit.

The Canadians were travelling in the tail of the monsoon and before the winter wind at the summit would blow too strong for anyone to stand. Camps would be established up the mountain in three steps. First, strong expert climbers would find a good route. Climbers would then "fix" rope along the route, solidly anchored by ice screws. Finally, climbers and Sherpas harnessed to the fixed ropes would carry up loads of food and equipment for provisioning the camps. From Camp 4 on, there would be no fixed rope. The strongest climbers and Sherpas would be roped together to break trail to the summit. The Khumbu Icefall would be crossed backward and forward to Camp 1 to carry loads that would be colour-coded for the camps higher up. Few people crossed the icefall without fear. It should be done as fast as possible. Aluminum ladders would bridge the deep crevasses. Sometimes rope ladders would assist the climbing of séracs. Altogether, five miles of rope would be fixed for the security of climbers, almost to Camp 4.

The trek to Base Camp would be taken slowly over three weeks to allow the Canadians to acclimatize. The climbers would not fly to Lukla, barely 30 miles from the mountain, but would take the long walk instead, from the Friendship Highway. They knew the theory that a slow approach – with the practice of going higher, then lower, then higher still and lower – was effective for adapting to altitude.

Bill March looked around the room. Any questions?

Some signs of altitude sickness, he confirmed, would be headaches, sleeplessness and breathing difficulties. Acclimatization happens by degrees, with a slow increase in the blood's red cells and hemoglobin content. To climb high during the day and then return lower to sleep, eat and rest was proven to maximize performance.

Camp 2 would be a place on the mountain to rest, find food and hot drinks and meet with other team members. And speaking of creature comforts at lower elevations, Peter Spear had gone on ahead with Dave McNab to create an efficient tent city for Base Camp from materials portered up into the clouds.

Blair decided to begin the trek with his colleagues and trust that his equipment would catch up. It was sad that the video seemed to be of so little importance to the team at this point. And the warm clothing promised by Advertel – would that arrive in time? He would be alright with the clothes he already had until they reached Namche Bazaar and it grew colder. Then he must have a proper parka and tuque. The next morning Blair sat on the hotel terrace, making plans and eating a huge breakfast he knew he would never work off. He wrote a letter authorizing Mountain Travel Nepal to pick up the radios as soon as they were released and have them portered to Base Camp.

Now he relaxed.

He had done all he could. Tomorrow the trek would begin.

Chomolungma, Goddess Mother, be kind, as good mothers should be.

JULY 26 · Blair was awakened at 4:00 a.m. by a smiling young Sherpa serving him tea in bed. This was to become a routine on the trail. Wake early to a cup of tea, breakfast of porridge, and out on the trail before the heat of the day.

He yawned and stretched. Around the hotel there was already bustle and excitement. Then laughter. Backslapping. After all their planning, the climbers were finally moving together toward the mountain.

The porters, Rais and Gurungs of Nepal's lowland tribes, had already collected the coloured boxes with the Canadian logo, sorted into 60-pound loads. They would carry them up to Namche Bazaar. Bending figures, men and women, some well-shod and some barefoot with splayed toes gripping the rough trail. All supplies were carried up on foot and by yak. It was a way of life.

The climbers gathered, one group with one goal: to reach the far mountains, remote and glimpsed above the clouds.

They travelled in a jolting vehicle, past rice paddies where seed-sowers, calf-deep in monsoon rain, followed water buffalo at the plow. But Blair had no camera. They jolted up and up, past fields of such bright green they dazzled the eyes. They crossed a river in furious spate near the end of the monsoon. And there the track abruptly ended. They left the vehicle and prepared to walk, when a Land Rover rocked dangerously up the rain-rutted trail that passed for a road.

"Blair, Blair! Good news, Blair!"

Dwayne Congdon's head peered out the window. He had stayed behind to supervise the porters' loading. Then Rusty Baillie looked out.

"We've got all your equipment. All your stuff! Tapes, batteries, tripod, camera!"

Blair's heart embraced the scene at that moment. The valley looked greener through the gathering mist. The light painted the rock above in myriad colours.

The men began to trudge uphill. After 700 feet they looked uncertainly at the darkening sky. The reason for the bright-green fields and the flooded rice paddies was clearly above them. It was going to rain. Forewarned, they carried umbrellas and had them ready.

It was as though someone in the sky turned a huge tank of water suddenly upside-down. The rain fell heavily, solidly. It came straight through the umbrellas. The path ran with water like a river. The climbers huddled, their heavy packs beside them. The rain went through the packs and plastic bags and everything now floated in a sea of mud. Tents were put up. The rain poured through them. Groundsheets floated like rafts.

Then it stopped abruptly. Tents were taken down. Dirty packs were slung over clothes that clung to sodden limbs like wet Victorian-age bathing suits. Water streamed from hair and into the men's eyes. In the heavy, humid air nothing dried. They sloshed along where the trail seemed to be.

The rain brought out the leeches. Blood-sucking, waiting for a warm body to fall on, clinging to the grasses and dripping rhododendron boughs. They could be extracted with a lit cigarette or salt shaker applied to their wiry, protruding tails.

A chang house selling tea and local beer appeared like a mirage in the desert, and the team dripped its way inside and onto the wooden benches. With thanks they drank hot tea.

Saddled up again, they looked up to the crest of the hill above. Once they reached it, they could see they would drop down again into the valley, losing most of the elevation they had just gained. They knew that by the time they would finish the slog through the foothills to Base Camp, they would have attained the height of Everest twice over.

Some walked in pairs, some singly, lost in their own thoughts. Some wondered what kind of a team leader Bill March would be. Others thought of John Amatt, responsible to the people who paid their bills.

Partway down the valley, on this first day, the climbers began to experience what they had known would lie in store: pain in the knees and calves. It was becoming almost intolerable. They prepared to spend the night in a village schoolhouse.

In the village, kids hung around for handouts. Somewhere in a house a man played a hand-squeezed organ. The clouds banked for more rain. Then came the downpour again. The valley steamed.

Hot supper was welcome. Well fed and tired, the climbers spread their sleeping bags on the floor and fell asleep to the sound of heavy rain on the roof. If this was the tail end of the monsoon, what must the middle be like? And it was likely to rain every afternoon!

JULY 27 · At 4:00 a.m. Blair entered the new day in his diary. The men were full of energy after a night's rest, and made an early start after breakfast.

They trekked through thick, cold cloud, then down into the bright-green damp of the valley, to push up, up again into the warmth of sunshine breaking through the mist.

Lunch was omelettes with onions and the best chips most of them had ever tasted. It was eaten around a large table with a white tablecloth, incongruous in such a setting! The climbers lounged, warm and dry in the sun, until the mist stole up from the valley and touched them with cold, clammy fingers. They looked forlornly at the creeping white fog, saddled up their packs and headed down into cloud, losing all the elevation they had just gained.

Blair finally had his lightweight video camera and a tripod. Now he must get the team used to it. He shot footage of them washing in the river, playing leapfrog. He filmed the seed-sowers in the rice paddies, a suspension bridge with wooden planks rotted through, and a small tea house amid bright-green marijuana plants.

At the back of his diary he methodically drew columns and wrote dates well into October. Beside the dates he recorded the subjects of the day's video footage, the times and locations. He photographed the river roaring down from the Khumbu region, and an old monk at lunch reading his prayer cards, the light streaming into a fire-blackened room.

Day Two, and trekking was already increasingly hard on the knees. Up, up over the rough trail in the cool air, then down into the warm river valley for a swim, hopefully followed by hot potatoes in chili sauce.

Life was falling into a routine. The team, usually sleeping two to a tent, woke to tea served in bed at 5:30 a.m. by Sherpas. Then a cool morning trek to a lunch spot, arriving about ten o'clock. They would relax among bright rice paddies and sharply ridged hills disappearing into mist and cloud. Then walk on, eat early, and in bed by about eight in the evening.

July 28 · The team was getting used to the camera. Although Blair described it as a "bit of a bitch," it was light enough to carry while he climbed. With altitude it would seem heavier, but perhaps he would reach the summit with it, as Teleglobe Canada badly wanted. No harm in dreaming. Then, sitting shaded from the heat by pine trees at the confluence of two cool rivers, he suddenly felt alone. Why was he so quiet and introspective? Debbie, his sweetheart, found it so easy to relate to people.

Speedy Smith came and sat beside Blair, telling him he felt a personal responsibility to Air Canada, their chief sponsor, to help produce a great film. Then they talked of the weather, how it was already turning cold at night. Warm clothing was being portered up for the other climbers. For him too, Blair hoped.

July 29 · Blair's confidence returned, and in the evening, when the hills grew dark and full of lightning, the rain came down solidly and he joined a group for a drink of Drambuie and a "puff." Water ran through the tent, and far from being cold, in the hot night in the valley they were all drenched in sweat and rain as the camera rolled and they laughed. They were full of suggestions for the film. "You'll get some good shots at Namche Bazaar," said Tim.

JULY 30 · Through rainforest and pine groves and up to mountain meadows, down into farming villages and rushing rivers to bathe in the eddies. The climbers came to a small town that they pronounced a metropolis. The law was represented by a police officer who carefully checked their permits, and the populace turned out to watch the Canadians file into the Geranium Arms for a beer.

Speedy produced a leech taped to a piece of paper. He wanted it photographed as a character in the video. But the sun had slipped behind the hills, the light faded from the window, and the picture of the leech was not a howling success. Never mind. There would be more leeches. In fact they could have a cast of thousands.

Back on the trail, the rain returned. Within minutes everything was wet. The men huddled under their umbrellas. The gentle stream they had just bathed in became an angry roar. Everywhere were leeches: no shortage for the film!

As more black clouds built, the Sherpas pitched tents in the courtyard of the home of a Gurkha officer who had offered the space. At 9,000 feet elevation, here was an opulent three-storey house, with glassed windows, tiled roof and thick stone walls.

JULY 31 · Blair woke to a lightning storm, rolled out of his sleeping bag and shook the rat droppings out of his shoes. At lunch he ate two boiled eggs, three boiled potatoes, a scoop of beans and bread with peanut butter and marmalade. After which he felt less like climbing another thousand feet than he had before the break. Blair sat with Don Serl, a young climber he had grown to like, and they were joined by Rusty Baillie, who talked of cinematic practices and transcendental experiences. Dwayne Congdon brought news: 30 porters had deserted. Although 21 loads still had to be carried up, the porters had earned as much as they needed. New porters had been found, but they demanded wages way above the standard rate. They clearly knew the law of supply and demand.

The team moved on, Blair carrying both his pack and his camera bag, which he now referred to as his albatross. The camera was tethered by a three-foot-long umbilical cord to a recording deck, and was awkward to carry. What was deemed lightweight at sea level was becoming a drag as he gained altitude.

In the evening he reviewed the footage he had taken so far. Sharing it with the team, he found enthusiasm was building.

AUGUST 1 · Tim Auger had developed tendonitis. Doc Jones, the camp doctor, had a back problem. Blair's knees were bothering him. Several people were suffering sunburn. In spite of this the climbers were irrepressible, talking of how many they might put on the summit of Mount Everest. When Blair joined a group before supper for a beer, he found himself referred to as the "Media" and Dave called "New Wave Dave" for his choice of music. All of them, each so different, felt themselves being welded into one unit.

AUGUST 2 · Carrying his "albatross," Blair walked through an enchanted forest of firs and rhododendrons. He was sorry the flowers were not in bloom, but the steep-sided hills were enveloped in their magical morning mist. He thought: "Whatever life might offer, or withhold, from this time on, I have been given this day."

AUGUST 3 · Last night's camp had been luxurious. In a room provided for trekkers by reservation, in the home of a wealthy family, the sleeping benches around the walls were draped with rugs, and a small shrine had been built into the corner. Tea was served in china cups.

The Canadians straightened themselves up and brushed their hair in recognition of such orderly surroundings.

It was turning cold and the Sherpas had been provided with warm parkas. One of the lowland porters was found to have stolen some of the parkas as well as 315 feet of expedition rope. Threatened with jail, he ran away with the parkas and left the rope.

In a beautiful valley Blair walked into a picturesque village with nuns at their prayer wheels. His camera rolled. In a trekkers' hostel where everyone stopped for lunch and the usual post-lunch relaxation, the sun sent a sharp ray of light into the smoke-darkened room. "It should be a study in black and white," Blair thought, but he had only the altitude camera, his "little bitch," and with it he rolled away.

AUGUST 4 · Blair and Tim crossed a bridge over a river and looked down into the valley 2,000 feet below where farms and houses clung to the hillside like miniatures and clouds unrolled like a grey carpet. They chatted about Tim's job as a search-and-rescue co-ordinator and how he had brought injured people down from the mountains. Sometimes bodies.

Blair smiled. He had picked up a few bodies in his time, working one summer for a funeral parlour when he was in university. "It's impersonal, though. It must be different if it's someone you know. I can't imagine it."

AUGUST 5–8 · The team was out of toilet paper and relying on leaves – in leech country! This would become serious as they climbed above the tree line. Some of the men were also beginning to feel a lack of energy in the thinning air. As they felt themselves flagging and breathing hard, Don Serl joined Blair and passed him a portable cassette player. Blair found himself walking through the next little village to the strains of Elgar's "Pomp and Circumstance." Then Bach, but that didn't go so well with the flow of the trail. As they clambered up through forests and past streams, he switched to Beethoven's Sixth, the "Pastoral." Just right. Then, up the hill to Beethoven's Fifth, perfect as they reached the crest. Down the home stretch he plunged onward to "Chariots of Fire," happily fantasizing that he was being greeted at home after making a praiseworthy film. "Oh sure!" But he was happy.

A Sherpa wedding party came up the hill dressed in traditional finery. According to custom, the bridegroom was supported by two friends while the pretty bride needed no support at all, apparently. They didn't mind the camera and everyone laughed, on a day when the gods were smiling. All, that is, except the Nepalese liaison officer who had joined them as a government presence on the climb. "Rules must be kept."

When the team found a cool eddy by the bank of the fast-flowing Khumbu River to wash away the day's perspiration, the liaison officer stepped forward to represent the law. "Nude bathing forbidden," he said.

The climbers must now be resourceful, and get dressed up for a bath.

This was the eleventh day of the trek. As they climbed higher into a changing atmosphere, the men realized they were getting slower. Blair and some others suffered bladder problems. The uphill slogs took longer, but he urged himself on with Elgar's "Enigma" Variations, and imagined himself sailing around the world with Debbie.

Sleep at night came slowly now because of a queasy stomach. Breath was short. The march uphill to Namche Bazaar was proving hard, but suddenly, on August 8, above the cloud came the first glimpse of Mount Everest. The narrow ledge of a summit caught the sun for a brief moment. The team was invigorated and Blair's camera rolled. The mountain seemed so close, but that was deceptive.

At Namche Bazaar, a flourishing Sherpa trading post at a road junction to Tibet, the lowland porters handed their loads over to altitude-climbing Sherpas with yaks. The new procession continued up the trail, a colourful caravan in bright shirts and baseball caps.

The bazaar was in full swing. The faces, the smells, the noise! Blair regretted that no photography could do it justice. But the camera rolled, and it still rolled as the team climbed up to Tengboche to rest for acclimatization and to receive a blessing from the head lama at the monastery that clung to the hillside. It was an impressive and sacred ceremony, to which the Sherpas added a talisman of a knotted nylon necklace for the protection of each climber. They had seen death on the mountain. When it happened it was the will of the gods and the Way of All Life. But apparently the wearing of a nylon necklace might please the fitful Chomolungma.

The climbers would rest here for two days. An acclimatization camp was pitched above the monastery. The immense south face of Nuptse rose above and yaks grazed in the alpine pasture.

AUGUST 9 · Early the next morning, Blair left the tent he shared with Rusty Baillie. He walked alone into the darkness to see the sunrise fill the sky with the light of the new day. He watched the mist lift briefly from the summit of Everest, and the sun flood with gold the upward-reaching arm of Ama Dablam. Turning, he could see as far as the big clouds that hung in the skies over India.

He could feel the beauty and majesty of this place enter his soul.

17 UPWARD TOWARD AN ILL-TEMPERED GOD

AUGUST 12 · Team Canada reached the little town of Pheriche, a barren, wild and rugged place of stone huts huddled against the weather. Surrounding were yak corrals. Here they paused again for two days to acclimatize. Blair and Don climbed up into the alpine meadow. They met no one, and got back in late afternoon before the rain.

Lying in their tent listening to the beat of rain on nylon, the two men talked of many things that become suddenly important in a place so wild and lonely.

Blair began to shiver. His stomach was upset and he was still in summer clothes. Don lent him a fleece vest and he felt better. There had been no warm clothing sent up for him with the video equipment as promised, and it began to get cold at night when the rain clouds rolled away and the sky was clear and full of stars. In Don's toasty-warm vest Blair slept well this night. He was happy, having learned that he was to be on the climbing team.

AUGUST 13 · The morning warmed and Blair's senses were alive to the perfumes wafting up from the valley after rain. Mountains were shrouded in mists that cleared to reveal rock scoured bare by the winds. The sun peeked through and lit the dark valley below. It was only two days ago that they had gained 300 feet but then descended 3,000. Then up again.

Pheriche had once been a place of juniper scrub among the boulders. But juniper is used for sacrifices to gods whose anger can flare in a moment, and it had been used up. Yak dung was spread on rocks to dry for fuel, though how it could dry in the monsoon rains seemed open to question.

In the late afternoon it rained still more and cloud dropped over the valley below, giving it a haunted appearance. The Sherpas told the climbers of the yeti, a bear-like creature with long hair. It walked on all fours in the moaning mountain wind. Only "the stranger" thought the yeti walked upright. It was possible to meet them on the mountain.

With this rain, it would be snowing at higher altitudes. Voices drifted by the tent where Blair and Don lay talking of different restaurants they knew. From the Sherpas' tent there was laughter. And then country music: "A good-hearted woman."

They were at about 14,000 feet. Tomorrow would be another rest day.

AUGUST 14 · Blair wandered alone in the direction of the Khumbu Glacier with his camera. To climb 1,000 feet and back again might help to keep his breakfast down. His stomach churned. His nose pinched but he put it down to the glare and brightness of everything around him. Alone with Creation, with Everest rising above, aloof, lost in cloud – Chomolungma and her white lion – Blair was absorbed with the mystery and magnificence of it all. At that moment he wouldn't have been anywhere else on earth.

Soon, he considered, the jet stream would drop to 26,000 feet, and the team must be gone from here before then. There was much to achieve.

Tomorrow they would climb up to Lobuche. It was a place that would be etched in everyone's memory.

AUGUST 15 · This morning the climbers were slower and later starting. They pushed themselves to tackle the boulder-strewn path that lay down a broad, sloping valley, then up a very steep hill and across a gully. By the time they reached the village of Dugla, a yak corral, they were on the terminal moraine of the Khumbu Glacier.

Lobuche lay beyond, on the vast expanse of boulders and ice that led to the heights above and almost to the edge of earth's atmosphere. Amid yak-keepers' huts, Lobuche boasted trade, and even had a Russian-designed solar shower. Among its huts was a teahouse called The Promised Land.

Higher up the glacier, Peter Spear had set up a Canadian tent village at Base Camp. He had sent warm sleeping bags and down-filled jackets to the climbers down in Lobuche. But there was none for Blair. No jacket or tuque, no warm underwear, no ascenders and descenders. He felt like a second-class citizen. Still the new boy without a uniform. John Amatt found him extra clothes, and Blair felt well enough taken care of in his borrowed parka and tuque.

Alone, he wandered up into the high meadows and picked some flowers, single ones of gentian blue. He put them gently into a fold of paper to send to Debbie as soon as he reached Base Camp.

Although his stomach still churned, he made himself eat lunch, and then in the clear freshness of the rarefied air he climbed up a little toward the snout of the glacier. His gaze travelled up to the icefall, a maze of crystalline blue pillars described by Hillary as "sheer rock buttresses, seamed with ice..." Blair stood and looked for awhile at the terrible beauty under a deep blue sky. He thought it looked like a Lawren Harris painting.

Climbing a bit higher now, Blair found the place of wonder he called his "cathedral," the place to rest if the pale horse should come. He would describe it to Debbie in the letter that would also enclose the little blue flowers, and he would explain the path he took to get there.

He descended to rejoin the others and found them puffing and panting over a soccer game. Suddenly a herd of yaks barged through the middle of the playing field. Fresh from delivering equipment to a nearby camp of Catalan climbers, the newly unburdened beasts careened happily around and through the Canadian camp. "Stupid yaks!" said their driver, peering from under a cowboy hat, pleased to show off the English he had learned from other climbers.

The soccer game was abandoned and everyone had hot tea.

It was a cold night with no moon. But a multitude of stars lit the clear sky, illuminating the peaks above, brighter than anything in the world below. The new down sleeping bags beckoned. The team slept well in its silent world.

AUGUST 16 · Dawn was an orange finger that touched the peaks of Nuptse and half-hidden Everest. Then the mountains themselves took on the colour of the sky. In the distance came the thunder of an avalanche, ominous, unusually early, before the slopes were warmed by the still-rising sun.

The trek from Lobuche to Base Camp was arduous, over ice and sliding scree, down into gullies with little lakes of emerald, up again, half climbing, half scrambling, leaping over boulders. At last they reached what appeared to be the dreariest place on earth: a tent city, with the Canadian flag snapping in the wind. Garbage and fecal matter never decay in Base Camp's year-round cold at 17,000 feet. Nor are they burned, since the gods would find such smoke offensive. Garbage was to be portered out. But Peter Spear and Dave McNab had wrought marvels in accommodation, with a dining tent that smelled of hot coffee, small tents for sleeping, and a small structure known as "the shitter."

Blair's tent had a view of the shitter. He angled it differently so that he looked at the Sherpas' prayer flags, each flap in the wind sending a plea to the unpredictable gods of the mountain.

On reaching Base Camp there was open rejoicing among the climbers. Now they were positioned to climb Everest herself. The Sherpas prayed and offered food and drink to Chomolungma, asking for protection from any misfortune. The ceremony was followed with Christmas cake and rum, and the Catalans invited the Canadians over for wine and olives. Afterward, drunk on alcohol consumed at this altitude, they staggered back over the unstable terrain for lunch, followed by total collapse into slumber. The rest of the day was not filled with activity. In fact, in Blair's diary, it was left blank.

In the next two weeks these men would run the gamut of emotions, but that afternoon they slept like children.

18 DEATH ON THE ICE

AUGUST 18–21 · Woken by Sherpas to a cup of hot tea before first light, Blair looked out of his tent at the new snow that had fallen during the night. He wrote the date in his diary and then recorded his thoughts on how the weather that day would affect his photography. ·

The monsoon was ending later than usual this year, with rainfall turning to snow by late afternoon as the temperature fell and sometimes continuing into the night. This meant the climbers would be working with more new snow than usual. All work on the mountain would begin before dawn, when the snow would still be hard and the risk of avalanches less. The climbers would rise at 2:00 a.m. and struggle into boots and mountain gear, wearing headlamps fixed to their helmets to light their way before the sun rose at about five. Everyone should be off the mountain by 9:00 a.m., when the sun could be expected to warm the snow.

As a general rule, the late morning would bring bright sun, followed by clouds after lunch and rain starting around three o'clock. No one would be on the icefall in the afternoon or evening. Over a mile long, it was, Bill March told them, a place to fear. It was up to each man to get on and off the icefall as quickly as possible. Squeezed between the flanks of Everest and its neighbouring mountain, Nuptse, the icefall was what Dave Read called a moving, groaning, living thing. The ice was always in grinding motion, creeping slowly, lurching suddenly, carrying and sometimes collapsing towering ice blocks, opening chasms of deep darkness.

Each morning's group of climbers would go a little farther than the previous day's carry, opening up the route, staking the ropes and spanning crevasses with the aluminum ladders. Sherpas and Canadians alike would bend under their loads, plodding, placing the metal crampons on their boots on the slippery rungs, picking their way in the early dark through the glitter of ice pillars caught like ghosts in their headlamps. Sometimes the path would lead vertically up the face of a pillar, or sérac.

Everyone must be back in the safety of camp before the sun would sap their precious energy and soften the snow. The afternoon would allow time for resting as well as checking and assembling the next day's loads.

Blair carefully considered the light and dark and shadow he would have to work with as he filmed. It could be interesting. He would also be making his daily load-carry up the 3,000 feet of fixed rope through the river of ice, helping as he went to deal with taut-stretched rope, twisted ladders and newly opened crevasses.

Shooting video, therefore, thought Blair, would be mostly in moon and starlight and at first sun-up, often in places spectacular in their terrifying beauty.

The team had permission from the Nepalese government to be on the icefall from August 20 onward in order to establish Camp 1, but it could not occupy Camp 1 until September 1. In the meantime there were plenty of chores around Base Camp. In unpacking and checking transported goods for damage, three oxygen bottles were found to have faulty seals. This was an important discovery to make before lives depended on them.

Blair had fixed up a long work table across most of his tent, with a packing case for a chair. He checked and neatly arranged his video equipment.

One morning Bill March started off with Dave McNab and Laurie Skreslet to search for a route through the icefall while Base Camp was coming alive with activity. The team was making good time and getting ahead of itself. Morale was high and there was excitement in the air. At this rate they might break records.

AUGUST 22 · The route had already been pushed with excellent speed to the top of the Khumbu Icefall and the day's carry team woke at 1:00 a.m. to make an early start. The task now was to cross the icefall and fix rope above it, on the route mapped by Bill to Camp 1. By 2:15 they were a line of moving, flickering lights attached to black dots in the vast whiteness that reflected the starlight above. Soon the sun rose over Pumori, Nuptse and Ama Dablam, rugged peaks that touched the sky with a wild beauty the world below could never know.

A virulent form of diarrhea with vomiting had caused severe dehydration and depleted the energy of some climbers. Blair felt the regular ascent and descent would help him deal with the thinning air that made a body deteriorate. Laurie, with a Sherpa, moved fast "up the hill" and Blair and the other Sherpas fell behind, plodding through cold, crisp snow.

Blair was dissatisfied with his performance, although by the time the day's work "on the hill" was completed, the team had built two bridges and put a fixed line beyond yesterday's high point.

As they descended to Base Camp the intense sun appeared, draining the energy out of the climbers, softening the snow and increasing their fear of an avalanche. They plodded down slowly. Just moving became an ordeal. Then they caught the sound of a chopper that might be bringing mail. It spurred them on.

When Blair staggered exhausted into Base Camp there was hot tea, Christmas cake and a letter from Debbie. The climb "up the hill" hadn't been so bad after all! Strength was flooding back already. He told himself he wasn't doing too badly.

John Amatt also had a letter, from the Canadian Broadcasting Corporation. It had bought the film rights to the climb and would send a senior producer and reporter to the production office in

Kathmandu. They would receive Blair's footage from the mountain. He knew he must be up to the challenge. He decided again that he must perform better than he had today. Since dehydration was a possibility, he would drink more.

That night before bed, John sat down with Blair to look at some of the footage he had so far. It seemed to represent what the sponsors wanted: perseverance, integrity, courage, challenge. Blair had also focused on moments of awe and wonder that would thrill the armchair explorers at home – the contrasts of light and shadow on snow; sunrises that turned the mountains golden and paled the fading stars; headlamps on snow against a black velvet night; aluminum bridges over dark-blue caverns; climbers front-pointing up ice towers; the moon over Nuptse.

AUGUST 23 · While the first tents went up at Camp 1, Blair and Dave Read surveyed what they had accomplished with the Sherpas since they began at 2:00 a.m.: more fixed rope and two more bridges. With the others they began their descent to Base Camp feeling confident.

Halfway down the icefall they passed through the Traverse, a place of towering séracs and yawning crevasses, some easily 150 feet deep, between the blocks of ice.

In the darkness came a distant thunder, louder, nearer – a roar, terrifying. Avalanche! It passed so close that it lashed the climbers with spindrifts of ice particles, sharp like needles. They were paying for yesterday's sun on snow. Perhaps there should be no carry tomorrow.

They were still descending when heavy wet snow fell from a low sky. As visibility closed down, they were guided back by the fixed rope.

In the evening the Sherpas clustered around a little altar to their gods, offering Chomolungma food and drink. They lit the juniper boughs that burned morning and evening, sending their prayers upward on the sweet smoke, begging for charity from this peevish goddess who they said jealously guarded her territory on the mountain.

The weather closed in. The decision was made to make no load-carries for several days.

As the days passed the team grew restless and anxious to keep going, while the sound of avalanches rumbled from the west shoulder of Everest.

No one was permitted on the mountain.

AUGUST 29 · It was good to be on the move again after being weather-grounded at Base Camp. The carry set off in the dark with three Canadians – Blair, Jim Elzinga and Dave McNab – and three Sherpas. Blair carried in his pack two oxygen cylinders weighing 39.6 pounds to be left at Camp 1 for carrying higher. About 100 loads had already been taken through the icefall, and in spite of unsettled weather the teams felt things were going well.

The Sherpas at the back of the line shouted suddenly. Those in front replied and ran back. They were edgy. The snow conditions in the icefall worried them. The climbers listened to their concerns and gave reassurance. The carry continued. Blair plodded on steadily, slowly but no longer nagging at himself for poor performance. The oxygen was heavy but the dawn was beautiful and the morning clear and cold. Mercifully today, the mountaintops didn't shine blindingly in the early sun. There was no sound but the voices of Sherpas drifting up from behind and the ring of crampons when the climbers crossed icy ladders over crevasses. There was not even a sigh of the wind. Silence and snow, and Blair's mantra the thoughts of his sweetheart far away.

By 8:00 a.m. they were back at Base Camp ready for hot drinks. It was now that Blair, still feeling dehydrated, began to doubt if he would fulfill everyone's expectations of getting near the summit with his camera. Yet he was told he was strong on the mountain. So self-assured. Maybe!

The team was doing well and was still ahead of schedule. Bill March, Dave McNab, Laurie Skreslet, Tim Auger and Al Burgess had gone beyond Camp 1 to probe into the Western Cwm and open a route to Camp 2. They had passed the final unstable mad jumble of ice and were comparatively safe, above the icefall on the moraine at 21,400 feet. Their first view of the Western Cwm, the valley of snow between Everest and Nuptse, was like stepping into the security of some inner sanctum with the knowledge that all was well. But after turning for Base Camp, they fought high winds and a dangerous whiteout. Unable to descend past Camp 1, they spent the night there, exhausted. At Base Camp, the sympathetic government liaison officer described this premature occupation of Camp 1 as "research."

Knowing there would be no carry from Base Camp if there was new snow in the morning, the five climbers collapsed to rest, and Bill informed Base he would take no calls until five o'clock next morning.

They slept deeply.

AUGUST 31 · At 2:05 a.m. Blair left his tent on the morning carry with a sack of static, or fixed, rope weighing 42 pounds. Today he would climb with six Sherpas, led by Pat Morrow and Rusty Baillie. There was no new snow and the stars were bright. Blair reached the already fixed rope in 30 minutes and began the climb "up the hill" to Camp 1 more than a mile away.

Then another early morning snowfall began.

Rusty had stopped to fix a ladder bridging a chasm near the threatening Traverse, and Pat and Blair had gone ahead in the pre-dawn darkness. Some distance back, Blair could see the headlights of Peter Spear, Bruce Patterson and a second group of Sherpas. As they neared the Traverse, the snow fell faster. It was thickening underfoot. In the lower valley Blair could see dark figures against the snow moving up by the ladders, before they vanished in what was rapidly becoming a whiteout.

Given the weather, Pat was thinking of aborting the carry and was anxious to know conditions ahead. He was on the radio to Camp 1.

There was no reply.

The snow was blowing into drifts now. Pat had to make decisions. It was still cold, and he and Blair were at the Traverse, with more climbers coming up behind them. Below, a moat separated the icefall from the face of the mountain, and it was thought that any avalanche would most likely be caught in this natural gully. The team was not unused to working in new snow. Pat thought it would be safer in these conditions to press on rather than retreat into a whiteout. But he wished he could raise Camp 1 for a weather report.

At Camp 1, the team of March, McNab, Skreslet, Auger and Burgess was just waking at 5:15 a.m. They quickly saw there had been heavy snow in the night, weighing on the tent roof, piling up outside and making a dark shadow against the tent wall. Surely the carry would have been aborted today.

Bill answered a radio call. It was Pat asking for help in breaking trail to Camp 1 through the thick new snow.

Bill was shaken. It had been agreed that there would be no carry if there was new snow at Base Camp. "There was no new snow at Base Camp," Pat reported. A call to Camp 1 at 3:00 a.m. to inquire about conditions was unanswered, he said. They were now two hours into the carry and needed help from Camp 1 to break trail.

At Camp 1 the tent suddenly trembled and then violently shook. There was a rushing sound of wind on snow. The air was thick with ice mist. The rushing grew louder until a roar filled the mountainside. The avalanche thundered down the gully as Pat had predicted, but an angry tongue licked out across the Traverse. Pat and Blair faced a wall of billowing snow.

Pat sheltered behind a sérac but the rushing air sucked him out again. Badly bruised, he staggered up, calling to Blair.

Blair had been knocked down and bashed with hunks of flying ice. The wind blasted past him so fast that he couldn't breathe it in, and now he lay in the ice gasping for air. He had an agonizingly sharp pain in his thigh where the rope stake-anchor above had pulled out and smashed him. When he heard Pat call he managed to raise his arm to show he was still alive.

There was sudden silence.

Some distance behind them, Rusty Baillie had been bashed and tumbled about 25 feet down the mountain. He came to rest buried up to his chest. Nearby, Peter Spear was buried alive. The snow pressed hard against his contorted body and began to set like cement. The rope, still attached, was binding. He couldn't move. He couldn't breathe. He couldn't call.

Rusty dug himself out. When he staggered to his feet he saw a foot sticking out of the snow above him. He and a Sherpa chipped away the ice already forming and brought out a freezing body that was Peter. He had pushed out a hand to make an air hole and was in tremendous pain from the tension on the rope, which Rusty quickly cut.

Radios crackled. The icefall now felt like a place to leave immediately, but Stephen Bezruchka was already hurrying up from Base Camp with other climbers to help. They passed Peter coming down with Rusty. Peter was wrapped in a warm parka that Rusty had carried in his pack as an extra, and Dr. Bezruchka thought that Peter, although badly shaken, would be able to descend to Base Camp and the care of Doc Jones. Dave Read, who had also hurried up from Base Camp, went back down with Peter. Rusty stayed to try to direct Stephen and the others to the place in the icefall where three Sherpas were last seen. They climbed up to a scene of total desolation. Somewhere in the mess of ice blocks and rock-hard snow in the Traverse, three men were buried. Blair and Pat and several Sherpas were searching. Those up at Camp 1 had hurried down and Tim Auger was directing the rescue attempt.

Pat and Blair, working together, dug along the fixed rope as the most likely place to find the missing Sherpas. There was a shout from those digging higher up. A hand was seen in the snow. They rushed up to join a small group of climbers chipping around the hand in snow that was fast becoming concrete. Pasang Sona was brought to the surface, and Stephen put the Sherpa in a warm sleeping bag he had brought up. He applied CPR and mouth-to-mouth resuscitation while Rusty climbed into the sleeping bag with Pasang to warm him back to life with his own body heat.

But Pasang Sona did not come back.

While the doctor worked frantically on the Sherpa, Blair and Pat continued with others to search for the two still missing: 40-year-old Darwa Dorje and 18-year-old Ang Chuldim. But by now the snow was so hard, they couldn't penetrate it. At 9:00 a.m. the search was called off.

Snow was still falling when the Sherpas strapped the body of Pasang Sona to a ladder and carried it, heavy and clumsy, down the icefall, down the mountain. In the still-falling snow, slippery on top of ice, he was carried to Base Camp, where Peter Spear, still in shock, had been cared for by Doc Jones. Pasang Sona was placed on an altar, where a Sherpa would stand guard through the night and burn sweet juniper boughs. The next day the body would be taken down to Lobuche for cremation.

Two Sherpas still lay under the ice. Their spirits would not be released on the sweet smoke of a funeral pyre.

As darkness finally came and the flames from the juniper boughs lit the night, three ravens perched on a ledge near the altar. Then a fourth raven flew down, signifying to the alarmed Sherpa on guard that further tragedy would follow.

In his tent Bill couldn't sleep. The Sherpas were his responsibility and three were dead. A Japanese ski expedition in 1970 had lost more. Six was it? Or seven? What did numbers matter? The Sherpas would say all life leads to death. It is The Way.

Bill got up in the darkness and left his tent. He walked over to where Pasang Sona lay on his altar. There he stayed a moment and prayed.

SEPTEMBER 1 · In the morning the Sherpas carried the corpse, wrapped in a sleeping bag cover and lashed to a ladder, down the ice and scree, through a gully, over the glacier rubble, down to Dugla, just above the stone huts and yak pens of Lobuche. After writing the official report of the accident and collecting Pasang Sona's few possessions to deliver to his relatives, Bill March also descended to Lobuche. Stephen Bezruchka and John Amatt went with him. John was to trek two more days to Namche Bazaar, where he could use the national park radio to convey news of the accident to Nepalese government officials in Kathmandu. As they left, they could hear the icefall cracking and groaning under the weight of the avalanched snow.

Pasang Sona's widow came up the trail from the clouded valley below. She led her daughter by the hand and they sobbed bitterly. Their wailing lasted for hours. Bill tried to comfort the sobbing mother, feeling guilty that her man had been lost on the mountain, but she would have none of it. It was no one's fault. It was The Way.

The father of one of the Sherpas still buried in the ice arrived. He was wizened and sat stoically still, except for silent tears. A lama came up from the valley with a porter, carrying the cups and pots needed for the cremation ceremony. He also sat expressionless beside the mourners. The ritual wailing was heart-rending. The meal was taken for ceremony, not for hunger.

SEPTEMBER 2 · The spilling of grief had gone on all night and Bill and Stephen, without sleep, felt tired and emotionally drained in the morning. The party took the body from one of the huts where it lay and carried it to a ridge beyond the village, where, in the mist, chortens to the memories of others who had died on Everest stood like sentinels. The lama took the body from its sleeping bag, washed it, fed it with ceremonial rice, and propped it in a sitting position against a ladder on the funeral pyre. Then, as Pasang Sona's daughter wailed and the lama chanted, the body and the pyre were soaked in kerosene. A match lit the wood. The wailing widow was held back from the flames. As Pasang Sona disappeared she wept uncontrollably. The smoke rose heavenward and as the earthly Pasang disappeared, his spirit was free.

Bill was spent. When an old man said to him "Let no more Sherpas die," he knew the words would haunt him. He must be a strong leader, stronger than ever, guarding every life in his care.

He turned away from the chanting, the smell of smoke and kerosene. It was at this moment that a runner came down from Base Camp with a note, and put it into Bill's hand.

* * *

The night before, those left at Base Camp, including Blair, had made an effort to get a message to Canadians who were following the climb, to say there had been an accident in the icefall. Blair's large radios were still impounded in Kathmandu. He took two smaller ones over to the Catalan climbers' camp to see if it would help to use their antenna. No success.

At Base Camp, the mood had been low as people reminisced about the dead Sherpas. Blair remembered Darwa Dorje especially. A middle-aged man in white hat and knickers, friendly, strong on the mountain. He was always smiling. Now he was dead. No juniper smoke for him to carry his soul up beyond all pain. The winter snows would bury him deep. Perhaps he would never be found.

The climbers held a small party to celebrate Don Serl's 35th birthday, with a cake and good wishes. Some were wondering seriously whether they would stay with the climb. But now they smiled for Don. Sombrely they sang "Happy Birthday to You."

Don had spent the day quietly, looking within himself. He thought that men had died up there on the mountain because the team had been too casual about the avalanche risk. In addition to the Sherpas, they had nearly lost Peter.

But climbing, surely, should be a joy, a contract between climber and mountain in which the climber bore the cost of his errors. Don was not sure he could accept a climb where three men died from risks they could not control and the rest simply carried on.

He believed he was through. He was going home. Happy Birthday.

September 2 dawned cold and clear, ideal for climbing. While Bill March was down at Lobuche, the team reported to Lloyd "Kiwi" Gallagher. A volunteer work party of Dave Read, Rusty, Blair and two Sherpas left camp at 4:00 a.m. to repair the damaged bridges at the scene of the disaster two days earlier. The icefall continued to moan under its new weight.

When the sun rose, it shone on dazzling new white snow under a blue sky.

Rusty and Blair operated close together on one end of a ladder over a crevasse. Dave and a Sherpa worked on the other end.

The sun crept in brilliant splendour down the west shoulder of Mount Everest, warming the air. It was 8:30 a.m. The work team would quit at nine.

Down at Base Camp Peter was busy organizing various chores. The old routine was operating again. Activity was good for them all.

Under the sun on Everest's west face, the ice cracked and fell in a solid piece half a mile across and 20 feet deep. It headed toward the Traverse like a wall that seemed as high as the sky. A section of the icefall buckled under enormous pressure and began collapsing in chunks of ice the size of houses.

Rusty, working on the ladder near the Traverse, felt a tower of ice fall past him, missing his face by inches. Instinct and adrenalin made him scramble each time the ice beneath him moved, and he leapt from one ice block to another.

After the roar and the shrill hiss of rushing wind on snow, all was suddenly, eerily, quiet.

Rusty stood looking at the mess. Hillary had described the icefall as "the shoulders of a malevolent god." It looked violent and angry. Blair was almost beside him, crushed to death by an enormous chunk of tumbled ice that may have been the one that missed Rusty by inches. Dave and the Sherpa had vanished.

194

Rusty seemed to be the only one still here. He moved as in a dream, with a feeling of unreality. It was a disaster that could not be true.

Dave had felt something like a quake beneath him, then the ice he stood on fell away under his feet. He was falling down a darkly opening crevasse. Ice blocks hurtled down with him until he was caught at the waist by the packed ice with his feet dangling in loose snow that gave him no traction to try to climb out. There was light somewhere above, where miraculously two huge ice blocks had cantilevered, leaning on each other like a roof. If they had closed flat above him he would have been entombed.

He had one arm free. He picked up a tuque lying near him, and was astonished to find it attached to the head of the Sherpa he had been working with. Dave pulled the head back so that the man coughed up choking snow. As the Sherpa came to life, he realized with panic that he was trapped at the bottom of a deep ice chasm. He used Dave to try to climb out and pushed him further under the ice. Dave yelled for him to stop.

Rusty heard a muffled cry and hurried over to the place it seemed to be coming from. He peered down and there was frantic movement in the darkness below. Dave saw Rusty's silhouette in the opening above.

"Thank God. You're alive!" called Rusty.

"I won't be if this Sherpa finishes me off," Dave shouted back.

Rusty lowered a rope, the Sherpa grabbed it, and Dave heaved him up with his one free arm shouldering the weight. The other arm stayed trapped in the ice.

Now Dave was alone in the dark, held in a painfully tight tangle of rope in a freezing chasm, wedged in ice that was numbing his limbs. With his free arm he was able to manoeuvre his knife and axe. Somehow, struggling more desperately than ever in his life, he cut himself free of ice and the rope that bound up his body so painfully. Rusty threw down the rope he had used to save the Sherpa, and slowly hauled Dave up.

Blinking in brilliant light on snow after the darkness, and shocked at the unbelievable mess of the icefall, Dave turned to Rusty. "Where's Blair?" he asked.

"I'm sorry, Dave. Blair's dead."

Dave blinked from tears and from the pain in his legs. The sun on the snow was agonizingly bright. Everything was chaos. Everywhere were tottering and broken ice pillars. They made their way over to where Blair still stood, pinned upright, crushed between two huge tumbled ice blocks, his head and shoulders free, one arm raised slightly against the inevitable. His face was calm. His blue eyes hadn't lost their light. He looked as though he might suddenly laugh and say, "It's okay, guys. I'm only joking!" But all joking was over.

This was horribly real.

Dave took the dead hand in his. "I'm so sorry, Blair," he said.

In shock, they turned to find a route down through the terrifying mess to Base Camp. The fixed rope danced in the wind some 25 feet above.

The icefall was now a place no one should cross. And yet Rusty and Dave, chilled and exhausted, believed that someone would be coming back. For Blair. To bring him down among his friends.

19 WHERE THE MOUNTAIN WIND BLOWS

SEPTEMBER 2 · At Lobuche Bill March read the note handed to him. It was from Peter Spear at Base Camp. Bad news. A major sérac collapse in the icefall at 8:30 a.m. had killed Blair Griffiths, and two others were nearly lost. Please call on the radio.

Bill received the news calmly. He had no emotion left. He radioed Base Camp. Peter said a party would carry Blair out of the icefall and bring the body down to the cremation site.

Bill, still in shock from the cremation he had just witnessed, reacted strongly. He was the leader. He would give the instructions. Three people had been killed. Now another. And they would risk more for a dead body? To go through all he had just gone through? They had no idea what a cremation was like. It was impossible. Morale would be shattered. His responsibility lay with the climb, with their sponsors and with those still alive. After a dignified ceremony on the ice Blair could be lowered into the nearest crevasse for a grave.

Bill gave his answer over the small radio: "Negative. Leave the body."

Now Peter was shocked. The men with him had made the decision together while fully knowing the danger involved. They wanted to honour their dead friend to the end. Bill's decision was met with a reaction. "We feel very strongly," Peter reported after conferring with the others. But Bill was adamant. If the men had to face a cremation he was sure the team would fall apart. In no way would the body be brought down.

Peter held the radio and talked again to the men with him at Base Camp. Feelings were running high.

Bill realized he was facing insurrection. He may not have known that strong feelings about the climb were under the surface even before Blair was killed. Some team members still smouldered with resentment about the exhausted leader's failure to wake up and take the 3:00 a.m. call about snow conditions at Camp 1 on the morning the Sherpas died.

Peter waited for his answer.

When Bill's voice crackled over the radio he asked for two hours to consider, and Peter's voice crackled back. They would wait for Bill's call.

Bill March was a teacher of team leadership at the University of Calgary. He had his own ideas about leading men. He could not let emotion rule. But now, in total weariness, he turned to gentle Stephen Bezruchka, who had been beside him as a doctor and friend through the Sherpa's cremation. Stephen thought the team needed catharsis and Bill might come across as too severe, when that was not his nature. Stephen knew Bill was thinking only of the climbers and how they were to carry on through a rescue of Blair from the icefall in its unstable state, and then witness a cremation as he and Bill had seen it. He firmly believed this would end the climb. But Stephen still felt that only a suitable ceremony for Blair, a dignified end, where his friends had done all they could for him, would give the men the strength to go on. It wouldn't do to throw the dead into the nearest crevasse and continue climbing. This was not war.

The team was wondering if Bill had become hardened and changed. But he was no monster. He was a tired, drained man trying to do his job. To save national pride. And to save other lives. Down at Lobuche he didn't know how strongly feelings were running up at Base Camp.

Some of the team had already decided to leave. Kiwi Gallagher, in charge as deputy in Bill's absence, had given orders to take down the tents at Camp 1 and put all equipment under tarpaulins.

The climbers waited for Bill's call from the cremation site.

Unwillingly, and fearful that other lives might be lost, Bill agreed that Blair's body could be retrieved and brought down to Dugla, the cremation site below Lobuche, where the memorials to men claimed by the mountain stood in silent watch.

He had given in, but he felt totally empty at the thought of men already worn down trying to make such a journey carrying a heavy body. He had seen how hard it was to carry the Sherpa over the difficult route, and Pasang Sona was small. Now they were looking at transporting a large man in his prime on a stretcher down slippery and rough terrain, and Bill was not sure that Blair himself would have wished this.

The team could not afford one more accident.

Tim Auger, who was to lead the retrieval of Blair's body, had already made up his mind to leave the climb when the rescue was over. He lay sleepless that night, listening to the mountain groaning. The strain on the ice was so great after the fall of the west face that other areas might give way. As a professional in mountain rescue he knew they were taking an enormous risk, but he felt the team owed this much to Blair.

Tim was afraid. He knew the odds were stacked against them. But in steely determination they would leave in the early morning dark to find Blair, trapped above in the ice.

SEPTEMBER 3 · At 4:30 a.m. Tim Auger, Al Burgess, Dave McNab and Don Serl left their tents with headlamps lit and started off in the moonless dark. The climbers at Camp 1 would meet them at the Traverse to help.

Séracs were leaning drunkenly in the men's headlights.

The last two days had been full of sudden death. They talked about possible hazards as they climbed, and made themselves more fearful. It was agreed once again to get on and off the icefall as quickly as they could. If conditions were impossible they would turn back.

The area they were climbing into, once familiar, had become unknown. They had crossed the icefall every day, but this twisted mass of ice blocks and séracs was a stranger. They hurried, breathing hard. At the Traverse they found Blair, still upright. He seemed to watch them calmly as Tim attacked the ice, hard as iron, with an axe.

A rope was tied into Blair's harness, and with an almighty pull the body came free.

Down below were new fault lines. Fearful still, they slid Blair's body over the ice, talking to him as they went. ("Sorry, Blair. It's a rough ride.") They lifted him, heavy and awkward, over obstacles ("Come on, Blair, we can do this together") and carried him across ladders, trying not to slip while negotiating their burden. Bringing him down the mountain might remain in their minds a feat beyond any they had yet attempted or probably would attempt.

Nerves were stretched. The way was steep. They were trying to rush to get off the ice. It was a mercy when they could reach a little plateau and wrap their friend in a tarpaulin to make the mission less searing and personal.

After a mile they made safe ground. The group coming down from Camp 1 had been delayed by the appalling conditions they met in the collapsed section of the Traverse. Laurie had fallen while repairing one of the twisted bridges and was in pain with broken ribs. He had been accidentally bumped by someone's pack and smashed against a block of ice. They were coming down slowly.

At the foot of the icefall Speedy and some others met the rescue party, lashed Blair to a ladder and carried him to Base Camp. Dave "Doc" Jones received the body and wrote a report that would serve as a death certificate. The end had come instantaneously with the crushing of the thorax and abdomen.

Blair was arranged with hands together for dignity and easier transport, and then placed in his sleeping bag cover, on a stretcher with a single wheel like a wheelbarrow. When all was ready, those at Base Camp, the Canadians, the Catalans and a team of New Zealanders camped nearby came together to carry the body in turns on its stretcher down the steep scree, through a gully, over slippery ice to the cremation site near the sentinel chortens to the dead. It was exhausting.

As they descended, Tim tried to raise Bill on the radio but couldn't. He wanted him to send up Sherpas to help. He went on ahead and found Bill at Lobuche in the teahouse called The Promised Land. He was staring ahead and looked empty of all feeling. His mind was on the climb. Let those who wanted to go do so, and quickly. There could be enough remaining to get at least one Canadian on the summit. The mountain was a hard place. He needed hard men.

But his team had nerves of steel in a different way. Some had even risked their lives in a kind of cold courage and magnificent skill equal to any, to bring Blair down from his prison alone in the ice.

In a cold mist they carried him to the meadow at Dugla. There a funeral pyre had already been laid.

They laid him tenderly in the rhododendron boughs. In the meadow where Blair had picked his flowers for Debbie, Dave McNab found shy blossoms, yellow and blue, and gently arranged them over Blair in his makeshift shroud.

Then they lit the pyre.

They prayed, led by Bill.

"Our Father, which art in Heaven," said softly, was hardly heard above the crackle of the flames. Voices were choked with tears and sweet smoke.

In the Sherpas' belief, the fire releases the soul, which spirals upward on the curling smoke. Dave McNab said: "A little bit of us goes with you, Blair. A little bit of you stays with us. Thank you for that."

Don Serl said: "I looked forward to more climbing with you, Blair. Now I shall go to my home and you will go to some home of your own."

Tim Auger acknowledged his quiet friend's love of poetry in a poem of his own:

> *This is the way of all eternity*
> *As we see him now so shall we be.*
> *When the time comes to follow him*
> *To where the mountain wind blows*
> *Go as he does, with a good heart.*

Rusty, the mystic, had a Chinese quotation: "I climb the road to Cold Mountain. The road to Cold Mountain never ends."

It was Rusty who stayed behind after the others had clambered, feeling lost, over the rubble of the glacier to Base Camp.

With Stephen, faithful to the end after two cremations, Rusty saw the last and gathered the ashes.

Then he too collected his things together, to leave the climb.

20 THE ANGER OF CHOMOLUNGMA

No news came from the mountain, and the public waited. The men who had done all they could for Blair were spent emotionally. Weeks earlier, before the Canadians had even reached the mountain, Roger Marshall had been asked to leave the expedition for breach of contract and had returned, angry, to Canada. Now, with no large radios at Base Camp to connect to Kathmandu, all the media had to feed their hunger for information were Roger's negative opinions, and rumour. What was appearing in the press at home greatly saddened the climbers' families, but the men returning to Base Camp from Dugla had no idea what was happening at home.

The boulder-strewn moraine above the cremation site was hard going as they pushed on, low in spirit. Back at Base Camp they now felt desolate. Each man had been passionately committed to the challenge of the climb, but some were saying now that if they had to die, let it be from their own misjudgment, not from the throw of loaded dice in the form of a moving morass of tangled ice blocks. Others said they owed it to Blair to go on. They had come to climb. And they also had sponsors with expectations.

On any other mountain, the icefall would be a site to avoid in planning a climb. But this was Everest, and until an easier way might open up through Tibet, this menacing, frozen jungle in Nepal was the main gateway to the mountain. Yet Peter had been buried in it, unable to move until Rusty dug him out. Three Sherpas were dead, two still buried. Rusty had saved Dave Read and a Sherpa from entombment at the bottom of a crevasse. And for Blair's quiet assurance on the mountain they now had only ashes.

"No mountain is worth this," Tim said. "Wrong mountain. Wrong time."

Rusty felt that the icefall simply didn't belong in professional climbing.

The Sherpas were demoralized. They had never seen Chomolungma so angry. The weather. The avalanches. Two refused to set foot on the icefall again. They all huddled around their offerings of food, sending up prayers on flapping flags and sweet smoke.

Now it was time for discussion. There was much to talk about. Had the team been living in a bubble of its own immortality? And had that bubble burst? It seemed time for a reality check. Time to talk with their leader.

But Bill sat alone in his tent. He had little left to give or to say. He was empty. The climbers had defied his initial instruction to leave Blair's body on the mountain, and he still believed it would have been the best thing to keep the team together. Now, some were getting ready to leave. Well, let them go quickly to save morale among the rest.

When Bill did emerge from his tent he presented an autocratic leadership. He told each man to look within himself. If he wanted to go he must go now. "If a climber loses faith within himself, he has no choice but to walk away from the mountain."

At the same time he was writing to Blair's family, gently, understandingly. "It must be hard to lose a son…. I have a son who grows more precious to me every day." Bill was more full of tears than anyone would guess from his unyielding front.

All the men on the climb had given fully what they could. Not one had lacked courage. Some were less afraid of what had already happened than they were about what they believed would happen again.

In the absence of discussion, questions became accusations. The lack of an early weather report from Camp 1 the day the Sherpas died still rankled. Jim Elzinga, who was talking about leaving after those deaths, ordered up six yaks, like calling for a taxi. They would take the gear of those wishing to leave the climb.

SEPTEMBER 5 · Tim Auger and Dave McNab departed with the yak team. They vanished into the mist, leaving a sense of loss at Base Camp.

SEPTEMBER 6 · Rusty Baillie and Don Serl left, with six porters carrying gear. Dave Jones, the Base Camp doctor who had prepared Blair's body for cremation, departed with them, never having completely overcome altitude sickness.

Those still left needed some final decision.

Avalanches and death were no strangers to Bill March in his climbing career. Now he felt alone with his responsibilities and his ghosts.

* * *

John returned to Base Camp. While trekking back up from Namche Bazaar, he had met the climbers who were leaving. At Base Camp he and Bill had a quiet meeting to decide whether the climb should continue or end now with dignity.

The remaining climbers must first be heard. A meeting would be called. Perhaps there could be some kind of closing ceremony.

SEPTEMBER 8 · When the Canadian newspapers arrived with a helicopter bringing the mail, the climbers left at Base Camp realized they had been so consumed with the events overtaking the expedition that they had forgotten the media at home. The public knew there had been deaths on Everest, but there had been no official details.

When the climbers heard that the team had been described as ineffective, and some at home were saying the climb should be called off, they felt abandoned. Pat Morrow remarked that if sensation was what people needed, there was enough sensation in the truth.

But the public wasn't hearing about it.

It was an urgent desire to know the facts that brought a CBC reporter to Base Camp in the helicopter. After he had tottered around with altitude sickness, and taped an interview with Bill March, he returned to Kathmandu with John Amatt, who spoke with journalist Barbara Frum on the CBC national newscast. John talked in a matter-of-fact way (because it was all so familiar to the team) of the fall of ice blocks the size of houses that crushed Blair, their CBC news photographer, to death. Listening to this disembodied voice on the radio from Nepal speak so quietly of death, Frum winced visibly on camera as though she could see the ice blocks coming. The public had no idea there had been bad weather owing to the late monsoon, no knowledge of the unstable conditions the Canadian team had faced in the icefall.

A letter had arrived for Bill March from Claude Taylor, CEO of Air Canada. It was a message of support for whatever course he decided to take. This, from their chief sponsor, left the option open to abort the climb.

Bill looked at the remnants of his team. How many did he still have? Laurie could be discounted. He was in the clinic in Kunde, waiting at lower altitude for his broken ribs to heal. There was no time to wait for him. Peter was a pillar of strength at Base Camp, but he'd survived being buried alive and the doctor did not consider him ready to go back on the icefall. Dwayne Congdon had decided to leave and had sent his gear down by yak with the others, but he was still at Base Camp in a state of indecision after hearing that his girlfriend had arrived in Kathmandu. Of those left, Bill counted Al Burgess, Speedy Smith, Lloyd Gallagher, Pat Morrow and the irrepressible Dave Read, all strong climbers – six counting himself – to climb Mount Everest for Canada. Was it enough?

Bill called the meeting. There was tension. The little band remaining at Base Camp sat quietly waiting for his message. He praised their efforts and courage. Then he explained that if the team members remaining were in agreement, it might be wise to end the ascent. Camp 1 was already under tarps and Base Camp could be fairly quickly dismantled.

Al Burgess spoke first. He was here to climb Everest and in the team's depleted numbers he saw only opportunity. The few left could continue the climb for themselves, and not for any public spectacle. There were 120 loads of food and equipment at Camp 1, transported at risk by those still left and those who had gone, including Blair. He thought a lightweight, alpine-style climb could still succeed. The team could take the Hillary route up the South Col instead of the unclimbed South Spur, which had been selected as a fitting objective for a team of such talented climbers, and one that would have put Canada on the climbing map. But there was time still, before the jet stream descended on the summit, to put at least one Canadian on the top of the world.

Pat said he felt more comfortable with a reduced team size, and he was prepared to go as high as he could with Blair's camera as well as his own. They all became more certain that it would be possible for so few of them to summit Everest by the Hillary Route. They were ready to try.

There were still difficulties, Bill said. A new permit for a change of plan must be obtained from the Nepalese government. If the Canadians were to change to the Hillary Route it would take them over the face of Mount Lhotse. The New Zealand expedition sharing Base Camp for its summit attempt on Mount Lhotse had exclusive climbing rights there until September 30. If the Canadians waited until the end of September to obtain their permit, they would be facing the edge of winter. If they were to climb now with the New Zealanders, all under the New Zealand permit, the national integrity of each team could be jeopardized.

"Well, why not explore this option before aborting the climb?" it was suggested, and Bill was ready to continue if he could negotiate with the New Zealanders. He wasn't at all sure that they would go for such a plan. However, the New Zealanders were making their ascent by the same route as Canada for quite a distance, travelling light without Sherpas because they were relying heavily on the Canadian team's Sherpas to carry supplies for the icefall and the Lhotse face. After the recent disasters they just might consider using some of the Canadian stores at Camp 1 to reduce the time they would have to spend crossing the icefall that was proving so unusually unstable.

Over the next few days Bill and John, who was in full agreement, worked out a contract for the two teams to climb together. The New Zealanders, at first reluctant, now agreed to share the effort to reopen the route across the icefall, using Canada's food and equipment and porters as needed, as far as Camp 3. Beyond Camp 3 they would go their separate ways, one team up Lhotse and the other up Everest. In return the Canadians would share the New Zealand climbing permit to cross the Lhotse face.

Al Burgess was particularly happy with this new arrangement, as his twin brother, Adrian, was climbing with New Zealand. And Bill, re-energized and satisfied that he had made the best contract he could and that he had his men with him, wrote to Claude Taylor at Air Canada: "I am absolutely convinced the expedition should continue, albeit with a changed objective." Then he went down to Namche Bazaar for six days to finish up administration and collect himself for the task ahead. While he was away the little band of climbers at Base Camp dubbed themselves CRASS, for "Canadian Remnant Attempt on Sagarmatha's Summit" (Sagarmatha being the name given to the Everest region by the Nepalese government).

Al got along well with the Sherpas. He told them Canada would continue to climb for awhile with New Zealand, a team that included his twin brother. Sherpas knew twins were lucky. This was new karma. No more bad karma.

Bill returned with more lama-blessed rice for the Sherpas and cord necklaces for good luck for the team from the monastery at Tengboche. The Sherpas were looking forward now to activity. Base Camp was coming alive again. Plans were made.

Peter would remain at Base to keep it organized and receive a daily radio message from the climb. The large radios had been released by the Nepalese government and were being sent up by porter. John would be stationed permanently in Kathmandu as liaison with Canada. He would receive daily reports from the climbers on the mountain through Peter at Base Camp, transmitting them from Base Camp to the Mount Everest Society by satellite.

Camps 1 through 4 would be established on the mountain, with Camp 2 as Advanced Base Camp. Supplies would be portered up from one camp to the next.

The monsoon had still not ended, and in the week since they had last been on the mountain, it had snowed constantly. The fixed rope would be buried. The avalanche and collapse at the west face and the resulting chaos at the Traverse had altered the route, twisting ladders and throwing some into chasms. The route would still lead through the narrow valley between Everest and Lhotse known as the Western Cwm. The steep mountain faces on either side were prone to avalanche. Emerging from the Cwm they would meet the full force of the mountain wind.

Climbers would be harnessed to the fixed ropes until Camp 4. From there the strongest climbers would proceed with two Sherpas to the summit, over the ice, over the steep Hillary Step, and up to the apex of the world.

SEPTEMBER 9 · An avalanche roared down the icefall, unnervingly close.

SEPTEMBER 10 · A trail-breaking team of Pat, Al, Speedy and Sherpas left Base Camp in the early dark, headlamps lighting the way like glow-worms. They were a few tiny creatures in a huge white world under a star-filled sky.

Al led the little group. They were all glad to be in action. The rope was buried under two to three feet of snow, and Al, without a burden, hand-pulled it free by sheer strength while those following fixed and anchored it, bending under loads. The stars faded and the sun rose over the mountains in a brilliant show of majesty.

The New Zealand team caught up and plodded on with the Canadians. Al's twin brother took a turn at hauling up the buried rope; together the twins were a strong team. Snow had fallen while they had been off the mountain, then melted in the sun and frozen at night. Some of the rope lay under thick ice. Some was beyond repair and was replaced.

Together the two small groups arrived at the Traverse, hit badly by the avalanche and still considered unstable. The route was unrecognizable. Séracs thrown in all directions stood, leaned and hung overhead. It looked as though Chomolungma had had a drunken party. New crevasses had opened. The icefall was still groaning in its disorder. Peter Hillary, Sir Edmund's son, who was climbing with the New Zealanders, remembered that his father nearly lost his life in the icefall. He said he would congratulate the old man all over again when he got home.

The clouds rolling up from the southwest were full of yet more snow, and blowing fast toward the climbers at the Traverse. The teams didn't want to be caught in a whiteout. They dug into the ice and buried their loads with a marker before heading quickly back to Base Camp in falling snow. As they went they fixed wands that would guide the next morning's start in the dark.

But at Base the weather closed in again, and for three days the team stayed in camp because of heavy snow. To raise everyone's spirits the Catalans invited the Canadians and New Zealanders to a party. Peter contributed an armful of whisky from Canada's stores, Seagram being one of the sponsors. There was Catalan hospitality, camaraderie and good food, including tinned quail. There was singing and happy backslapping. It began to matter less how much it snowed.

SEPTEMBER 14 · The evening was cold and clear, with a promise of good weather. But it was decided to wait just one more day to be sure. It was September 16 before the Canadians with their Sherpas and the New Zealanders, rested and ready, prepared to push up from Base Camp to Camp 1 in one day.

Rising at 2:30 a.m. on a clear morning, the same team of Pat, Al, Speedy and Sherpas ate porridge and dressed quickly. Their loads were already at the Traverse, so they travelled light, harnessed to the newly repaired fixed ropes, now snow-laden. They progressed well by their headlamps until they reached the Traverse at daybreak. The half-light picked out the impossible aftermath of disaster. Séracs loomed like huge spectres.

The men dug up the buried loads and entered their "valley of death." They climbed over avalanche debris where they could, detoured where they couldn't. They fixed and replaced rope, past the places where six Canadians and Sherpas, their comrades, had been killed or injured just a couple of weeks before. Buried in the snow they found loads dropped by the Sherpas at the sound of the avalanche that killed their colleagues. The climbers were unable to carry those as well as their own loads, but would come back for them.

Where a rope ladder had once taken the climbers up to a small plateau, they now went up on their front crampon-points to the upper part of the icefall. At a crevasse some 30 feet across, a ladder had fallen in. It was fished out with an ice axe on a rope, but another ladder that lay at the bottom was lost in the abyss.

They found a way into a section that was honeycombed. From the groans and cracks it seemed that this part of the icefall was falling apart. It was necessary to find a way around it.

The sun rose high in the sky. The clothes necessary for the early start became too hot. The honeycomb of ice sparkled and dazzled as they skirted a steep-walled valley bottomed by a massive crevasse. Tired, having worked 10 hours, they plodded on through knee-deep snow, up, up, until they reached Camp 1.

The men had opened a passable route through the icefall and they were thirsty, with lips and noses tender from snowburn and throats dry and parched.

There was no comfort at Camp 1. It was in shambles. Equipment had been left by men who expected never to return. Snow had fallen day after day. It took an hour's digging to free the tents and make a cold, wet shelter. The cooking equipment was found under a snow-covered tarp. Some got a propane stove going and melted snow for a drink.

They made themselves at home.

The day closed freezing cold and the sun went down in a vivid flood of crimson that dyed the snow red on Mount Pumori. Alone with Creation, the little team lay down to sleep. They had re-established Camp 1.

SEPTEMBER 17 · In the early morning, under the stars, the same trail-breaking team left Camp 1 to open a route to Camp 2. At Base Camp the remaining Sherpas left with the last of the loads.

With the route now well marked, the Sherpas reached Camp 1 in good time. Resourceful, they transformed the heap of rubble into livable stores from which equipment would be carried higher up the mountain.

Led by Al, the climbers repairing the way to Camp 2 arrived after a hazardous climb in the dark. Staked out earlier, it was a safe place for Advanced Base Camp, at the head of the Western Cwm, on the moraine at the edge of the glacier. But it was full of the garbage of past expeditions, in the growing heat of the high valley. The climbers felt it was a site from Hell, in a reflective oven on bottomless ice. They were glad to drop their loads and descend the newly opened trail back to Camp 1 for breakfast.

While they were away, Camp 1 had been transformed. The kitchen tent was in full operation. The Sherpas were in good spirits, boasting that on the next trip to Camp 2, they would each carry a load and a half and shorten the climb.

After breakfast, the Sherpas sat in the sun and dried out their boot liners, drinking tea happily amid the rubble. They were anxious to get moving again. Some of them hoped for the status of reaching the summit.

As the sun rose, the small climbing team was consolidated at Camp 1, and Camp 2 was re-established at the head of the Western Cwm. Bill March had declared the icefall closed for danger. There was no retreat. Whatever happened, they had to go on.

SEPTEMBER 18 · By the next day Camp 2 was also bustling with activity, a tent village beginning to look like Advanced Base Camp. A main tent was set up as a meeting place, the walls lined with boxes for seats. Smaller, brightly coloured tents had sprung up all around, and the kitchen was a source of comfort and good aromas.

The Sherpas began to search the garbage heap with the enthusiasm of a group of anthropologists exploring an ancient midden. All sorts of surprising things emerged: delicacies, pieces of useful equipment. Finders keepers. Goods to be sold to trekkers.

Back at Base Camp below the icefall, Peter was in charge, aided by Stephen Bezruchka. When Laurie arrived from Kunde, his broken ribs still tender but almost healed, he was greeted by the doctor. Laurie was rested and, despite his ribs, perhaps in the best shape of any of the climbers who were slowing and hurting in the thinning air above.

Full of enthusiasm, Laurie was ready to join the climb, but the icefall was closed. Peter had to tell him it was impossible. No one was permitted to cross. Laurie raised Camp 1 on the radio. He was desperate to join the climb. He said firmly he was coming up.

The call was taken by Kiwi Gallagher, deputy leader.

Kiwi forbade Laurie to come. The icefall was definitely closed and had not been maintained. A call was made to Bill at Camp 2, and he also firmly forbade Laurie to cross the icefall.

"I'm coming anyway." Laurie's voice crackled over the radio.

"At your own risk," crackled back.

SEPTEMBER 19 · Laurie started off alone in the dark. He carried a radio but was aware that if he ran into trouble rescue might not be possible. Harnessed to the fixed rope, he made good, strong progress. There was only one light, it seemed, in all the world, and that was his headlamp in the blackness. Shining the lamp inside a crevasse as he crossed on a ladder would reveal only bottomless blue-green ice.

On the icefall he met the challenge of warped ladders and ropes pulled from their anchors. There was no sound but the wind and the groan and crack of ice, ever-moving, and the crunch, crunch on the icy ladders as he carefully fitted crampons over ladder rungs. If he slipped there was no one to pull him out of the crevasse underneath.

Alone in the half-light of the coming day Laurie entered the "valley of death," past the places of disaster, past white séracs like ghosts. A human voice would be welcome. He tried to turn off his worry switch. To be full of fear, all the time, all the way, would be too much.

Then he came to a crevasse that had widened, leaving the bridging ladder sticking out from one side like a diving board. Laurie estimated the gap between the free end of the ladder and the far side to be about five feet. The other side offered a patch of solid ice for a footing if he should try to leap it, but it was too far. And he would have to jump from the free end of the ladder, instead of being able to take a run at it. It was hopeless.

Laurie turned away. He considered that he would have less than a 50–50 chance of survival. He looked for a way around but there was none. After about an hour that brought daylight, he returned to peer into the crevasse. He thought it must be at least 100 feet deep.

Laurie turned to go back to Base. He had given his very best to the climb. His ribs ached. He thought he understood how Jim Elzinga must have felt after reaching Base Camp with a torn ligament and then turning around after giving the mountain his very best.

But a voice inside Laurie wouldn't be still. It was asking him to give this expedition something beyond his best. Gingerly, he walked out to the free end of the ladder. From a crouch, he took a flying leap and drove his axe into the lip of the crevasse on the other side, his body hanging down the wall of ice, and kicked in his crampons. In an adrenalin rush he gradually hauled himself up, up, up over the edge. He stood in the early light of morning, not daring to think what he had just done. But he was safe and the sun was magnificent on the mountains. He plodded up until at last he could see the yellow tents at Camp 1. He pushed on to Camp 2, where most of the other climbers had waited in anxiety after hearing of the crevasse leap on the radio. He wondered how Bill would receive him after he had defied his leader.

But at Camp 2 Bill rushed out in relief to greet his friend. Laurie was safe. And now he had another strong climber on the team.

Camp 2 was shared with the New Zealanders. Both teams wanted to get to the Camp 3 site and on their separate ways. Both teams would fix rope on the lower Lhotse face the next morning and come back to rest in the afternoon.

But there was no rest on the afternoon of September 20. The heat was too great in the oven between mountainsides, even with the men stripped down to underwear. It seemed urgent to move on up. But the pattern of ascending and then descending to rest and acclimatize must be strictly followed.

Sungdare, the tallest and strongest of the Sherpas, knew how hurrying too much could cost in the end. In 1979 he had accompanied a German woman and an American guide, Ray Genet, to the summit. But they had pushed themselves beyond their limits, and not far below the summit, Genet collapsed. Sungdare made a dugout to shelter them from the wind, but Genet died. The Sherpa, determined to save the woman, went down to get more oxygen to strengthen her enough to make the descent. But she was too weak to go far, and when the oxygen was used up she also died. Her frozen body lies between the South Summit and Camp 4, scoured by the mountain wind.

In that rescue attempt, Sungdare's feet had frozen, and he later had to have his toes amputated. Now the Sherpa was climbing Everest again, but this time without the advantage of an intact pair of feet.

The team became conscientious about taking rest days. At night, in their tent, the Sherpas would sing. They were a people of the high mountains. Gradually the Canadians felt part of the altitude as well. Dave Read saying "This is where I live!" became the cry of men who had found a sense of belonging. Laurie's raised, gloved fist became a signal of success. Perhaps it was used with less dignity than intended when Pema Dorje, searching for treasure in the rubble at Camp 2, found a tin of anchovies.

In spite of the heat, Camp 2 had grown into a worthy centre of operations. Below lay the infamous icefall. Above, the jet stream was already in descent. At its lowest it would scream over the mountain below the summit, as low as 26,000 feet. And there was a long way still to go to the top. Time was becoming an enemy.

While hundreds of feet of rope was being fixed along the lower Lhotse face to Camp 3 the climbers had other new enemies to contend with. They battled the risk of snow blindness, sunburned lips and general weakness in spite of rest and good food.

Laurie said he felt as if he had been at a party for three days and three nights. Pat said on top of that, add a dose of flu. Bill said he felt

20 years older, bent and plodding. Strangely, some of the men began to look alike: the same beards, same brown, drawn faces.

As well as his own camera, Pat was carrying Blair's video camera, his albatross. But Pat, a professional photographer, recorded the climb faithfully in both video and stills. He got shots of spindrift ice flying against dark rock from a frozen sea of snow. He took pictures of bending figures ascending with the sun shining silver on their goggles, oxygen-starved muscles making painful steps, red jackets against blue-white ice. He photographed brightly coloured tents and yellow oxygen bottles waiting for portering to Camp 3. The cumbersome video camera rolled as Pat ascended the Lhotse face. He carried it all the way to Camp 4. But then the tape froze in the camera. He pried it out with the tip of his ice axe. From then on he captured their white world in stills.

From the Western Cwm, Everest seemed close. But this was deceptive. Laurie found that to think about the climb as a whole was becoming "just too much." He started telling himself "the big push is for just another five minutes. Then stand and breathe. Another five minutes. Then rest. And breathe." When even putting boots on became exhausting, he revised his climbing drill to "one step at a time."

From Camp 2 to Camp 3 – which was only three tents that would store provisions for climbing higher – they must run fixed rope to over 23,000 feet. The New Zealanders ran rope for only 450 feet beyond Camp 2 before they came back with news of extremely strong winds blowing over the summit of Mount Lhotse, where they were headed. The Canadians faced a wind at the end of the valley that was blowing snow and waves of spindrift as from a frozen ocean in a storm. Both teams retreated to Camp 2, where Bill opened a bottle of Canadian Club for the birthday boys, Al and Adrian, and the Catalans sang Happy Birthday over the crackling radio.

SEPTEMBER 25 · Against the full force of the wind, Camp 3 was established high on the face of Mount Lhotse, just below a rock known as the Geneva Spur. The wind tore at the tents as they were erected. Over the summit ridge above them it roared and snarled like a wild animal. Chomolungma rode her white lion.

As the Canadians parted from the New Zealanders and set their faces toward the Everest summit, Lord Hunt, leader of the 1953 Hillary expedition, sent his good wishes, and Peter relayed them on the now unclear radio channel from Base Camp.

The team was glad to receive all good wishes. The traverse from the frozen Lhotse Face to Camp 3 had been difficult. The ice was so hard that it was a challenge to get a screw into it. The wind was gusting to 60 miles an hour, threatening balance. A slip would mean pitch and tumble down to Camp 2, with little hope of survival. A spare video camera pressed into action proved too much for anyone to carry. Laid down, it was soon buried under a three-foot drift of snow.

The climbers had to dig themselves in and out of the tents as the snow piled up. It was essential now to put on oxygen masks, but the newfangled cylinders that released oxygen on demand according to the rate of breathing didn't work well.

SEPTEMBER 26 · The wind worsened. It must be blowing 100 miles an hour up above, they thought. Everyone had descended into the "alley," or Camp 2, to rest and drink copious cups of tea to battle that other enemy, dehydration.

In the meeting tent at Camp 2 they considered what to do. They couldn't climb against this kind of wind. Some felt that if they could go down to Base Camp for a few days the wind might drop and they would be strong enough to climb back and even higher.

Lloyd Gallagher was temporarily taking the leadership. He looked at his men, sitting on food boxes around the meeting tent. They had been three weeks above 18,000 feet, the altitude at which the body deteriorates. They were so wasted that he knew if they went back to Base Camp they wouldn't make it up again.

Lloyd took a gamble. Tonight would be the full moon. A full moon could bring a change in the weather. With the wind still screaming, he spoke quietly.

"Everyone stays on the mountain."

As evening came and the moon came up, flooding the valley, the wind dropped. Speedy Smith looked out of his tent. He must be dreaming. But no, it was real. All was still, silent, the sky bright in the thin air, the wind a whisper. The peak of Nuptse was half in shadow under the moon. The moonglow was silver and the stars were out. Rock crags projected from snow slopes, looking like medieval castles. The mountains were blessed with a fairy-tale beauty.

Laurie stayed up later than the others, drinking in the silver scene in the valley that lay between glistening walls of ice. Everest loomed on one side, Lhotse on the other, and Nuptse at the head of the Cwm. Blair would have seen it as a study in black and white.

Cloud began to roll into the valley. In the new stillness a wisp of vapour curled straight up into the sky. It hovered there, halfway up Nuptse, and Laurie thought it formed itself into a figure with arms outstretched toward the camp.

He was not a religious man. He attached no meaning to this vision. But the mountains are a spiritual place and he felt the team was being kindly watched over. He looked around quickly to see if anyone in the tent was awake to look up at the sky. They were sleeping deeply.

The Sherpas in their tent were singing and dancing. There was no time to run across and tell them to look upward.

The ethereal figure stayed still in the sky above, then slowly faded and dispersed, leaving only heavy cloud down in the valley. Laurie felt a deep inner peace. He hoped his visitor would stay with him to the top.

He slept well.

The next morning the team would be back in its old routine of resting to acclimatize, and deciding who would do what as they climbed higher the following day.

The storm was over. But not quite.

OCTOBER 3 · The wind gusted up again as Al, Sungdare and Lhakpa Dorje started off in the early morning. Then it blew harder. As they moved across the Lhotse face to Camp 3 they were cut by spindrifts of ice crystals, and with their goggles so ice-encrusted that it was difficult to see, they leaned against the wind, breaking trail and fixing rope up the mountain to Camp 4. Then they picked their way down again to Camp 2.

Al was more weary than he had ever been. Everything was ready now for his ambition, to reach the summit, but he knew he couldn't make the final climb.

With Al needing rest, Bill tackled the difficult task of deciding who would now attempt the summit. Dwayne Congdon had remained with the climb but had so far seen himself as a support climber, and he had been unsparing of himself to give that support to others. Laurie was ready for the summit and Lloyd Gallagher and Dave Read also wanted to give it a try.

The number that could go up depended on the oxygen supply at Camp 3. The depleted Sherpas had found it increasingly difficult to carry up heavy oxygen cylinders.

The team considered all matters from a practical point of view, and decided Laurie should go up to Camp 4, and Lloyd and Dave would follow, all three supplementing their oxygen supplies at Camp 3 from that recently delivered there by Sherpas.

Bill wrote in his diary his feeling of privilege at being on the mountain with this group of men. "Here is comradeship, sharing, caring, danger, careful judgment toward a goal, and hard work. Perhaps this is the answer to what life is all about." Down in the world below was bustle and friction. Wasn't the mountain more the reality?

OCTOBER 4 · Laurie left Camp 2 at 3:00 a.m. with a team of Sherpas carrying equipment to the site of Camp 4. It was blowing hard again as they reached Camp 3 at daybreak, and they dug down into the snow to cut an entrance into a tent. Their job was to pick up oxygen and continue to Camp 4, so that Laurie and two Sherpas could be in position for the summit. Laurie put on an oxygen mask from the provisions, but it didn't fit his face. He felt as if his nose was being cut off. But he wore the mask as they continued on to Camp 4 against a wind that beat them with rock and ice.

The fixed rope stopped here. Camp 4 was quickly assembled from the loads carried up, and most of the Sherpas left to go back to Camp 2. Sungdare and Lhakpa Dorje stayed with Laurie, to go to the summit the next day.

Laurie considered the oxygen supply Whatever he could find would be precious. He investigated some used bottles that had been discarded by past expeditions, testing them to see if any still had air in them. He wanted a supply for sleeping, to save the full bottles for the climb. But they were empty. He tied them to the tent cords as extra weight and anchors against the wind.

Inside the tent, Laurie cleaned the snow off his boots, cleaned off his clothes and made himself comfortable. He snapped a frost liner to the inside of the tent, fixed up the hanging stove, melted snow for tea and zipped up the tent. Home sweet home.

Outside, the Sherpas fixed a shell over the tent to protect it from wind-blown rock and ice chunks. Then they came in for lunch at 2:30 p.m. Laurie couldn't eat. Tomorrow would be the climb of his life.

The radio crackled. Lloyd and Dave would arrive about 5:30, bringing oxygen picked up at Camp 3. In the late afternoon Laurie looked out to see if they were coming up.

No. No sign of them. Lloyd and Dave had evidently turned back.

The wind had died. The weather was now perfect. Laurie felt he couldn't ask for better conditions and felt ready for the summit in tomorrow's early dark. He made tea for himself and the Sherpas to rehydrate them all. Then he melted more snow, made more tea and filled a Thermos flask for the next day. If he got everything ready for the morning and went to bed early, he could get eight hours' sleep.

He wrapped up his boots and put them into his warm sleeping bag with his mitts inside. Then he put the insoles into his down sleeping booties. All would be warm and dry for the start.

The radio crackled with an urgent message. Had Dave arrived at Camp 4?

"Negative," Laurie returned.

Then it seemed he was lost between Camps 3 and 4. The order came: "Prepare to search."

Laurie abandoned his plans to reach the summit. If precious oxygen were to be used in a search, there wouldn't be enough for the climb to the top. All chances to make it to the roof of the world flew away.

The team had come so close.

But out there in the freezing night was a life that was more important.

Lloyd had staggered back into Camp 2 in a weak state. He had left Camp 2 with Dave, but both had had difficulty with the delivery-on-demand oxygen system. They discarded the equipment to climb without oxygen to Camp 3, where they would pick up a supply from stores. Dave, going strongly, passed Lloyd. Plodding upward, Lloyd found the oxygen cylinders that should have been at Camp 3 half-buried in the snow, where the Sherpa carrying them must have dropped them in exhaustion. He knew that without oxygen equipment, he lacked the strength to porter them further himself. Disconsolate, he turned back and began his descent in the moonlight, slowly, trusting the fixed rope. To the relief of the team beginning to organize a search, he arrived at Camp 2.

So where was Dave? Alone somewhere in the dark? Laurie had found no sign of him.

At about 6:00 p.m. Dave almost fell inside Laurie's tent at Camp 4, gasping for oxygen and covered in hoarfrost. Laurie seized a precious oxygen bottle and clamped the mask over his teammate's face. After he had scraped the frost off Dave, he wrapped him up and put him in a warm sleeping bag. Then he removed Dave's oxygen mask just long enough to give him hot soup and tea. Dave slept deeply under oxygen. But Laurie stayed awake, checking on his mate and scraping the ice off his own oxygen mask from time to time.

OCTOBER 5 · Dave woke early. He was positioned for the summit. This would be the biggest day of his whole life!

Laurie had to tell him the reality. There was only enough oxygen left for one of them to reach the top. Dave could see that Laurie was stronger, so he made soup and tea for him and the Sherpas. He helped Laurie with his equipment, drew a happy face on his oxygen canister, and earnestly wished them all good luck.

A message crackled through from Bill at Camp 2, also wishing Laurie luck and begging him to go with extreme caution. "I'm worried about you," Bill said.

"I'm more worried about you," Laurie replied. "If I don't come back my girlfriend will kill you." At 3:00 a.m. Camp 2 received a radio message from Dave saying that Laurie, Sungdare and Lhakpa Dorje had left for the summit. The message went down to Base Camp on the small radio and was flashed by Peter to the climb's production office in Kathmandu. There, a Pilatus Porter airplane was readied to fly over the summit and photograph the three on the top of the world.

The temperature was 30 below, lower with the wind chill. There was no fixed rope now. Laurie and the Sherpas must break trail in the dark, roped together, relying on each other. There was still some moon and the stars were out. Sungdare led and Laurie's headlight shone on his bending back. Lhakpa Dorje followed. There was some six feet of rope between them.

Over snow on top of blue-green ice they pushed on together. Slowly upward a few steps, rest, then up again into wind-crusted snow up to their knees. Pull a leg out of the snow. Test where you will put your foot next. Then cautiously take the step up. Rest. Heave the leg up, heavy, slow, give the test kick, put the leg down, rest, ignore the fatigue and pain of oxygen-starved muscles. Another step up against the fresh new wind. Rest. They climbed laboriously for two hours, breaking trail.

Deep in the snow one of Laurie's feet went numb. He couldn't feel the test kick, or where he was stepping. He couldn't go on. Although he was thirsty he needed both hands to try to warm his foot. He gave the Sherpas the Thermos of hot tea.

Working on his foot he began to feel a tingling in his toes. Then a feeling like needles. His foot came to life and they started off again as the sun rose over the Tibetan plateau in a light dawn that indicated fair weather. Daylight revealed the true majesty all around them and their spirits rose. They took off their headlamps and laid them on a rock.

Above them now lay the mound of Hannelore Schmatz, the frozen woman. They paused in silence, paying tribute to a fellow climber in her place of rest. Then they pushed on past her, toward the South Summit, opening a trail. As they climbed Laurie would push with his knee and then ram his leg through the snow. Lhakpa Dorje was a short man, and was having a harder time than the others. He was tiring. He wasn't sending his ice axe right in deep. He didn't kick-try each step first.

Laurie watched him anxiously. They were all in trouble if Lhakpa's ice axe didn't hold.

They climbed laboriously for two hours, breaking trail, past the South Summit. Now they were on the narrow ridge, often so close to the edge that their axes went through the lip of snow that curled in a huge cornice beyond the ridge, fragile, deceptive. Through the holes they could see the steep drop into Tibet.

It became difficult for Laurie to watch Lhakpa through both the goggles and oxygen mask. The goggles fogged up, but without them the white glare was too much for the eyes, and snow blindness at this altitude would be a disaster.

Now their final hurdle: the Hillary Step, a steep, 25-foot pitch of snow and rock. An experienced climber at lower altitude would tackle it easily, but at 28,000 feet, it had broken the hearts of many climbers in the last stages of debilitation. It was essential now that Lhakpa Dorje use his ice axe properly, for all their sakes.

Slow and tired, they concentrated. Nothing else mattered but where to put their feet next. Nothing else existed. The day was clear. So close. Almost there.

Sungdare, still strong, led the difficult pitch, with Laurie and Lhakpa Dorje following on the rope. Now they continued on easier ground to the summit. A few hundred feet still to go.

Sungdare reached the narrow summit a second before Laurie. He gave the Skreslet salute of the gloved fist and Laurie drove his axe into the ice to lever himself up beside the Sherpa. The ice broke and he fell to his knees.

Not there yet.

With an effort he tried again, sinking in the axe. Again the ice curling over the lip of the rock gave way. This was dangerous.

On the third try he stood on the summit of Mount Everest, nothing above him but the cloudless sky of the deepest blue in the thin atmosphere. Then Lhakpa Dorje joined them.

From this patch of snow no bigger than a kitchen table, they looked down in all directions at the curve of the earth, down at the summit of Mount Nuptse, down at the peaks rising from the Tibetan plateau. The air was so clear they could see for at least 100 miles in every direction. They took photographs with Laurie's Leica. The

Sherpas with the Nepalese flag. The Sherpas against the blue of the sky. Pictures through cloud gaps of a world that would be waking far below. They took pictures until the film ran out. Then the Sherpas photographed Laurie with his Minox camera, but it was found later that the camera had frozen, and the precious record on the Minox was lost.

It was Sungdare's third time on the summit of Everest; eventually he would become the first person in the world to reach the top four times, a feat commemorated with his portrait on a Nepal postage stamp.

Today, the summit was pristine. The wind had swept away all paraphernalia left by others. It was as if the three climbers were the first ever to stand up there in space.

But these things occurred to them later. On the summit they were absorbed with thoughts of getting safely down.

It was about 10:00 a.m. when they began to descend. A plane flew overhead, low over the summit, to photograph the climbers, but they were gone and there was nothing there but an empty oxygen bottle left as a gift for the gods.

The way down revealed small crevasses. Laurie fell into them twice and was glad to be roped to the others and helped up again. Tired, not fully grasping what they had achieved, they descended over the ice, over the Hillary step, slowly, one step at a time.

At Camp 4 Dave had melted snow and heated the water to have hot tea ready. They talked on the radio to the team members waiting at Camp 2. Almost at once the news was reaching Canada from Kathmandu.

The three continued their descent, going strongly. At Camp 2 Lloyd met them with congratulations and a message from Laurie's girlfriend.

That night while the team celebrated, Laurie walked alone in the moonlight, treading the even snow in the valley of the Western Cwm. He reflected on one incredible day in his life. Then, back at Camp, the media were on the radio with questions. They wanted to know what it

GEORGE AND HIS SISTER EILEEN

GEORGE GRIFFITHS

MARRIED

KAIROS HEAVILY LOADED IN THE CARIBBEAN

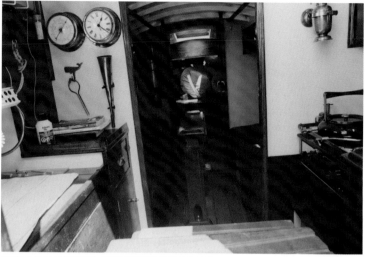

KAIROS, THE INTERIOR. ON THE LEFT, THE CHART TABLE. ON THE RIGHT, THE GALLEY.

BLAIR AND GEORGE

MARK WITHOUT HIS RED BEARD

GEORGE GETTING A SUNSHOT

MARGARET PREPARES DINNER

THE FIRESIDE. THE ANIMALS ON THEIR CUSHIONS.

MARGARET AND GEORGE

KAIROS

THE SHERPAS WERE AN INTEGRAL PART OF THE TEAM

DISCUSSING PLANS AFTER THE ACCIDENTS AND TEAM SPLIT

PETER HILLARY CONTEMPLATES LIFE FROM HIS PERCH ON A SÉRAC NEAR BASE CAMP

BLAIR CHECKS THE RADIOS USED ON THE MOUNTAIN

DR. STEPHEN BEZRUCHKA CAREFULLY CROSSES THE KHUMBU ICEFALL

THE TEAM CARRIES BLAIR ON A STRETCHER BELOW BASE CAMP

APPROACHING THE CHORTEN SITE JUST BELOW LOBUCHE

THE CREMATION

GEORGE AND MICHAEL MAKE THEIR ARRANGEMENTS

THE BUS TO JIRI

THE NEW SHERPA HOTEL

A PLAQUE MARKS THE SITE WHERE THE ASHES WERE LAID

was like to be the only Canadian to stand on top of the world. Laurie said the memory of another Canadian, Blair Griffiths, was with him at the summit.

"Yes," he told the *Vancouver Sun* reporter, "I took Blair's memory to the top. I hope he will be proud of what the team has done."

"And what will you do when you come back?"

"Get cleaned up. Get some sleep. Get some sun."

With their mission accomplished, some climbers now wanted to get off the mountain and go home. But with the fair weather and the fixed ropes in place, others felt ready for a second attempt on the summit. Al was rested now, and ready to go up with two Sherpas, Pema Dorje and Lhakpa Tshering, and the others felt Al deserved a chance at the summit. Pat said he would go with them as high as he possibly could, to take photographs. With the political objective of the climb met, this day was purely for the joy of the climbers, and the weather was ideal, without a breath of wind.

But there was no oxygen left at Camp 4.

Dwayne Congdon decided to make a second attempt possible by carrying oxygen from Camp 2 to Camp 4, returning the same day, all without using oxygen himself. This was a remarkable feat.

Then Pat, Al, Pema Dorje and Lhakpa Tshering positioned themselves at Camp 4 for an attempt on the summit.

OCTOBER 6 · The alarm clock rang at 3:00 a.m. at Camp 4. Al looked happily at the weather. This was to be his day. He had so nearly achieved the summit with a British expedition only a few months ago but was turned back by the wind. But today was perfect. He had slept without oxygen, and felt well and, in fact, quite hungry. He drank tea, and shared noodle soup with the Sherpas, fastened an oxygen bottle to his pack, and was ready for the summit.

Pat had slept badly. Someone had accidentally punctured his inflatable sleeping pad with crampons, and he was lying on the empty oxygen bottles that acted as ballast helping to hold their shelter on the mountainside. He stuck his head out of the tent and realized the weather was ideal for photography. But the others had taken all the oxygen that Dwayne had portered up. There was none left for him.

Outside, in the world's highest junkyard, he scrounged around as Laurie had done, looking for any oxygen that might have been left by a previous expedition. Laurie hadn't succeeded in finding any, but Pat found two old bottles that proved to be half full. Now he too was ready. Carrying a double burden of oxygen canisters and camera equipment, Pat started off roped to the others.

They set off in the dark and bitter cold. With so much weight, Pat fell behind and unroped himself to go his own pace in the deep snow. Al started strongly but then had trouble breathing. He and the Sherpas had climbed about 1,200 feet when he became quite sure there was something wrong with his on-demand oxygen supply.

Pat, however, had felt a sudden spurt of strength and didn't know where it could have come from. He had passed Al and the two Sherpas and waited farther up, not knowing that Al's oxygen was possibly frozen. There was none left at Camp 4, or Camp 3.

Al was popular with the Sherpas, and Lhakpa Dorje offered his oxygen. Al shook his head. Now Pat was tiring and unlikely to go much farther, said the Sherpa. Al shook his head again and turned to go back, waving toward the summit and telling the two Sherpas, who wanted so much to reach the top, to continue without him and good luck.

Pema Dorje addressed the mountain in his best learned English.

"Shit!" he shouted, and the wind carried his voice away. Then they continued upward to catch up to Pat.

Al radioed Camp 2 to say he was turning back. All the men there wept for him. Pat tied himself into the climbing rope with the Sherpas and took the lead. He was enjoying his surge of new strength. It grew as he pushed on. It amazed him. He was moving well and enjoying the climb. Over Tibet the sun burst into a bright morning that painted the mountains, and the higher they went the stronger Pat became. He called it his gift. It seemed to be something outside himself. His new energy and obvious skill inspired the Sherpas.

At 11:30 a.m. Pat astonished everyone at Camp 2 with a radio call that he was already on the summit. The cheers of the team came over the line. What was it like up there? "Rocks and snow," he reported. Then he added that it was like being in a stationary aircraft looking down on the world with nothing but sky above and all around. Mountains, wind-scarred, sloped below. There was a bank of cumulus cloud lying across the sky about 8,000 feet down.

As the three stood in a place of indescribable remoteness and grandeur, Pat took his camera out of his pack and photographed the two elated Sherpas on the narrow platform on top of the world. Then he asked Lhakpa Tshering to take his picture. The professional photographer, he struck the right pose, then suddenly took off his goggles and oxygen mask for a few brief seconds. Lhakpa Tshering snapped a photograph that went around the world.

The Sherpas told Pat they must leave a gift for the gods. Searching his pockets he found a Kit Kat candy bar. They tucked it into the snow. Then they began their careful descent.

Pema Dorje tried to remove the ice encrusting his goggles so he could see. But it was thick, and he took them off to quickly scrape them. And then he could see practically nothing. In a matter of seconds Pema Dorje had become snowblind.

They stood near the summit, three small dark figures in a vast white wilderness, facing the perils of a descent along a ridge no wider than a tabletop. And one of them couldn't see.

They started down, tightly roped together. Pema Dorje, at the bottom end of the rope, slipped and the others saw it coming and drove their axes into the ice to brake the fall before it could gather momentum and take them all over the edge.

Just below the South Summit Pema Dorje slipped again, and again the other two felt the fall coming in time to brake it. At the South Col, they attached themselves to the fixed rope and continued down carefully, helping the blind man over the friable rock of the Geneva Spur, feeling a warning tug and weight on the rope as the Sherpa would falter and quickly try to steady himself while the others guided him.

Gradually they climbed down in the footsteps they had made on the way up.

At Camp 2 Pat and the two Sherpas were greeted with cheers. All the men prepared to spend the night together at Camp 2 and then return to Base Camp.

The next morning, Al led Pema Dorje slowly and carefully on a single rope like a dog lead, step by step down to Camp 1. Bill guided him from there to the Traverse, with the Sherpa groping blindly as they slowly repaired and crossed the icefall. It was all the more dangerous for having been closed for three weeks. At the Traverse, Sherpas who had climbed up from Base Camp took over the care of their comrade who had made it to the summit. At Base Camp he was delivered into the care of Stephen Bezruchka until his sight returned.

Within two days Pema Dorje could see, and was now happy in the glory of success. The Canadians had achieved their goal. The tents were taken down at Base Camp. Equipment was ready to be carried away.

Debbie, having travelled from Canada, reached the camp in time to collect Blair's ashes. She had been expected, and there had been anxiety that she might not arrive before the team had to leave, but she and Blair's friend Steve Rendall had hurried. Now Debbie carried what was left of her sweetheart in a small box, bearing him faithfully to Blair's cathedral in the sky, following the description in his letter.

There she laid ashes and mountain flowers together on a ledge while Steve carefully placed the rock that he had wired to the memorial plaque. In the bitter cold they said farewell as some of the ashes caught the mountain wind. Then they turned to walk down to Lukla, to catch a plane to Kathmandu and then home.

Sherpa women driving yaks came up to Base Camp to transport loads of equipment down to Namche Bazaar. From there the gear would be portered to Kathmandu. Base Camp felt empty, like a home when all the furniture has been taken out and voices fall silent. Saddened, the Canadians heard that both the New Zealand and Catalan teams had been turned back by weather and strong winds without reaching their goals. It had so nearly happened to the Canadians.

The Canadian team also went down to Lukla soon after Debbie and Steve had left, to board a plane to Kathmandu. They stopped on the path at Dugla where chortens were being built to the memories of Blair and the dead Sherpas. Each climber found a rock to be made a part of Blair's chorten. Peter joined them after closing Base Camp, and draped the camp's Canadian flag over the finished chorten to honour their fallen comrade. The words were already roughly hewn into the rock: "G. Blair Griffiths, aged 33, killed on Mount Everest." Peter wondered if Blair knew they'd made it to the top. He believed he did.

In Kathmandu there was a cocktail party. The noise of so many voices was strange to them all, perhaps like coming into port after a long sail. The climbers were used to saying only what was important. Small talk had been a waste of time and breath. This contact with the world was too sudden.

"What was it like?" came the question. The hardships, the grief, the triumph. It was all so personal. A journey within. What could they say in reply?

The team flew home from Kathmandu. As October ran its course the jet stream descended on Mount Everest, sweeping the summit clean, blowing away the Kit Kat bar offered to the gods, burying the old oxygen bottle. Eventually it, too, would be driven from the summit. Chomolungma would claim her own.

Climbers and Sherpas dispersed to their loved ones and picked up the threads of their lives.

It was almost as if the climb had never been.

Except that one of the men who left Canada with them three months before was not going home.

And the rest would never be the same again.

22 THE WIND ON THE WATER

NOVEMBER 1984 · The night wind blows easterly, off the water. The moon sends a shaft of silver over the sea from a gap in the clouds. A place I swore never to leave again is shrouded in winter, and while embracing everything I see here, I am mentally preparing to go away. I've said I would never leave here.

But I have to go.

I am grateful to know Blair's story, and to have gone in my imagination with his colleagues to the mountaintop. And I thank Laurie Skreslet for his visit with me, and for saying that Blair's memory went with him to the summit.

But I carry a load of anger against myself. It is probably quite irrational, but it weighs heavily. I had introduced Mark and Blair to climbing when they were teenagers. It became Blair's passion. And it killed him.

I know the reasons he climbed were his own. The experience, delight and challenge he crammed into his 33 years were what he sought. But now I must go and stand where he stood, in his cathedral of ice and glacial rock in the sky, the place of awe that he selected for himself if the pale horse should come.

Debbie covered his ashes with flowers from a mountain meadow. If the meadow is still in bloom I shall gather flowers for my own offering of love and thanks for all the years.

That is the reason I must go.

I look toward the nearby hill known as Galiano Mountain, which is a thousand feet high. I must climb over seventeen times as high in ups and downs that can break the heart and almost break the knees. Oxygen-thin air can burn the lungs. And I realize I am an old man.

But I must go.

I told Margaret on our daily walk with the dogs, choosing a favourite cedar grove to stop and talk. She knew, of course. She hadn't been blind to the maps of Nepal spread over the kitchen table where she wanted to roll out her pastry.

"How high do you have to go?"

"About seventeen thousand. Look, I may be an old fogey, but I think I can still handle this."

As we walked on she said, "Blair talked of an airstrip partway up the foothill trek. Couldn't you fly in and out?"

"Yes, I could fly out, but going in I need to climb very slowly into the thinning air. I couldn't do it suddenly by plane. I'd risk being ill."

The dogs ran back to see why we had stopped and we obligingly walked on.

Margaret said, "I do understand why you're going."

And I nodded. "You see, I didn't say goodbye."

We still walked on, feeling close, not talking, under cedars with boughs dripping bright moss from the winter rains. Then we turned back.

This evening, by the fireside, we were relaxing in easy non-communication, each with our own thoughts. The dogs lay together on their bed by the fire in a warm and happy coma, rousing to turn occasionally in a canine choreography. A stray cat that had reported to the front door awhile ago sat on a cushion in the warmth of the logs by the hearth. Margaret seemed to be dozing but she suddenly said: "I looked it up, and you don't qualify."

"Qualify for what?"

"Fogeyism. A fogey is someone advanced in years but behind the times."

I became suddenly alert to this piece of research.

"You can be fogey-like. That's having the characteristics of a fogey but not the real thing," she explained. "And you can have fogeydom, which is group fogeyism. Like the Canadian Senate."

"You don't think I'm a fogey?"

"No, of course not. People who leave the fireside to climb 17,000 feet at the end of a monsoon should be called something, but they're definitely not fogeys."

I was so glad to be released from the burden of being old-fashioned that I became eager.

"I could go in the spring, before the monsoon, instead of waiting until after."

"If you have to train you might need more time. Better to wait." And I agreed.

Margaret has already gone to bed. Before she went she seemed to be choosing her words carefully as she slowly said, "You're undertaking quite a lot, you know. Sometimes you may be tired, sometimes disheartened. You might even have to turn back with altitude sickness. I wish I could be with you but I couldn't make it. My thought will always be where you are."

"I shall need you there." That was the most necessary part of my leaving.

Now I am standing alone at the window watching the night change as the wind off the sea blows clouds across the moon.

This is my place. And part of me has already left it.

DECEMBER · The island is shrouded in winter. The heron stands still on the point in a morning frost, waiting for a shadow on the sea that will mean breakfast.

Christmas is sweeping in with bright wrappings and wonderful smells from the kitchen. Christmas cards go out and Christmas cards come in.

I keep up a regular morning climb to the top of Galiano Mountain and down. It's a hard slog and coming down hurts my knees terribly. The trail is muddy with the winter rains. But my speed is improving.

I had hoped the bulldogs would come with me. I have a new goal that gives me energy for the goal. The bulldogs have no goal. They make it clear they are not in training. If it's raining, which it often is when we take the last walk of the day before bed, down the lane that leads to the house, the bulldogs stand in the shelter of the carport.

When I call them in vain and turn back, not pleased, they greet me ecstatically. "Did you have a good walk, George?"

And when I return from my morning climb they welcome me home as though I had been away for a month. "We've been waiting for you, loyal and faithful as we are."

I train alone.

Margaret has a lot to do. Last night she plumped down in her chair and scribbled a haiku.

> *"All is bustle,*
> *A fat saint in scarlet.*
> *But the message comes in silence."*

I string the Christmas lights.

JANUARY 1985 · Standing under a wind-torn sky looking up at a silver sliver of a new moon, I made only one New Year's resolution. I am becoming tedious in my single-mindedness. My resolution is to prepare thoroughly for the ups and downs of foothills trekking.

On Galiano Mountain the mud is still awful and I train a lot inside with wrist and ankle weights attached with black belting held by Velcro.

Margaret's grandson Sean is visiting, with his younger brother. He wears the black-belted weights around his young waist, and after a few karate kicks he acknowledges the cheers of the crowd. Then he demolishes New Year's leftovers, his karate performance having been strenuous.

FEBRUARY · The old day lingered in the light of a white landscape, with myriad silver twigs feathered in snow. Maples with grace in their branches stand against straight dark fir trees.

Dave Morgan over at the sheep farm says it's going to get colder than a well digger's ass. With the wind in the southeast from the sea, bringing an extra chill, he has put his sheep in the barn.

In the blowing snow Margaret and I and two unwilling bulldogs walked a way together, but the ground proved too difficult to go far. Now it's the evening of my birthday. Seventy-one.

Margaret gave me a new recording of *The Valkyries*, which she knew I wanted because I told her. Her card warmed my heart. There were presents and family phone calls and gifts from the animals who were duly thanked and dismissed it as nothing.

Early in the morning more birds than usual came to the feeders outside the kitchen window, finding a good supply of seed sprinkled above the snow. Standing on the window ledge a junco looked in at me through the glass.

"Happy Birthday, George."

Between feeds they stood in a row, light as the feathers they wore, unmoving on the snow mounds along the deck rail, conserving energy.

The heron found his icy place on the point uncomfortable, and kept his sentinel watch from the top of a fir tree.

Now in the evening, the log fire crackles. We have finished my birthday dinner, and the animals' inert bodies are sprawled on the floor in positions of collapse from warmth and birthday leftovers. I tell the bulldogs they would both have been eaten by now if they lived in the Philippines, and they just listen, stretch and yawn.

"It looks as if a bomb dropped," Margaret mutters as she steps over three sprawled bodies to sit beside me. Then she announces, "I think you should take some long johns with you to Nepal." This seems apropos of nothing, but she may be feeling concern for Dave Morgan's well diggers, and that has prompted her train of thought.

I say, "I'm not going high enough," but this she disregards.

"You can get nice silk ones that don't take up much room in a backpack."

"Trekking with silk undies?"

But Margaret ignored such flippancy.

"I've looked it up," she said. "When you're moving in a thinning atmosphere you become slower and don't circulate much warmth yourself. You must keep in what you have."

All this made sense and I knew I should follow such good advice, but I didn't want to. I'm taking the minimum to carry, and I hope a longish warm coat may be enough.

Outside there are no stars and no moon over the hard, white landscape. The only lights are the beacon in the bay on Collinson Rock and the yellow, rippling light on the sea from Dave Morgan's barn. The snow piles up against the window panes.

The room is warm and full of music. Wagner. My favourite. It's been a good birthday.

MARCH · The two pairs of eagles that raise their families each year in stout fir trees across the bay are busy refurbishing and restoring the old nests. One male eagle was found injured some weeks ago and was taken to a wildlife rehabilitation clinic on Salt Spring Island, travelling in a box on an islander's boat. When he was brought back and released from the beach below the house he flew straight home. His mate may have said, "Where on earth have you been?" He may have replied, "You'll never believe it." And perhaps she didn't.

Now he is bringing the ritual piece of evergreen to the nest to rekindle the old flame, and together once more they ride the air drafts over Galiano Mountain.

The winter pansies outside the bedroom window lay their heads very low. I use the southeast wind for my daily climb, a push from behind going up and a brake coming down.

Margaret's grandson Michael came to visit. He has been special to me since he was a little boy. In maturity he is quiet, well read, with a sense of adventure. Now 19 and exploring the world, he has served in a Buddhist monastery in Thailand and plans to trek in India, travelling light with a pack as he always does. He can be away for months with one spare shirt and a toothbrush.

I told him of my own plans, to climb almost to Everest Base Camp.

He commented: "You'll be going higher than any point in the Canadian Rockies." Then he didn't smile, or deride me because of my age. He just said quietly, "I'll come with you."

Margaret was concerned. "You'll go too fast, Michael. You're young and George will exhaust himself trying to keep up."

The reply was confident: "I'll go his pace, and maybe help when the going gets rough."

So we have a pact, Michael and I. He will come through from India to Nepal, arriving in Kathmandu at the beginning of October. There I will meet him, obtain the services of a guide and get the necessary permits. We will go together to a rock and ice cathedral in the sky.

APRIL · Spring came in on a wind from the water that scattered the blossoms on the crabapple trees. Then the breezes blew softly with a perfume of seaweed and spring flowers.

Realizing that time is passing quickly I have become business-like and rummaged among my papers to find a card I was given by Debbie. "G.B. Ranjit," it said in important letters. "Rainbow Travels, Kathmandu, B. Comm., MSC (Moscow)."

I wrote to Mr. Ranjit very politely, inquiring about reasonably priced and clean accommodation in Kathmandu. And could he direct me to a guide who could speak English? I also wrote that I understand there is a clinic on the route to Everest Base Camp. I am in good health according to recent medical checks, but seek more information on altitude sickness.

In a very short time Mr. Ranjit replied. He can find me good accommodation nearer the time of arrival. He knows a man who speaks English who may be available as a guide. He encloses some frightening information on mountain sickness and remains my humble servant. I shall be in touch again.

Kairos is straining at her lines. She always comes out of the water in May for refitting. But I am finding this scraping down and oiling every year more than I can manage as time is going by. So I have asked Phil, who owns the boatyard at Bird's Eye Cove, to give the hull an epoxy shell. It won't be visible but will be very durable and protective. This means that the money left over for my Nepal trek will be a very small amount. My long walk will clearly differ from Blair's as described in his diary. No Sherpas laying white tablecloths in the wilderness for Michael and me!

MAY · Margaret and I sailed *Kairos* to the boatyard in a steady prevailing wind from the southeast. It felt so good! We spent the night in Sidney, on Vancouver Island, then turned northward the next day to Bird's Eye Cove. There we oiled the cockpit, and while the hull was given a facelift at the yard we worked on the mast in a shed. Then we dawdled pleasantly before bringing the boat back home again.

As I tied her up in the marina in Montague Harbour I promised *Kairos* we would sail together through the summer. "Don't fret, old lady. I'll never be too busy to share my life with you."

JUNE · My regular climb up Galiano Mountain in the freshness of the morning has become a joy. Below, the world is small and ships in the Pass are like toys. It is completely silent.

There are different kinds of silence. The silence I share often with Margaret is effortless, companionable, never empty. There is no reason to fill it with words. The silence of the cedar grove is a natural cloaking of the trees in their own quietness. But up here, solitary, above the sound of the sea, is a place of truth, beyond the tyranny of the petty, a place of the wide horizon and the call of the eagle. I call back, "Where are you?"

I left the house early this morning to climb up here to see the sun come up over the sea, to watch the morning embrace the new day and clothe it in pink and lavender-blue gauze. And I give thanks for the morning.

JULY · The garden is still perfumed with Margaret's antique roses, which began flowering in June. This is their last flush and they will not flower again this year, but now their scent comes in through the open windows.

We sail *Kairos* in short summer trips that won't interfere too much with my training schedule. Erik sails with us, harnessed on a short rope to avoid accidents. There will be no meeting with friends at Port Townsend, across the American border, or in Desolation Sound, where we have glided silently with no noise but the dipping oars of the dinghy, and the sheer beauty has made Margaret brush tears from her face. No sailing this year through the night with Margaret in her bunk and me at the tiller, singing under the stars.

My exercise routine is my priority. "There will be other years," I tell the little ship.

The stream that gushed through the woods, over the waterfall and down to the sea is dry now. We are into a hot summer with little rain. In fact, from the middle of July to October is usually a time of sun-filled days, wells running perilously low, and gratitude for tanks of water stored from the winter rains.

Michael has sent me a letter from India. He will definitely meet me in Kathmandu in the first week of October.

AUGUST · At the end of a dry, rainless month, with the garden irrigated from the water tanks, the maple leaves are turning golden early. Some are already falling, drifting onto the sea. I make my climb up the mountain at sunrise now, to be back before the heat of the day. Watching the dawn is always my joy, Omar Khayyam's roses, scattering petals on the ocean.

At night the sky is spectacular. We take our sleeping bags out onto the deck and watch the night with its show of shooting stars at this time of the year, and hear the occasional rustle of a deer coming through the grass to eat the fallen plums. In the morning Margaret spreads the sleeping bags over the deck rail to dry off the heavy night dew.

SEPTEMBER · I wanted to take Margaret away for her birthday at the end of this month, but she would rather stay quietly here.

We made a last sail on *Kairos* and then covered her with her winter tarpaulin. I explained, "I'm very sorry, old girl. I know it's early to go to bed. But you see, I'm going away."

Michael wrote to say he is on a journey that leaves me reaching for my atlas. He has come from Manali through Zanskar to Leh with two American friends and a guide with a horse. I am thinking that his trekking at these elevations will really acclimatize him for our slog upward and down through the Himalayan foothills. I hope I don't hold him back. From Leh he will be travelling by bus and train to Kathmandu, where he will make his own hotel arrangements and wait for me. I must look for him at the airport, for he will definitely meet my plane, which arrives on October 4.

I feel almost guilty for travelling in comparative comfort by air via Hong Kong!

Now I am making last-minute lists of things I will need to carry for a very basic life. I have lots of advice from friends who have friends.

"You must take an umbrella," said one.

"Why? I'm hoping the monsoon will be over."

"Calls of nature above the tree line."

I don't think the elevated landscape will be crowded, and decide against the umbrella. I'm sure to leave it somewhere anyway.

I have an argument with myself about the long johns. I decide against carrying more stuff and will probably regret it.

Now Margaret and I sit outside as the slow autumn sun goes down behind Galiano Mountain and leaves a long twilight. September is already slipping into October. I tell her "I'll write from Kathmandu but that may be the only letter I can send. After that I'll keep a daily journal to show you when I come home. Everything is ready. Nothing can go wrong."

"I'm not worrying," she says.

The evening is soft and we watch the stars come out.

"When did your hair turn silver?"

She smiles and says, "Last night."

23 THE OLD MAN AND THE BOY

OCTOBER 8, 1985 · I am in Kathmandu. My hotel is not quite Blair's cool marble floors with a scent of flowers, but my room is ensuite, with a bathroom with a pull chain over the toilet and a wash basin. A lightbulb hanging above the bed serves me well until the power goes off.

The room is noisy, looking onto the street, and I am open to the curiosity of passing people carrying heavy loads, monks in saffron robes, and sacred cows that struggle to survive on what they can find in the rotting garbage piles in the street.

After a dreadful flight here, I arrived late on October 6 instead of October 4. Leaving Seattle six hours late, my plane was bound to miss the Hong Kong connection to Kathmandu. Michael had worked things out and was at the airport, such a welcome and encouraging sight after my struggle to get here. He had arrived a week earlier and was in lodgings in a humble part of town. He found the taxi ride from the airport a luxury after the simple nomadic life he has become accustomed to. After we had a meal together he returned to his own lodgings, which he wishes to keep, and I arrived here in time for the grandfather of all post-monsoon thunderstorms.

We have explored the town, Michael and I, photographing, but not wishing to look like tourists.

The country is governed unequally in the flow of profits from tourism. It seems an administration courting rebellion. The royal family, perhaps not fully aware of the changing world pressing through the isolation the mountains have offered through the centuries, lives in imported luxury rivalled only by the Sheraton Hotel. Nearby, in a narrow road with a community water trough, people live one family to a room open to the street except for a piece of cloth over the door. A Mercedes Benz drives by. Children sell what they can on the street. One young child offers to weigh passersby on a pair of bathroom scales. A young boy in jeans and western jacket, a new leather satchel on his back, walks past on his way to private school.

Animals and humanity seem to be burdened under loads that are too heavy. A sad-eyed buffalo pulls a cart impossibly overloaded. A man walks by with a large piece of furniture on his back, his leg muscles standing out like thongs. Tourist money has brought a building boom. A young girl, born to hardship, stands ready to receive a load of bricks on her back to carry them up a rickety ladder, followed by a lad who is weighed down by a "carrier" of wet cement, staggering, groping for the ladder rungs.

The ugly Hindu god of chaos sits opposite the law courts. Beautiful Hindu shrines are in hidden courtyards.

Not far from the god of chaos a Buddhist temple in the centre of town points heavenward through the 13 steps to enlightenment, and in four different directions the compassionate eyes of the Buddha watch with blessing the struggles of humanity.

Michael and I have been busy getting our trekking permits and employing a guide. We asked for someone who can speak English, and were introduced to Krishna. I thanked him for offering his services, and he smiled and said, "No problem." It was a short time after I signed him on that I realized that those two words are the only English he has, apart from a couple of obscenities.

Tomorrow the three of us, Michael, Krishna and I, take the bus to Jiri to start the upward trek.

Margaret said her thought would be always with me. Those words will be my mantra.

OCTOBER 9 · We caught the bus to Jiri! I started off briskly from my hotel, clean, shaven, carrying a full pack to meet Michael and Krishna at the post office, where the bus stops.

I strode past tourists, monks, women walking and chatting, with bundles of washing on their heads and babies on their backs. I passed street sellers, walked past the hole dug in the road that I have nearly fallen into twice, past a man asleep on the sidewalk in all the noise of the waking city. Michael and Krishna were at the bus stop along with a huge crowd catching the same bus. Everyone carried their belongings, backpacks, ducks in cages, bags of rice. I mailed a letter to Margaret.

When the bus pulled in there was a surge forward to board. Those who couldn't grab a seat stood packed together. Those who couldn't get inside climbed on the roof. Michael and I stood with Krishna, swaying, jolting, jerking, until eight o'clock that night. Each time the bus came to a hill, everyone got off and walked up, otherwise the bus wouldn't make it.

The smell, the heat, the noise, the diesel fumes mercifully ended for us when the bus could go no farther and neither could I. It was dark as we came to the end of the road and I wanted to book into the first guesthouse we came to.

Madame who ran the guesthouse was shrewd. Michael thought she was asking too much to board us and I got the same signal from Krishna. I was tired out and suddenly handed to Krishna all the money I had allotted for accommodation on the trek. It was up to him to bargain with the locals in their language. Michael looked anxious and Krishna saw no problem. I knew he would cream off his profit, but that was his due for shared responsibility.

I didn't eat. My bed was hard. I didn't care. I would never again have to take the bus to Jiri.

OCTOBER 10 · Today was beauty in the morning, then deadening pain, and a party in the evening. So goes the magic of this place.

We slogged upward in the cool crispness of the new day. We are 2,000 feet above sea level and getting close to winter. Jiri began to look small down in the valley, and the high, terraced hillsides were lush from the monsoon rains. We climbed up, up, across a river in spate that cascaded under a swaying suspension bridge. Then we lost all the height we had gained in a knee-breaking slog downward, perspiring as we came into the warm valley.

We had trekked for eight hours with little actual progress and I couldn't go another step. And so Krishna booked us into a tall stone building on the trail with a courtyard that was the centre of activity. There the maize and barley were dried, there the cooking and eating and dishwashing all happened together.

In the quiet of the late afternoon, in this sheltered courtyard, I slumped down while Michael and Krishna explored the surroundings. I had trained for a year with climbing, descending and weights, and this was our first day on the trail. Muscles I didn't know I had were in agony. How far could I go?

I felt very low.

As the day darkened a young Canadian came in. He and his friend from England sat with me in the courtyard.

"I'm Steve. This is my friend John."

"I'm George."

They sensed that all was not well with George. Their conversation was cheerful, lights were brought, wicks in whisky bottles filled with kerosene. The little flames flickered in the dark in the cool of the early evening, after the sun had set in splendour over the foothills.

Four Israelis arrived and Michael and Krishna wandered in. Then two Swiss. In the lamplight under the stars we ate duck and rice, exchanged stories, talked of other lands and finally went to bed with the bedbugs.

OCTOBER 11 · Today felt like playing hooky. Michael and I left Krishna with our packs on the trail and climbed up to a cheese factory nestled in the hills. We sat at a table in a bright, clean guest villa and ordered tea and a helping of the local cheese. Then we returned to Krishna and the hard slog, taking up our packs again.

The trail has Buddhist stupas and carved mani stones to guide people in prayer as they climb. They must be passed respectfully on the left. It is the rule, like the rule for modesty in dress.

As we came to a stupa beside the path in the gathering mist, a young woman wearing very short shorts passed the sacred stone on the wrong side.

I said, "Hello. I often forget too that we pass the stupa on the left."

She looked at me coldly, an old man, probably a fogey.

"Shit," she said and walked on.

Krishna grinned. I think his vocabulary is larger than he lets us know. But I felt hurt. The country's innocence is being torn away. Something pure is violated. I stopped by the stupa and said a line from Psalms. "May the mountains bring peace to the people." Then we trekked up to the pass in the hills.

We were at about 9,000 feet, above the valley in thickening mist, when I began to cough badly. Then mist turned to rain. I could have been coughing from altitude or because all the beds are damp.

We found a guesthouse and put down our dripping backpacks. When I collapsed still clothed on the bed, I didn't help the damp bed problem.

OCTOBER 12 · This may be as high as I can go without feeling discomfort from the thinning atmosphere, although we are nowhere near the 18,000 feet at which the body begins to deteriorate. So I enjoyed this morning especially. I had a good wash in a clear running river and the air was like wine. We crested a hill and began the inevitable descent into the valley. Coming up was a little girl with weary eyes and a load on her back. She would put her burden down on the hillside for a moment, then take it up again and struggle on. I felt miserably guilty for not appreciating enough the difficulty these people have feeding trekkers like us, in country where no wheels can go.

Down in the valley amid lush vegetation we found a pretty village centred by a stupa, with Buddha's compassionate eyes offering understanding and forgiveness below the 13 steps to enlightenment. I felt better. On the hillside, tucked away, was a small monastery.

In this atmosphere of profound peace we booked into a guesthouse, and too late found the table a mass of flies. Dinner was being cooked: buffalo meat and rice. I saw a buffalo head covered in flies in a butcher's shop in Kathmandu. It had one mournful eye, and one ear missing. Since then I have been off buffalo.

I went outside because my stomach was heaving. Michael was already out, talking to Steve from Canada and John from England, who had just arrived. They saw me. "Aha! The Old Man and the Boy!" They took us to their superior guesthouse for a meal, followed by Ceylon tea from the supply in John's backpack.

We were all happy together, but I was happiest because I realized that we are keeping step with the two young men. I really believe I am going to make it to the cathedral of rock and ice in the sky.

OCTOBER 13 · I am coughing badly. Today my camera bag with nothing inside but two small cameras and lenses weighed very heavily and Michael took it on his own shoulder. My backpack is lighter as I begin to put on most of my clothes.

As we continue to climb, the stones underfoot become loose and slippery. I begin to catch my breath. The atmosphere is changing.

Coming down into the valley mist I started to shiver and sweat. Krishna became concerned and signalled to Michael that there would be no more huts or houses for some time. He led us into a shelter where a happy baby played on the dirt floor among the chickens.

I felt ill and couldn't eat. The walls of the room were lined with sleeping benches with soiled rattan covers, on which slept a huge Tibetan mastiff. We moved in, and Krishna took a leech from his leg in the half-light of the room. I took off my shirt, damp with sweat, and put on a warm New Zealand wool one. Keeping on my down jacket, I lay down with the dog and listened to the rain on the roof.

OCTOBER 14 · I woke at cock crow. I could hardly do otherwise as the cock was standing beside me. Michael and Krishna shuffled off their benches and the fire was lit for breakfast.

Getting ready to join the breakfast table took very little time. I was already wearing most of my clothes and there was no spare water to shave. I carry my own mug for sanitary reasons but it's beginning to look most unsanitary. I decided to stop at the next river and get cleaned up.

As we slogged up the trail an old monk passed us with his acolyte. He smiled and saluted me in my dishevelled state, holding his hands together. I thought I had been blessed, but Michael said he greeted me by saying: "We're a couple of old ones." I should have shaved.

The trail led up to 11,500 feet, and inevitably down again, into the Khumbu Valley, the home of the Sherpas who brought Buddhism from Tibet as an immigrant people. As the Buddha was born in Nepal, I suppose it might have been a kind of homecoming.

Climbing on up the slippery, muddy trail, I fell. I put out my hand to stop myself and got up bleeding, to the concern of the others. I wagged my wrist to show it was alright. I don't want to break anything up here.

We were down in the valley by early afternoon, back in the damp mist that creeps along the valley bottoms, and found a place to stay at Junbesi. There was running water here from a nearby stream, and we washed and showered. I cleaned up my mug. I was about to give this place five stars when I discovered the lock on the privy door was on the outside. I pointed it out to Krishna and he didn't say "No problem."

Clean and sparkling, the three of us sat down to a spread of noodle soup and fried rice washed down with hot chocolate. We were all very happy until joined at the table by a young Israeli with an upset stomach, and a depressed Spaniard whose friend had gone home with mountain sickness. I sympathized, but they were miserable and determined to stay that way.

A French couple stayed the night on their way to Jiri. By the light of the lamp I wrote a quick note to Margaret and they promised to mail it.

OCTOBER 15 · Writing that note made me think of home all the way up the tough slog to Ringmo. I wondered if the rain had set in on the island after the hot dry summer. The little stream through the wood would be running fast past where the bright yellow skunk cabbage blooms in spring. Almost as fast as the river here that runs down from the mountains. I found myself wondering why the Nepalese don't harness this power to sell electricity to India. Perhaps at home we could get enough electricity from our waterfall to heat the house. Such musings took my mind off the hard climb. Then, with aching muscles, lunch at Ringmo was our reward. In a clean little town with apple orchards we had a very pleasant meal.

We should have stayed there. But, feeling better than I had for the past few days, I was all for pushing on until we reached a most depressing little town, and there we took a room.

In the kitchen a bowl of precious water on the floor, hauled laboriously from the river, served to wash hands, dishes and glasses. The resulting mixture resembled in consistency the Sherpa stew that was placed before me. I took it quietly outside and gave it to a grateful dog.

We spent the evening sitting at the table with an Israeli lady with the unlikely name of Violet. A young girl sat with us, nursing a five-day-old baby. When she was called to work in the kitchen, the young mother handed the infant to Violet, who rocked it gently while telling us of her travels.

As we were going to bed a crowd of porters came in, ready to forget their aching muscles and weary backs by knocking back chang, the local beer. Above the noise Violet was yelling from her bed that if they didn't tone down she wouldn't pay her bill. I fell asleep in the uproar.

OCTOBER 17 · At dawn Violet appeared in the kitchen and seemed surprised to see me up. Kind and motherly, she gave me some stomach powder and a big kiss. Then she was away in her lone descent to Jiri, sturdy legs in thick woollen socks, heavy pack on her back, a strong, vigorous figure on the downward trail.

I went outside as the first light tinted the high, snow-covered mountains in a shade of orange deeper than I had ever seen before. I reflected that, living in the mountains, it might be easy to become a buddha, meaning any person who has completely awakened from ignorance and discovered a lasting and deathless happiness and peace in the cycle of life and rebirth, the cycle they call "The Way."

Living as high as the Sherpa does, he can compare our true nature and potential to the sky, and the confusion of the human mind to the clouds. Some days the clouds obscure the sky, but cannot touch or stain it. Above the clouds everything is limitless and clear.

I believe I am learning something as I climb. Given time I feel sure I could become a buddha.

Today was hard, but rewarded in the afternoon when we reached the crest of a hill and obtained a clear view across an intervening valley to the airstrip of Lukla. Built by Sir Edmund Hillary, to the considerable benefit of the Sherpa people, it brings tourists and money on each 30-minute flight from Kathmandu. People needing slow acclimatization, as I do, climb the foothills.

As we stood staring at the high ridge beyond the next valley, where planes were coming in to land, Krishna got excited and signed that they had electric light over there.

I began to shiver and cough, and Michael insisted we book into the nearest guesthouse, where those already there kept their distance from my sneezing.

OCTOBER 18 · I have a heavy cold and I'm beginning to tire. I have my first real doubts that I will make it to my goal at the foot of the Khumbu Glacier. I don't want to tell Michael, nor do I want to be a drag on the others. But I do make heavy going now of the upward trail, muddy and wet with rivers from the mountains flowing over it.

Today we made only 1,500 feet by the time we had descended to the valley and up again.

But we are in Lukla, the place of airplanes and electric light, a place of restaurants belonging to the few guesthouses. A place of fresh food coming in by plane.

After the gate to the airstrip was permitted to be opened we crossed to the Buddha Hotel. We have only just booked in but already I am reflecting that in the search to become a buddha, creature comforts hold us back. Faced with this luxury of cleanliness, good food and electricity, how easily enlightenment can slip in our priorities!

OCTOBER 19 · This place has mirrors. I saw myself today. I wish I hadn't.

My clothes need to go to the cleaners, and me with them. My eyes seem to have sunk into my head. My reading glasses are broken and held on with a rubber band I found in my pocket.

From the many planes landing come tourists, clean with well-pressed clothes, long socks carefully pulled up over the bottoms of hiking pants. They all have cameras slung over their shoulders, and clean boots.

Regardless of my appearance we visited a restaurant that was filled with a party of elderly Japanese. They were polite when they saw us and wanted photographs! Perhaps we were the first real characters they have seen in the hills since leaving the plane. Smiles, camera flashes, bows. I bowed. Michael bowed. Krishna bowed very low. No problem.

John and Steve have kept pace with us and I told John I feel very shabby. He sympathized and gave me a better rubber band for my glasses.

OCTOBER 20 · After a day's rest at the Buddha Hotel and a good breakfast this morning we have moved to the Himalayan Hotel, a little farther from the airstrip and quieter. Here every possible effort has been made for the comfort of tourists and the décor is almost ritzy.

Michael and Krishna chose the dormitory. But the Old Man went mad on luxury and, with Krishna's help, got himself a room with a double bed. The privacy! The dazzle of electric light! The wonder of a hot shower!

I got into bed and reached out to the lamp on the bedside table and turned it off. Then I turned it on again, just for the hell of it.

OCTOBER 21 · I reflected this morning, as I showered, shaved and brushed my hair, that Michael shuns luxury and extravagance. Perhaps I might too if I were his age, but that double bed last night was wonderful.

It was today, as I started off relaxed and rested, that I began to fall sick.

We made it to the crest of the hill. Steve and John were there ahead of us looking with awe across the valley. Here was our first clear glimpse of Everest. Chomolungma of rugged windswept rock and ice high in the sky, Chomolungma who rides her white lion snarling into the wind.

I felt nearer at last to my goal. Steve and John went ahead again, walking toward Namche Bazaar, the Sherpa capital and market town, and we were following along the trail. Suddenly I stopped. I began to cough and vomit, choking, hardly able to draw breath, and everything turned black. I was falling. But there were strong arms there for me and I was grateful for Michael and Krishna.

Just as suddenly, I felt well again, and insisted we climb all day. When darkness came we still had a long way to go to Namche Bazaar.

There was no moon. I was shivering and stumbling. The stones under our feet were frosted and slippery. We picked our way carefully.

Then the moon came up, almost touching the mountains, and it seemed that every star in the hemisphere twinkled in the wide sky. My friends the stars, they lit our way to shelter.

Namche Bazaar, a meeting point of trade routes, is a town set in scenery of breathtaking beauty. But that night it was above all a haven. At the first inn we came to, I collapsed for the night on a bench without inquiring where the others would sleep. I suggested the next two days should be a holiday to rest. Michael agreed. Krishna saw no problem. Then I slept deeply on my bench with the whole clientele of the inn passing me to get to the toilet.

OCTOBER 22 · I rose early in my position by the toilet and looked for Michael. He was having breakfast in the smoke of the kitchen and planned to spend the day reading. Krishna was bored and pacing. Unable to read or write and scarcely able to communicate, days off made him restless.

I couldn't face breakfast and decided to enjoy the morning with my camera. I felt I should take Krishna with me, making the excuse that he could carry the camera bag. But I really wanted to be alone.

I skirted the back of the town into Sagarmatha National Park, where Blair had first felt the magic of the mountains. The early light was soft on the most beautiful of the Himalayan Ranges. Ama Dablam stretched her arms in a blessing for all humanity below, watching over a waking world. The sun was gently touching Nuptse in an orange glow. Everest was hidden.

The whole scene energized me. I felt whole again after feeling so ill. I started busying around, looking at maps. Above us was a hard clamber up the trail to Tengboche. My muscles were becoming oxygen-starved and aching. Besides my cough I had bladder problems. Michael and Krishna were acclimatized, Michael from his trek in India. And Krishna worked this trail regularly; it was his job. I didn't want to be falling behind. I would do my best.

At breakfast the second day I had the pleasure of meeting Reinhold Messner, who had climbed Everest without oxygen. And here was I, puffing and coughing and not yet at Base Camp.

I told him my mission, and my doubts that I would make it. He had heard of Blair and understood.

"Don't push yourself, George," he advised. "Rest when you need to. You'll make it."

I found a little store where I could buy snacks that wouldn't upset my stomach, and wandered around the town. In the evening John and Steve came in through the smoke in the kitchen. "The Old Man and the Boy again!" John had also been to the store and we rummaged through each other's supply of snacks like kids going through the others' lunch boxes at school. We exchanged four packs of peanut butter cookies for two packets of trail mix.

"How are you coping with the altitude, George?"

"I'm fine. But things become more of an effort. I'll just be careful not to push it."

With increasing bladder difficulties I was glad to return to my bench by the toilet. With the lack of privacy these things were becoming part of the general conversation.

OCTOBER 23 · I tried to block from my mind the pain of the steep climb to Tengboche by thinking of home. This is always a good escape. The wind would probably be blowing up onto the beach and there would be high tides dumping driftwood. Perhaps an east wind, full of bluster. Or perhaps a soft wind from the west, shaking the pine tree outside the kitchen window. Margaret would have brought the tender plants inside the house. She felt very close to me as I struggled on.

The mountain trail at the back of Namche Bazaar led first down into a valley and then to the steep weary walk up again that I found so hard. It was when I felt I could go no further that I was confronted suddenly with the full scope of Creation's magnificence opening up on the hillside. Under a sky rendered deepest blue by the thinning atmosphere, a monastery clung to a ridge. Beyond, Ama Dablam appeared and then hid herself in blowing cloud.

We found rest and quiet in a restaurant and chang house near the monastery. There I found a book of black and white photographs taken in the mountains. On the inside page was a verse by New Zealand poet James Baxter:

> *Alone we are born and die alone*
> *Yet see the red gold sunset over snow mountain shine.*
> *Upon the upland road ride easy, Stranger.*
> *Surrender to the sky your heart of anger.*

In some way the poem gave me peace.

In a guesthouse we booked into for the night I sat at supper beside an American lady who was coughing badly. After the meal I proffered my little packet of throat lozenges, my Fisherman's Friends. She said thank you and took the whole package.

I was affronted.

"I still need some," I protested.

She gave me two from the package.

"You have those two and I'll take my package back," I said.

She gave me three more.

We were above the tree line and the law of survival had kicked in.

OCTOBER 24 · Through barren boulder and juniper scrub we began the climb up to Pheriche. At 12,700 feet I realized I was going well. Everest could be glimpsed but was mostly behind Nuptse. We were bending under our packs, going slowly. My breathing was heavy. Coughing would come in short sharp attacks.

Porters were moving up the trail under heavy bags of rice carried on their backs, held steady by a band at the forehead, trying to fill the needs of the visitors.

A little before evening we reached Pheriche, a cluster of stone huts and empty yak paddocks, the animals having been taken lower for the winter. One stone hut was a guesthouse with three tiers of shelves for sleeping. With my bladder problems I secured a place on the ground near the exit, reserving it with my backpack. Michael and Krishna wanted the top shelf. Perhaps it was warmer there.

There were people moving up the trail and we were glad we had come early. As the sun slipped behind the mountains, preparations began for the evening meal. In the kitchen the yak-dung fire was stoked. Black smoke twisted and curled out of the door. People moved silently in the smoke. It was Dante's inferno!

I coughed uncontrollably.

I didn't go in to supper but sat in my place on the shelf near the ground. As I became sleepy I stretched out, fully clothed, in my sleeping bag, beating together my gloved hands to keep warm. I marked the exit carefully and put my flashlight beside me.

The places on the shelf near the floor were in demand, and the bodies were expected to lie fairly close, with the head of one toward the feet of the next. A middle-aged lady stretched out beside me, her feet to my head, and we smiled politely. People began to come in after supper and fill the shelves. Darkness came and the inside of the hut was as black as the inside of a sweep's hat and smelled of boots and socks.

I fell deeply asleep.

OCTOBER 25 · I woke a little after midnight with an urgent need to relieve myself. The hut was in darkness. My flashlight wasn't there. The lady beside me had rolled on it.

My need was great. If I groped under her legs would she understand that she was lying on my flashlight? If I were to lean over and whisper in her ear, "Excuse me, mada ..." No. She would wake and not even give me time to finish the sentence. My need became pain.

A wavering light appeared at the other end of the hut. Someone else had an urgent call outside. Man or woman seeking privacy, I was going with them. I struggled out of my bag and followed and stumbled after the dark figure with the light. My movements were terribly slow, my need urgent. Outside, an understanding young man heard my tale of woe as we stood shivering in a deep frost under a starlit sky. He lit my way back to my place on the shelf. The woman next to me moved a little and snuffled. The people on the shelves stirred. They made me think, as I lay sleepless, of an aunt I loved years ago, the one who gave me a toy sailing ship.

"Aunt," I had asked her as a small child. "How did we get navels?"

"Well, dear," she said, "God made us from the clay of the earth. Then he put us in the warmth of a kiln, an oven, to make us human and kind. When he took us out he laid us on shelves side by side to test us. Then he went along the shelves prodding us, and saying: 'You're done, you're done, you're done.' So our navels are God's fingerprint."

I lay in the dark, my legs not aching so much when I lay flat, thinking of a friend, now long since dead, who had heart surgery in its early stages of research. He finished up with his navel some two inches off centre. It ruined him psychologically.

I slept 'til first light, when people began to move off the shelves. The lady beside me was rolling up her sleeping bag.

"Is this your flashlight?" she asked. I scarcely thanked her.

Michael was beside me, asking me if I'd slept.

"Not much," I told him.

"If all this lot are going up to Lobuche I'd better go ahead to book us in. They're likely going up to Gorak Shep to get a clear view of Everest."

I coughed when I sat up. My legs were heavy. What oxygen there was in the hut had been used, even with the entrance open to the outdoors. I knew I had to let Michael go on. I would follow very slowly with Krishna.

It was an enormous effort to get my boots on. I felt as if I had rheumatism all over. The hut serving breakfast was belching smoke. Again I marvelled at the ability of the young to adapt and eat breakfast there. Michael ate and left for Lobuche, and Krishna stayed in the warm kitchen eating watery porridge. I lay on my shelf at the floor level, deciding to consult a doctor at the clinic established here for the summer to serve trekkers who ran into difficulties. Perhaps this was the end of the road for me.

The clinic was in a tent labelled "Himalayan Rescue." It offered services until the end of October, when the trekking season would end for safety reasons.

I reported to this tent, which was practically and sparsely furnished and a bit unwelcoming. A young American doctor beckoned for me to sit by a table.

I didn't want to talk. Words use energy and breath. I was brief.

"I can't go on but I must. I can't stay here in this smoke."

"What exactly are the symptoms bothering you?"

"Breathing. Muscles aching. Tired. Bladder. Stomach. Headache. Cough."

"Are you sleeping?"

"Not much last night."

"Was it stress? What were you thinking about?"

"Navels, mostly."

I had his interest. He was young enough perhaps to want to do a study of the effects of altitude on the elderly.

"Just navels?" he was being kind and encouraging.

"There was a lady beside me..." My voice trailed away. I was too tired to go into it all. The flashlight, the pain. I couldn't be bothered.

The young doctor was beginning to look at me uneasily now. I must look at least 90.

"Why do you have to go on?" he asked, taking my blood pressure.

"My son died on the icefall. There's a memorial."

I didn't tell him about the plaque in the cathedral in the sky. He probably thought I was talking about the stone chortens built to remember those who have died on Everest. He took my temperature, and sounding me with a stethoscope, he gave me some antibiotics.

"I think you can make it," he said, "but come straight down to lower altitude after your visit. Take today off and eat. You can't climb without fuel. There's a little store here, selling things that were left over from climbing expeditions, things not worth carrying down. They give them to the Sherpas and they're people of commerce and make good money from them."

I thanked him and gave him a contribution to Himalayan Rescue. I wasn't going to take a day off, but I would take it slow.

In the little store my spirits rose, like a desert traveller who finds an oasis. There were tins of fruit juice, and I did have a can opener. Among all the non-perishables there were hard-boiled eggs. Jars of marmite stood on a shelf under a scrawled direction to "spread it on your chipate" (*sic*). They must have been left by an Indian expedition. I went shopping and then had myself a feast, sitting on my shelf. I washed down hard-boiled eggs with fruit juice and antibiotics from the clinic.

Krishna came looking for me, and I signalled I was ready to go on. Michael had left me the camera, knowing I would be passing the place where Blair's chorten stood. Krishna picked up the camera bag firmly and put it on his own shoulder and would have taken my backpack too, but it was light now that I was wearing most of the stuff it had contained.

We started off on the rough, freezing path to Lobuche. An arrow pointing upward advertised the New Sherpa Hotel. That spelled luxury.

Muscles ached and I was slow. Krishna held back to go my pace. A few steps. Stop and breathe. A few more steps, sliding on the icy path, and a few more. At this pace we reached Dugla, the place of the chortens, below Lobuche.

I stood on this ledge of memories. The mist was creeping over the ground, cold as it touched me, the way it does in the Scottish Highlands. All along this dip in the upward slope stood stone pillars in sad company with each other. One after another, through the years, they had been built. Every chorten held a story of fear and human endeavour. Blair was remembered with the three Sherpas, their memorials standing close. His memorial was near that of the Sherpa whose lifeless body he had helped to dig out of the snow. A circle of stones marked the cremation site.

I knew now why Michael had gone on ahead. I needed to be alone here. Krishna kept a polite distance. I must not weep in front of him.

I paid my respects to the three Sherpas, and thought of their unsatisfactory goddess and the prayers that had begged her not to kick down the avalanche. The offerings of food and drink and sweet juniper smoke. The pleas on flapping flags. A curse on you, Chomolungma, ruling the summit and approaches of Everest, claiming a territory in men's minds.

When I stood before Blair's chorten I didn't know how I would be. I was surprised to feel anger. At Everest. Not the most beautiful mountain but the highest, drawing us like a magnet. We have to touch her. Some she will permit and some she will kill. It's all the same to Everest as she pulls people to her from all over the planet.

I had so much to tell Blair that I hadn't said. Why couldn't I have told him before the climb that I love him? Because men don't talk like that. Now I know better. And it's too late.

I couldn't find Blair in this cold heap of stones. I could feel his free spirit better in the wind or see it in the mist and the cascading rivers.

It was cold standing still. I signalled to Krishna that I was ready to continue on the path, and his face was gentle.

We walked slowly on. Everything was silent under a big sky. I seemed to stumble more and Krishna gave me his arm where it was steepest. We came into Lobuche in early afternoon, having eaten all the hard-boiled eggs on the way.

Lobuche had one road of mud. Yak dung was spread on rocks in the hope it would dry for fuel. One of the few huts was labelled the New Sherpa Hotel, and we turned in. I collapsed on a bench and signed to Krishna that it was the end for me. He didn't say "No problem," but vanished into the "hotel" and got me a drink of water.

Behind the huts I could see the peak that was most likely part of Blair's cathedral. I had come almost 80 miles. What if I couldn't go the last four or five? What if I really couldn't go any higher? I moved to a sleeping shelf in the dormitory, my pack beside me, and my New Zealand wool shirt acting as a pillow. I felt lower in my soul than I ever remembered.

Michael came in. He had gone alone to the peak to find the plaque that was wired above the ledge where the ashes had been laid, but he found no sign of it and the trail ended in a high heap of boulders. If the wire had broken, the plaque would have been swept away by the mountain wind that tolerates few mementos.

We all went into the warmth of the kitchen in the evening, when the frost was biting hard and the stars were coming out. I flavoured my boiled rice with marmite and ate it with some enjoyment.

A group of Spaniards was tenting in the village near the New Sherpa Hotel and they came into the kitchen for warmth. I began to cough in the smoke, and one of the Spaniards, full of concern, did the only thing he could think of to make things better for me. With a bow he gave me a large slice of chocolate cake. It was a kindness I shall remember always.

I went to bed on the shelf near the exit, my flashlight safely beside me. Michael stayed by the fire, reading in a distressingly bad light from a lamp on the table. Krishna curled up in a surprisingly small ball on my shelf.

Full of antibiotics and chocolate cake, with my woollen hat pulled low over my ears and my scarf over my mouth for warmth, I slept a deep sleep of sadness.

OCTOBER 26 · At 5:00 a.m. I awoke from the noise of people moving off the shelves and out of the hut. Michael and Krishna had already had breakfast and were leaving without me to find the cathedral in the sky. They knew, and I knew, I could go no further. They were off to explore the peak behind the huts by a different route. They would be back by afternoon.

I stood outside and watched them go. They were going for me to Blair's last resting place, where his ashes were laid by the girl he loved.

I couldn't go with them. It had been an effort to get off the sleeping planks. I saw them climb, Michael bending forward on the wind, young and slender, black wool cap pulled well down; and Krishna, tall for a Nepalese, dark-skinned and broader but sturdy, both now slowing in the thinning air. Krishna was Hindu. I wondered how he felt about the peevish Chomolungma. Perhaps he felt closer to the Hindu god of chaos on these guided treks.

Left behind, I was unsure whether my body was aching more than my soul. I lay on my shelf in my sleeping bag, thinking of Michael and Krishna on the upward slope. I prayed for them both. In the middle of my prayer I had a vision of a currant bun. This was terrible, and delicious. In my infants' school the Jesuits had taught me that it would be a mortal sin to eat, or even imagine, anything sweet and tantalizing while praying. They had emphasized toffee after I had been caught at prayer with a bulge in one cheek, but they didn't mention dreaming of buns with butter in the middle.

All my life I have loved currant buns and have eaten them with a sense of guilt for reasons quite apart from the Jesuits. As a boy I once consumed, in a helpless submission to temptation, every bun on a dish that had been prepared for afternoon tea and was waiting on the kitchen table to be carried into the living room. My mother told me I was greedy past redemption in this world and that it was doubtful about the next.

But now, where some people who are fed continually on rice at altitude imagine juicy steaks, here, for me, was this vision of a currant bun. I wondered where such dreams come from. I knew that my God was benevolent and smiling in the darkest times. Perhaps sometimes he laughs to help us along. I began to feel new energy in a sudden burst, but then promptly fell asleep. I slept until early afternoon, with my scarf again over my mouth to warm the air I was breathing. My cozy New Zealand wool shirt still served as a pillow. I didn't wake until the crunch of boots on the cold stones outside and the sounds of voices heralded the arrival of new people coming to book in for the night. They bustled inside the hut to reserve a place with their backpacks, and I lay resting, ignoring them. My visions still kept coming. I was beyond currant buns now, and into mussels cooked in wine.

I left my sleeping bag and pack to reserve my place. A day of antibiotics and acclimatization appeared to be working. I went in search of a little water to drink, wash, shave and clean my teeth. I valued each drop that had been carried up through the hills. In the kitchen I found Michael and Krishna. Returned, they had been unwilling to disturb me.

Michael was delighted. They had found the cathedral in the sky.

They had taken a more direct route up the peak, and when the path seemed to fade out and they were uncertain which way to go, they met an Indian party coming down. Had they seen a plaque wired to a boulder, Michael asked them.

"Yes. In memory of a young man who died on Mount Everest."

Their directions were vague, and when the path later branched, Michael and Krishna had stood in uncertainty. They decided to keep to the most direct route up the peak and suddenly, among the boulders, they came to a little plateau. There, still wired to a rock, was the plaque.

"It isn't far," Michael was telling me.

"We'll start off first thing in the morning," I decided, my mind purposeful at last. However, my body was giving me a different message, and I didn't know how on earth I was going to do this. Rest was important. I said goodnight and Michael stayed up reading, saying he would wake me just before dawn.

OCTOBER 27 · After we left our packs with Krishna and climbed through the early-morning dark, the sun rose in a burst of glory and dyed the mountain peaks deepest crimson, a warm light that flooded our world.

For me, every step on the upward trail was difficult. When I coughed, or gasped to take in air, the cold hurt somewhere inside me. We went carefully, step by cautious step, over the rubble at the snout of the Khumbu Glacier. We didn't stop to search the meadows for mountain flowers, survivors of autumn's bloom. All my energy was for the plod upward. Threading our way among the boulders on an uncertain path, I followed Michael. All around was wild loneliness. The only sound was that of our boots crunching.

In my labouring steps I thought of Margaret. She said that in thought she would always be with me, wherever I am. I put out my hand for her.

The path became more indistinct and branched. Michael, confident, so close to our goal, took the way that lay straight up. I stumbled on, puffing for air.

Suddenly I seemed to be going well. I had energy beyond my own, helped upward by a power that was not mine. Or was it just the wind gusting up?

We came onto a narrow plateau. Tiny in the immensity all around was a plaque I had last seen propped up against the kitchen window on the day Debbie brought it to show me. Through the glass behind it I had watched the maple leaves drifting into the sea. It seemed right to me then that summer had ended.

I stooped over and read the inscription, although I knew it by heart:

I CLIMB MY BODY IS PAST EXHAUSTION
AND MY MIND IS MOVING UPWARD,
HAND IN HAND WITH MY SOUL.
I'LL BE FRIGHTENED IF YOU TAKE MY LIFE.
I'LL UNDERSTAND THOUGH,
YOU ARE NOT MY SERVANT, I AM YOURS.
I AM A GUEST IN YOUR HOUSE
AND IT'S MORE THAN I DESERVE.

— J.F.S.

G. BLAIR GRIFFITHS

1949–1982

KILLED ON MOUNT EVEREST

I clutched the ledge beneath the plaque where Blair's ashes had been laid under a love offering of flowers.

Hidden from the world, far from the Jesuit teaching that boys don't cry, far from the stiff upper lip of the Royal Navy when men drowned in the cold Atlantic, I wept. I wept for all the grief I had ever known. I wept for my child grown to maturity with his life over too soon, like the maple leaves falling before the coming of winter. I may have wept because I was cold and tired and sad and had brought no flowers.

I crouched on the rock. The rock, jewel-studded with ice particles, fell steeply away to the world below.

"Do you know that I came, Blair? I said I would."

With no tears left to weep, I turned away from the grave to look up at the sky. But there was no need to look up. I was part of the sky, part of the mountains that shone above in the reflected light of the early day. In glitter and shadow they faded softly into infinity. I could almost hear them echo an unearthly orchestra that reached a crescendo of celebration and joy in Creation. Insignificant, I was part of the dance of the ages, beyond mortality. I sought for words but when they came they were borrowed from a book of photographs in a restaurant at Tengboche. I had forgotten. "Ride easy, Stranger, and leave your anger in the sky." I knew I had misquoted. It didn't matter. They were written for me and people like me.

I answered, hardly audibly, in reverence and awe: "Thank you. I too am a guest in your house. And it's more than I deserve."

It was too cold to stay. I turned back to touch the ledge. Michael crouched with hands together and head bowed in an Indian gesture of farewell. I whispered "Blair, I still cannot say goodbye. I am an old man and will soon come to where you are. It is The Way."

Michael took the camera bag and we went down carefully through the icy scree and boulders, along the path down to Lobuche.

We said little on the way back. There was little to say.

We had both been to eternity and back.

The Morning Light

It's 10 years now since I found my peace on a mountain ledge in the sky. Michael went on for further trekking before coming home to go to university. Krishna returned to Kathmandu to find another group to guide on the upland path. I flew from Lukla, back to Margaret, the bulldogs and the island.

These have been years of content.

Galiano Island is a spine of rock of great beauty. To describe my last peaceful days there as Margaret and I walked down the years together, I borrow from Thoreau: "The true harvest of my daily life is somewhat as intangible and indescribable as the tints of morning or evening. It is a little stardust caught..." Margaret and I have sailed *Kairos* for many summers in the light winds around the Gulf Islands, near steep, wooded hills dipping to the sea. One summer we sailed to Malcolm Island, and the wind was strong and the whales spouting. On to Bull Harbour, where the fog came in like a thick white carpet unrolling on the water. We picked up the Pacific swell and crossed to the Queen Charlotte Islands. When we came home we had to part with *Kairos*, my friend and sea partner. I had been diagnosed with cancer and could not continue the work of maintaining a wooden boat.

For years now cancer has been my shadow. At first I confronted it firmly, as one in control. "You shall not keep step with me. I will not have you." The cancer retreated, responsive I believe, to my prayers and meditations, and to an immune system nourished by the peace I share with Margaret, and by the blessed sound and perfumes of the woods, the rhythm of the sea outside my window, and by dark shapes of clouds and birds against the dawn.

I lived fully. Even after I was told the cancer had become active again I walked slowly with the dogs, and laughed, travelled a little and played bridge.

I loved colour as I had never loved it before – the roadside buttercups, the new, fresh green of the spring buds and late-season red of the vine maples, the tricks of light on water. I caught on film the delicacy of garden flowers and made close-up studies of Margaret's old-world roses. And then I knew I must get ready to leave it all, to prepare myself for what may be the greatest adventure of them all, that last walk for which the Plains Indians fitted their dying with new moccasins.

Margaret and I went quietly away to a hotel by a lake ringed by mountains. There we knew the closeness of those who must soon part. We strolled together in the quietness of early morning, and in the afternoon I tried the luxury of a sauna while Margaret read. She became anxious when time went by and I was still lying in a steam bath. Meeting a man wearing nothing but a towel she asked him, if he was headed for the sauna, would he suggest to her husband that he might be spending too long in there.

"His name's George," she said. The man proceeded to the sauna.

"Anyone here called George?" he asked. "Your wife says you've had enough."

I joined in the laughter with the friends I'd made in the steam, and came out feeling weak and delighted in this last glorious relaxation.

In the evening there was dinner and dancing. The band was made up of three young men and a girl who sang with a sweet voice. They played an oldie for the oldies.

I said to Margaret: "May I have this waltz?"

We slowly circled.

When I grow too old to dream,
I'll have you to remember.

And when I grow too old to dream
Your love will live in my heart.

I was reminded of my fantasy, half-waking, half-sleeping, when I was in the harbour in Bequia and imagined we danced, Margaret and I, higher and higher into the sky.

I said: "The music will never end," and she remembered, and told me: "When I join you we'll dance on the clouds."

After we came home my world gradually shrank to a corner of the couch where I could watch the sea, and the birds at the feeder, and Margaret would bring fresh garden flowers and put them in a bowl on the mantel.

I began to have flashbacks from which I would emerge with a jump. They usually came after dozing, when I was neither asleep nor awake, but sometimes even in the middle of talking I would find myself in some other place. I put it down to the morphine. Often I would be again on *Kairos*, feeling the motion, hearing the wind in the shrouds, and I would sing with it. But I made no sound. Other times I would hear men calling from dark water, and then find myself in the security of home but very cold. I tried to cut out this sorrow of the war. On the destroyers of the Atlantic convoys, it was forbidden to slow down to pick up survivors in the water after an enemy attack, for fear the rescuing vessel itself might be targeted and sunk. The convoy must close up in tight formation. I tried but could not stop these hallucinations. But the minutes they gave me on *Kairos* were a gift.

One morning in July, I suppose it was only a week ago, I dressed in my best light jacket and pants, chose my shirt with care, and wore my shoes with leather laces. We were leaving for Victoria. I didn't look in a mirror. I knew how my jacket hung on my shoulders. They say the departed whom we have loved will welcome us as we ourselves pass over. Blair, will you recognize your old Dad? I'm really a bit of a sight! But the spirit is still strong! Here I come!

It was early and still only half light when we left the house. I patted both the old dogs, who would be cared for by a housesitter. Then just a quick last look through the window. Dark clouds were banking over the sea and the tide was coming in. There were three eagles circling in the sky, riding the summer air currents, primary feathers spread like fingers as the earth revolved below them. Strange there were three. One was probably from this year's fledging.

Margaret drove us to the wharf and aboard the ferry. The wind was fresh and smelled of kelp. There were many people I knew heading for the stairway as Margaret and I moved slowly to the ship's elevator.

"Hello, George!"

"Hello there."

"Going into town?"

"That's right."

"Coming back this afternoon?"

"No, I have an appointment."

In the cafeteria people were lining up for breakfast and there was a smell of toast and coffee.

"Not eating, George?"

"No. Not hungry."

I watched each landmark fall behind us, places I had seen so often.

Margaret drove us from the ferry to the hospital. We had brought roses to give to the admitting staff who had been so kind.

"Hello, George!" Roberta greeted me from the reception desk. "Roses! How lovely!"

"They're from a sailor. Tell your husband."

That must have been only a few days ago. It seems longer. It's doubtful now that I shall live long enough to be transferred to the hospice. I've embraced those I love and wish I could see Erik grow to full manhood. With Margaret in a cot close beside me I watch the night through the uncurtained window of our room. Soon I shall see that blessed first flush of dawn that delights my soul, before the city wakes.

A bright crack of light comes through the door, left open a little. Outside in the passage are the noises of Ward 4 South. A trolley is being wheeled by. Soon the nurse will come in, smiling, encouraging. "Just a needle for pain, Mr. Griffiths."

I have put a slip of paper under my pillow. Perhaps it will be found later and be discarded by the cleaning staff. They must find a lot of funny things stuffed under pillows. I don't really need it, for I know the words. I don't remember whose they are, but they bring me out of the drabness of the dark into the transforming beauty of the light.

> *"Lord, in the watches of the night*
> *Keep thou my soul! a trembling thing*
> *As any moth that in daylight*
> *Will spread a rainbow wing."*

I lie here waiting for the morning light to flood the sky with glory.

George Griffiths died in the early hours of August 1, 1995. Mark placed his ashes in the ocean as he had requested. Erik put a memorial stone in the Galiano cemetery, on a grass bank sloping to the sea. Facing east, it catches the first light of the morning.